Computer Optimization Techniques

WILLIAM CONLEY
University of Wisconsin-Green Bay

Computer Optimization Techniques

PBI
a petrocelli
book
new york / princeton

Library of Congress Cataloging in Publication Data

Conley, William, 1948–
    Computer optimization techniques.

    Includes index.
    1. Mathematical optimization—Data processing.
2. Integer programming—Data processing. I. Title.
QA402.5.C64   519.7′7   79-24452
ISBN 0-89433-111-6

Dedicated to my Family and Friends

Also dedicated to anyone who has ever wanted the
solution to an optimization problem in five minutes or less

CONTENTS

INTRODUCTION

Computer science has advanced to the point where it is possible to greatly simplify integer programming. This book is an attempt to do just that.

This simplification takes many forms. It frequently allows us to solve integer, linear, and nonlinear programming problems, that were solvable before, in a much easier fashion. The technique is easier theoretically, easier on the programmer, and cheaper in actual dollars. The simplification also allows us to solve integer, linear, and nonlinear programming problems that were heretofore unsolvable. These solutions are as easy to obtain as ones from theoretically solvable problems. The complexities or nonlinearities of the objective and/or constraint functions will not make any difference to the computer, even though they completely ruin the traditional simplex algorithm approach.

But, how difficult is this approach really and how useful is it? These are valid questions which should be answered. It is necessary to have a knowledge of FORTRAN (we used FORTRAN IV) up to the point where the programmer understands DO-loops. A knowledge of subscripted variables would also be helpful, especially for the optimization problems with hundreds of variables.

Absolutely no mathematical background is required other than knowing that an equation is something with an equals sign and variables connected in some fashion through addition, subtraction, multiplication, and division signs. It is never necessary to analyze the particular equation to see if it meets certain conditions such as linearity. The system of equations and constraints never needs to be tested for redundancy or cycling as in traditional methods. In fact, the less a person knows theoretically about the system to be optimized the better. That way there won't be the temptation to try other methods.

This does not mean to imply that the very considerable, elegant, and useful mathematical programming theory developed to date is not useful. On the contrary, this area has been one of the most useful and practically productive areas of mathematics for years. Certainly anyone who is an expert in these techniques should continue to use and develop them. However, this book can help the expert by providing a method for obtaining a good answer quickly to the numerous theoretically unsolvable problems that arise in applications.

Also, the computer technique that is explained and illustrated in this book should make available optimization solutions to people who have little or no time to develop theoretical expertise in mathematical programming, specifically, business managers, beginning business students, advanced business students whose expertise is not in quantitative areas, engineers who don't concentrate on optimization, administrators, accountants, scientists, researchers, small businessmen, decision makers working on any quantitative project, and people who never liked mathematics because it was too difficult.

This book is not an attack on theoretical mathematics (my favorite subject) but merely the result of a realization that computer technology has made possible, in just the last few years, the simplification and advancement of an extremely complicated and useful area of applied mathematics by taking a different philosophical approach to mathematical programming.

This book is divided into two parts. Conceptually, they are almost the same. Part One allows us to solve problems with a small number of variables, while the second part allows us to deal with problems that have a great many variables. We will write many programs in Part One to illustrate the technique and obtain the solutions to our stated questions. This will also serve to reinforce the technique and show a variety of applications. However, it is really only necessary to understand one problem somewhere along the way because the technique is the same in each case. We are letting the computer do the difficult work. The same is true in Part Two. One really needs to understand only a few programs (dozens are presented) to understand the technique.

Lastly, an attempt is made to explain everything completely, thoroughly, and repeatedly. This is to make the book and the solution of mathematical programming problems accessible to most everyone. Therefore, readers having an extensive background in mathematics and programming can just move at their own pace through the discussion.

In fact, it is quite possible to understand this book completely in a short period of time. But, in these days of increasing sophistication and complication, maybe this will be helpful. I hope so.

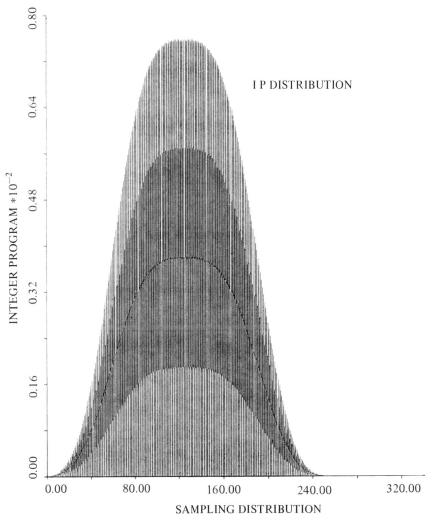

I P DISTRIBUTION

SAMPLING DISTRIBUTION

of $P = x_1 + 3x_2 + 4x_3 + 5x_4 + 12x_5$ subject to $0 \leqslant x_i \leqslant 10$ $i = 1, 5$

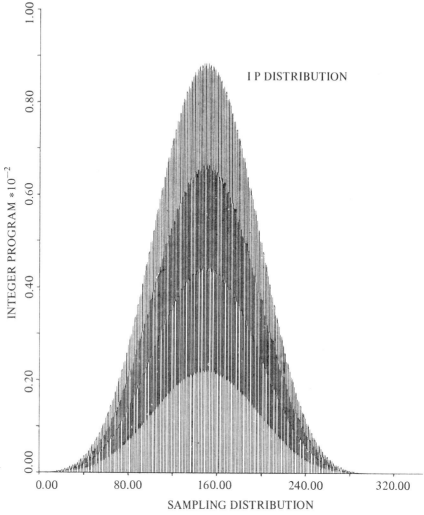

I P DISTRIBUTION

INTEGER PROGRAM $*10^{-2}$

SAMPLING DISTRIBUTION

of $P = 4x_1 + 5x_2 + 6x_3 + 7x_4 + 8x_5$ subject to $0 \leqslant x_i \leqslant 10$ $i = 1, 5$

Part One

CHAPTER 1

Optimization in the Computer Age

Mathematically, at least in our context, optimization means to find the maximum of a function or process that we want to maximize or to find the minimum of a function or process that we want to minimize. For example, we might wish to maximize a profit function or an output function of a process. Or, we might wish to minimize a cost function. Let's look at a few examples.

Suppose a company manufactures two products, A and B. Let x be the number of units of A produced and y the number of units of B produced. Suppose further that each unit of A returns a profit of two dollars and each unit of B returns a profit of three dollars. Therefore, the profit function would be written

$$P = 2x + 3y$$

where P is the profit in dollars.

Now, the question might naturally arise, how do we maximize this equation? Well, as stated the equation allows any values for x and y, therefore, it is only necessary to produce as much of A and B as possible to maximize P. P becomes infinitely large as either x or y or both go to infinity.

However, let's add a few restrictions to the variables x and y. Let's assume that the company's position is such that x must be between 0 and 10 inclusive, and y must be between 0 and 10 inclusive. In symbols this is $0 \leq x \leq 10$ and $0 \leq y \leq 10$. Let's further assume that x and y can only take integer values. This means that each possible x and y value must be a counting number or the negative of a counting number or zero. Equations to be optimized whose solution coordinates are restricted to integers (usually nonnegative integers in practical problems) are called integer programming problems. If we allow solutions that are not integer valued, like $x = .666, y = 7.5$, then we have a linear programming problem or a nonlinear noninteger programming problem. We, of course, can have a nonlinear integer programming problem. This is a problem in which either the function to be optimized and/or the constraints (conditions or restrictions) on the variables are nonlinear (they have squared and cubed terms, etc.). Also, in a nonlinear integer programming problem only integer coordinate solutions are allowed.

This book will deal mainly with integer programming problems (whole number coordinates for the solutions). But, fortunately, most applied problems require integer solutions. These are more difficult and sometimes almost impossible to solve theoretically. Later we hope to present a case for using integer solutions even in most cases where noninteger solutions are acceptable.

Getting back to our function to maximize, let us state the integer programming problem as maximize $P = 2x + 3y$ subject to $0 \leq x \leq 10$, $0 \leq y \leq 10$, and x and y must be integers. Therefore, let's look at the x and y pairs that are possibilities for the optimum. The following points are the only ones that satisfy the constraints:

(0,0) (1,0) (2,0) (3,0) (4,0) (5,0) (6,0) (7,0) (8,0) (9,0) (10,0)

(0,1) (1,1) (2,1) (3,1) (4,1) (5,1) (6,1) (7,1) (8,1) (9,1) (10,1)

(0,2) (1,2) (2,2) (3,2) (4,2) (5,2) (6,2) (7,2) (8,2) (9,2) (10,2)

(0,3) (1,3) (2,3) (3,3) (4,3) (5,3) (6,3) (7,3) (8,3) (9,3) (10,3)

(0,4) (1,4) (2,4) (3,4) (4,4) (5,4) (6,4) (7,4) (8,4) (9,4) (10,4)

(0,5) (1,5) (2,5) (3,5) (4,5) (5,5) (6,5) (7,5) (8,5) (9,5) (10,5)

(0,6) (1,6) (2,6) (3,6) (4,6) (5,6) (6,6) (7,6) (8,6) (9,6) (10,6)

(0,7) (1,7) (2,7) (3,7) (4,7) (5,7) (6,7) (7,7) (8,7) (9,7) (10,7)

(0,8) (1,8) (2,8) (3,8) (4,8) (5,8) (6,8) (7,8) (8,8) (9,8) (10,8)

(0,9) (1,9) (2,9) (3,9) (4,9) (5,9) (6,9) (7,9) (8,9) (9,9) (10,9)

(0,10) (1,10) (2,10) (3,10) (4,10) (5,10) (6,10) (7,10) (8,10) (9,10) (10,10)

Let's solve this problem by listing the 121 possible ordered pairs with their resultant P value in each case and then merely select the one that gives the largest value for P.

Possible points (amounts of A and B to be made) are sometimes called feasible solutions.

Points	$P = 2x + 3y$ value	Points (continued)	$P = 2x + 3y$ value (continued)
(0,0)	0	(8,3)	25
(1,0)	2	(9,3)	27
(2,0)	4	(10,3)	29
(3,0)	6	(0,4)	12
(4,0)	8	(1,4)	14
(5,0)	10	(2,4)	16
(6,0)	12	(3,4)	18
(7,0)	14	(4,4)	20
(8,0)	16	(5,4)	22
(9,0)	18	(6,4)	24
(10,0)	20	(7,4)	26
(0,1)	3	(8,4)	28
(1,1)	5	(9,4)	30
(2,1)	7	(10,4)	32
(3,1)	9	(0,5)	15
(4,1)	11	(1,5)	17
(5,1)	13	(2,5)	19
(6,1)	15	(3,5)	21
(7,1)	17	(4,5)	23
(8,1)	19	(5,5)	25
(9,1)	21	(6,5)	27
(10,1)	23	(7,5)	29
(0,2)	6	(8,5)	31
(1,2)	8	(9,5)	33
(2,2)	10	(10,5)	35
(3,2)	12	(0,6)	18
(4,2)	14	(1,6)	20
(5,2)	16	(2,6)	22
(6,2)	18	(3,6)	24
(7,2)	20	(4,6)	26
(8,2)	22	(5,6)	28
(9,2)	24	(6,6)	30
(10,2)	26	(7,6)	32
(0,3)	9	(8,6)	34
(1,3)	11	(9,6)	36
(2,3)	13	(10,6)	38
(3,3)	15	(0,7)	21
(4,3)	17	(1,7)	23
(5,3)	19	(2,7)	25
(6,3)	21	(3,7)	27
(7,3)	23		

Points (continued)	$P = 2x + 3y$ value (continued)	Points (continued	$P = 2x + 3y$ value (continued)
(4,7)	29	(2,9)	31
(5,7)	31	(3,9)	33
(6,7)	33	(4,9)	35
(7,7)	35	(5,9)	37
(8,7)	37	(6,9)	39
(9,7)	39	(7,9)	41
(10,7)	41	(8,9)	43
(0,8)	24	(9,9)	45
(1,8)	26	(10,9)	47
(2,8)	28	(0,10)	30
(3,8)	30	(1,10)	32
(4,8)	32	(2,10)	34
(5,8)	34	(3,10)	36
(6,8)	36	(4,10)	38
(7,8)	38	(5,10)	40
(8,8)	40	(6,10)	42
(9,8)	42	(7,10)	44
(10,8)	44	(8,10)	46
(0,9)	27	(9,10)	48
(1,9)	29	(10,10)	50

We can see that, as expected, the optimum solution (the one that maximizes the profit is $x = 10$ units of A and $y = 10$ units of B.

This may seem like a lot of work to obtain this rather obvious result. However, it should be noted that conceptually it is an easy approach, namely, just examine all possible points. Also, it will always lead to the correct answer. This will be especially useful when the function to be maximized or minimized and/or the constraints are sufficiently complicated so that the solution is difficult to obtain either by inspection or through mathematical theory. This is frequently the case in applications.

Of course, the approach we take, namely, listing all possible solutions, is extremely tedious for people even though it is straightforward. However, a computer just loves repetitive, tedious work and will produce the answer in seconds. And as the speed and capacity of computers increase this technique will become more and more practical.

Let's look at another example. Try to minimize the cost equation $C = 2x^2 - y^2 + xy$ where x can take the values between 0 and 5 and y can take the values between 0 and 5, and x and y must be integers. The possible points meeting the constraints are as follows:

(0,0) (1,0) (2,0) (3,0) (4,0) (5,0)
(0,1) (1,1) (2,1) (3,1) (4,1) (5,1)
(0,2) (1,2) (2,2) (3,2) (4,2) (5,2)
(0,3) (1,3) (2,3) (3,3) (4,3) (5,3)
(0,4) (1,4) (2,4) (3,4) (4,4) (5,4)
(0,5) (1,5) (2,5) (3,5) (4,5) (5,5)

Let's list the possible points (combinations of x and y) along with the corresponding $C = 2x^2 - y^2 + xy$ value and take the points which produce the minimum. There are 36 possibilities:

Points	$C = 2x^2 - y^2 + xy$ value	Points (continued)	$C = 2x^2 - y^2 + xy$ value (continued)
(0,0)	0		
(1,0)	2	(1,3)	-4
(2,0)	8	(2,3)	5
(3,0)	18	(3,3)	18
(4,0)	32	(4,3)	35
(5,0)	50	(5,3)	56
(0,1)	-1	(0,4)	-16
(1,1)	2	(1,4)	-10
(2,1)	9	(2,4)	0
(3,1)	20	(3,4)	14
(4,1)	35	(4,4)	32
(5,1)	54	(5,4)	54
(0,2)	-4	(0,5)	-25
(1,2)	0	(1,5)	-18
(2,2)	8	(2,5)	-7
(3,2)	20	(3,5)	8
(4,2)	36	(4,5)	27
(5,2)	56	(5,5)	50
(0,3)	-9		

We can see that the optimum solution (the one that minimizes the cost) is $x = 0$ and $y = 5$. This yields a C value of -25.

Now, let's try to maximize $P = 3x^2 - 2y$ where x and y must be nonnegative integers and, further, they must satisfy $y \leq -.5x + 5$ and $y \leq -2x + 10$. A graph of the related equalities is given in Figure 1.1. The shaded region shows the area that satisfies the inequalities. Generally speaking, with an inequality of the form $y \leq mx + b$ the solution is the half plane below the line $y = mx + b$. This is the case here. Let's now list the integer combinations that satisfy the constraints along with their corresponding function values and take the coordinates that give us a maximum P under the constraints:

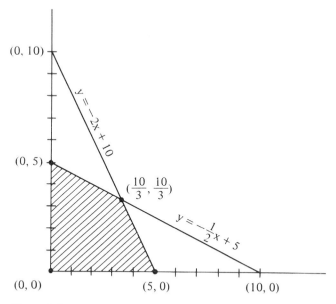

Figure 1.1

Points	$P = 3x^2 - 2y$ value		Points	$P = 3x^2 - 2y$ value
(0,0)	0		(1,2)	-1
(1,0)	3		(2,2)	8
(2,0)	12		(3,2)	23
(3,0)	27		(4,2)	44
(4,0)	48		(0,3)	-6
(5,0)	75		(1,3)	-3
(0,1)	-2		(2,3)	6
(1,1)	1		(3,3)	21
(2,1)	10		(0,4)	-8
(3,1)	25		(1,4)	-5
(4,1)	46		(2,4)	4
(0,2)	-4		(0,5)	-10

We can see that the maximum of P occurs at (5,0). We get a P value of 75 for that point. Therefore, this is the solution to the integer programming problem:

Maximize $P = 3x^2 - 2y$ subject to

$x \leq 0, y \leq 0, y \leq -2x + 10$ and $y \leq -.5x + 5$

Now, let's consider the integer programming system $P = 12x_1^2 + 17x_2^2 + 37x_3^2 + 18x_4^2 - 29x_5^2 + x_1x_3$ subject to

$x_1 \geq 0, \, x_2 \geq 0, \, x_3 \geq 0, \, x_4 \geq 0, \, x_5 \geq 0$

$x_1 + x_2 + x_3 + x_4 + x_5 \leq 400$

$x_1 + x_2 + x_3 \leq 200$

$x_1 + x_4 + x_5 \leq 300$

$18x_1^2 + 17x_5 \leq 1000$

Conceptually, we can take the same approach as before. This problem is extremely difficult, if not impossible, to solve theoretically. However, we could just list all the sets of five nonnegative integer points that satisfy the above constraints and evaluate P for each of these and take the set of five points that produces the largest value for the solution. So, conceptually, this is just as easy as the other examples although it might take dozens of hours to check and list all the right points. However, we can write a FORTRAN IV program in about five minutes that will easily search all of these points. And with the speed of computers increasing and the cost of computing time dropping dramatically, this is certainly one of the best approaches to take with these types of problems. It didn't used to be a practical approach but it is now.

We have available quite inexpensive minicomputers that sit around for hours each day not being used. They could be put to use solving these types of problems for virtually no cost at all, and the beauty of the approach of checking the points is that you always get an answer.

For those readers who may be thinking about what can be done if there are 20 or 200 variables with just too many feasible points (or feasible solutions) to check, Part Two will show how to get an answer to those problems, too.

Let's also keep in mind that we live in a world that increasingly puts constraints (inequalities, etc.) on our production or other operations. Therefore, it is more necessary to operate efficiently, and hence integer programming problems become very relevant and important. Also, this technique will increase even the efficiency of solving integer programming problems by making the very fast, efficient, and inexpensive computer do the inefficient part of the work. This will ultimately cut costs.

Review of FORTRAN IV

FORTRAN IV is probably the most popular and best version of FORTRAN, and it is the computer language that will be used in this book to solve integer programming problems. Therefore, it is recommended that the reader either be familiar with FORTRAN or, if not, become acquainted with it through one of the many fine texts available on the subject.

However, just for the purposes of review, and to try to illuminate our goals, let's discuss a few of the details of integer programming problems. We will also mention here that any language with loops, IF statements, and a random number generator would work in place of FORTRAN.

First of all, FORTRAN is short for *formula translation*. Its chief usefulness is its ability to evaluate any function or formula very quickly. It can also evaluate any formula for a large number of possible values in a very short time.

Therefore, let's assume that we have a profit function $P(x,y) = 7x^2 + 3x + 2xy - y^2 + 8y$ that depends on which combinations of x and y that we choose to use. Let's further assume that x can take the values 0, 1, 2 and 3, and y can take the values 0, 1, and 2. Therefore, there are $4 \times 3 = 12$ possible combinations that we can try in our effort to find the combination which yields the maximum profit.

The combinations are:

(x,y)
$(0,0)$
$(0,1)$
$(0,2)$
$(1,0)$
$(1,1)$
$(1,2)$
$(2,0)$
$(2,1)$
$(2,2)$
$(3,0)$
$(3,1)$
$(3,2)$

Now, it would take a bit of work to evaluate the profit function $P(x,y)$ for the twelve combinations of x and y. However, if we do this we can then compare the twelve resulting $P(x,y)$ values and note which one is the largest. We then can maximize our profit function by choosing the ordered pair (x and y combination) that yields this maximum profit value.

A computer programmed in FORTRAN could do the same thing we are attempting to do by hand, and it can do it about one million times faster than we can. So if the computer had to search 12 points or 12 million points for the maximum, it could do it quite easily. Also, with the revolution in minicomputers bringing 24 hours a day of computer power to the desk top of any manager, this idea of searching all possible points (or combinations) or a great many points is suddenly practical for the first time. The cost of this approach is essentially only the electricity required to run the minicomputers for the length of time necessary to find a good optimum value.

As an illustration, a typical integer programming problem that we worked out in the text checked 160,000 combinations of four different variables and calculated and stored the optimum solution in 18 seconds. The cost involved is so small it is hardly worth discussing, but the technique is.

Getting back to the profit function with the twelve possible combinations of x and

y, let's write a FORTRAN IV program to solve this question, while reviewing the rules of FORTRAN IV and keeping in mind that this approach can be adopted to any integer programming problem.

FORTRAN IV is a language that consists of a series of statements arranged vertically and executed sequentially from the top to the bottom, unless this order is interrupted by a command or control statement which orders the computer to proceed to a statement other than the next one. If this happens, the computer jumps to the statement as ordered and then proceeds sequentially until the direction of flow is changed by another command or it reaches the STOP and END statements at the conclusion of the program.

Any letter can be used for a variable. In fact, any sequence of up to six letters, numbers, and the dollar sign character can be used as variables. Equals signs are also used in FORTRAN IV. They order the computer to evaluate the function or relation on the right-hand side of the equals sign and assign that current value to the variable on the left. Also $+$, $-$, $/$, $*$, and $**$ are used for addition, subtraction, division, multiplication, and raising a variable to a power (exponentiation), respectively. Parentheses are used where necessary as in algebra. For example, if we wanted to evaluate $P(x,y) = 7x^2 + 3x + 2xy - y^2 + 8y$ for $x = 1$ and $y = 2$ and print x, y and $P(x,y)$, we could write it as follows in FORTRAN IV:

```
X=1
Y=2
PXY=7*X**2+3*X+2*X*Y-Y**2+8*Y
WRITE (6,3)X,Y,PXY          Just controls the form of the output.
3 FORMAT ('0',3E15.7)        Not essential to the logic
                             (see a FORTRAN text).
```

This would cause the computer to output 1, 2, and 26 which is the value of P for $x = 1$ and $y = 2$.

Now we would like to write a FORTRAN IV program to systematically search all twelve combinations of x and y and compare the $P(x,y)$ values and store the maximum value along with its x and y coordinates until the end of the program, and then print the optimum xy combination and the corresponding largest $P(x,y)$ value.

We will now write a complete FORTRAN IV program to do this and then go over it, introducing the few new statements used in it. The idea is this: we initialize a variable (call it PMAX) to be some very small value such that $P(x,y)$ will be greater than that value for all possible combinations of x and y. Then, we go through all possible combinations of x and y storing the combinations and P (the $P(x,y)$ value) when they produce a $P(x,y)$ value larger than all the previous values. When the program is through, it prints the x and y combination that produced the maximum plus the maximum $P(x,y)$ value which has been stored in the variable PMAX.

The program for this example is as follows:

```
INTEGER X,Y,PMAX,P
PMAX=-999999
DO 1 I=1,4
X=I-1
DO 1 J=1,3
Y=J-1
P=7*X**2+3*X+2*X*Y-Y**2+8*Y
IF(P.GT.PMAX) GO TO 2
GO TO 1
2   IX=X
    IY=Y
    PMAX=P
1   CONTINUE
    WRITE(6,3)IX,IY,PMAX
3   FORMAT('0',3I10)
    STOP
    END
```

Statement 1 declares x, y, pmax, and p to be integer variables. This means that only whole number values will be assigned to them. Any fractional or decimal part of the number will be dropped. However, the function deals only with whole numbers and its $P(x,y)$ values are only whole numbers for the 12 xy combinations, therefore, no accuracy is lost.

Statement 2 initializes pmax to be an extremely small number so that the first calculated $P(x,y)$ value (called P in the program) will be larger than the initial pmax value.

Statements 3 through 13 comprise a do-loop. Essentially, this tells the computer to proceed sequentially from statement 3 to 13 (of course, jumping around as ordered, also) four times. In other words, with I = 1 the computer goes from 3 to 4...13. Then with I = 2 the computer goes from 3 to 4...13. Then with I = 3 the computer goes from 3 to 4...13. And finally with I = 4, the computer goes from 3 to 4...13. While this is taking place, there is another do-loop inside the above outer one. This runs from statement 5 to statement 13. The effect of this loop is that it forces the computer to go from statement 5 to 13 (for J = 1,2 and 3) three times whenever it goes through the outer loop once. Therefore, the inner loop gets done 4 times 3, or 12 times. This allows the program to check all ordered pairs for the optimum profit value.

Statements 4 and 6 arrange to have x be 0, 1, 2, and 3, while y is changing from 0 to 1 to 2 as desired in our question.

Statement 7 evaluates the function in fortran iv and assigns the current value to P.

Statement 8 checks to see if the current value of P is greater than the current value of pmax. If it is, then it is a possible maximum value and it follows the command go to 2 and jumps to the storage space

```
IX = X
IY = Y
PMAX = P
```

which stores the current value of *x,y* and PMAX (possible optimum points). Then, it proceeds with the next loop. However, if P is not greater than the current value of PMAX statement 8 is false; therefore, the command GO TO 2 is ignored and the program goes to the next statement, GO TO 1, which skips over the storage space (statements 10 to 12) and continues with the next loop.

The result is that all 12 ordered pairs are checked to see if they produce a $P(x,y)$ value larger than any previous ones. If they do, the *x* and *y* and current maximum P value are stored in IX, IY and PMAX, respectively, as follows:

```
IX = X
IY = Y
PMAX = P
```

So at the end of the program, the current optimum solution (which is stored) is the true optimum because all points have been checked.

Statements 14 and 15 arrange to print the maximum solution.

Statements 16 and 17 just stop the program. These are used at the end of a FORTRAN IV program.

Now, if the conditions of the practical problem were such that *x* could take the values $0,1,2,\ldots,3999$, while *y* ranged through the values $0,1,2,\ldots,2999$, then we would have 12 million points to check instead of 12. This could be accomplished by changing DO 1 I = 1,4 to DO 1 I = 1,4000 and changing DO 1 J = 1,3 to DO 1 J = 1,3000. That's all that needs to be done.

The thoughtful reader may be wondering about this approach if we had, say, 20 variables and 100 possible values for each variable. Then we would have 100^{20} combinations of 20 variables to check. Even on the world's fastest computer this would take years. This is a valid question and the second part of the book will demonstrate how to get a solution in those cases. There are ways around that problem. Although this was not the case a few years ago, today if you can write the optimization problem down on paper, it should be a simple matter to optimize the function in question. This text will devote itself to that subject.

CHAPTER 2

Solving Integer Programming Problems by Looking at All Possibilities

Now, let's look at an example, write the FORTRAN IV program, and actually run it to get the solution. We will run our programs on an IBM 360-65 computer. However, virtually any minicomputer or regular computer could do the job.

We seek to maximize $P = 3x^2 + 2y$ subject to $x \geq 0$, $y \geq 0$, and $3x + 12y \leq 50$. Notice that it is not necessary to analyze the function or the constraints. Merely write the program and let the computer do the work. The program should consist of the following parts:

Declaration statements

Initialization statements

DO-loops to check all the points. One loop for each variable

The constraints

Objective or profit function

Line to compare this profit value with the maximum so far

Storage for the current optimum solution

Printing statements to output the answer

Maximize $P = 3x^2 + 2y$ subject to $x \geq 0$, $y \geq 0$, and $3x + 12y \leq 50$:

```
      INTEGER X,Y,PMAX,P
      PMAX=0
      DO 1 I=1,51
      X=I-1
      DO 1 J=1,51
      Y=J-1
      IF(3*X+12*Y.GT.50) GO TO 1
      P=3*X**2+2*Y
      IF(P.GT.PMAX) GO TO 2
      GO TO 1
    2 IX=X
      IY=Y
      PMAX=P
    1 CONTINUE
      WRITE(6,3)IX,IY,PMAX
    3 FORMAT('0',3I10)
      STOP
      END
```

```
THE PRINTOUT IS

16    0     768
```

The solution is:

$x = 16$, $y = 0$, and maximum $P = 768$

Statement 1 declares x, y, pmax and p to be integer variables (they take only whole number values).

Statement 2 declares pmax to be initially a value so small that at least one (and usually about all) P value will be greater than pmax causing statement 9 to be true and hence storing a solution in the storage area

```
IX = X
IY = Y
PMAX = P
```

The thing to avoid is setting pmax initially equal to a value that is larger than the true maximum. This would ruin the program. Therefore, always make pmax very small in a maximization problem.

Statements 3 through 14 set up a double DO-loop (one for each variable) to examine all the ordered pairs $(0,0)$, $(0,1)$, $(0,2)$, ..., $(0,50)$, $(1,0)$, $(1,1)$, $(1,2)$, ..., $(1,50)$, ..., $(50,50)$ to find the optimum solution. It was decided to check the numbers from 0 to 50 because the constraint $3x + 12y \leq 50$ immediately rules out any number larger than 50. Statement 3 fixes I at 1, and statement 4 changes this to $X = 0$. (DO statements must start with a nonzero whole number.) Then with X fixed at 0, Y goes from 0 to 50 as the inner loop (statements 5 through 14) is executed 51 times. Each time Y has a different value, namely, $0, 1, 2, 3, \ldots, 50$. Each time at statement 7 the program checks to see if $3x + 12y$ is greater than 50. If it is, then it doesn't satisfy the constraint $3x + 12y \leq 50$ so the program goes to statement 1 and continues with the next Y value.

If $3x + 12y$ is less than or equal to 50, then statement 7 is false and, therefore, the computer just proceeds to the next statement and evaluates the P function for that particular ordered pair. Then statement 9 checks to see if this current value of P is greater than the current PMAX value. If it is, then the computer jumps to the storage area and stores this solution in IX, IY, and PMAX, because this is the largest P value so far. If P is less than the current PMAX value, then it is not a candidate for the true optimum; consequently, when statement 9 indicates this by being false, the computer proceeds to statement 10 which tells it to jump over the storage area and then the program continues with the next pair. Each time a new value for X comes up in the outer loop, the inner loop is executed 51 times (for $Y = 0, 1, 2, \ldots, 50$) allowing the computer to check all possible ordered pairs. This is a little like the inner loop being the tenths register and the outer loop being the miles register on the odometer in an automobile. The inner loop is performed 51 times every time the outer loop is done once. Therefore, because the outer loop is done 51 times, the inner loop is done 51 x 51 times, checking all possible ordered pairs from $(0,0)$ $(0,1), \ldots, (50,50)$.

Statements 15 and 16 output the solution from the storage area

```
IX = X
IY = Y
PMAX = P
```

The storage area always stores the current optimum (the best solution so far). Therefore, at the end of the loops when the WRITE statement outputs the "best solution so far," it is the true optimum because all possibilities have been checked before the program ever gets to the WRITE statement.

Notice that the actual equations and constraints don't have to be checked for degeneracy or redundancy or nonlinearity which might interfere with traditional theoretical methods of solution. We quite literally just put the integer programming problem in the program and let it run. Not much analysis is required.

If we want to consider the constraint $3x + 12y \leq 50$, notice that 3 into 50 equals 16.67 so x can't be any larger than 16 or $3x + 12y$ will be greater than 50. Similarly, 12 into 50 equals 4.17 so y can't be any larger than 4 or $3x + 12y$ will be greater than 50. Therefore, we can shorten the loops on the preceding problem to 17 for X (for $X = 0, 1, 2, \ldots, 16$) and 5 for Y (for $Y = 0, 1, 2, 3$, and 4). We present the program below:

```
INTEGER X,Y,PMAX,P
PMAX=0
DO 1 I=1,17
X=I-1
DO 1 J=1,5
Y=J-1
IF(3*X+12*Y.GT.50) GO TO 1
P=3*X**2+2*Y
IF(P.GT.PMAX) GO TO 2
GO TO 1
2   IX=X
    IY=Y
    PMAX=P
1   CONTINUE
    WRITE(6,3)IX,IY,PMAX
3   FORMAT('0',3I10)
    STOP
    END


THE PRINTOUT IS

16    0    768
```

The solution is:

$x = 16$, $y = 0$, and maximum $P = 768$

This cuts the execution time to about 3 percent of the time in the previous run. However, in this case both execution times were a very small fraction of a second so the efficiency steps weren't necessary. Later, in problems with many variables this analysis and efficiency procedure might save much computer time. It was presented here for that reason.

Let's now maximize $P = 10x + 4xy + 9y^2$ subject to $x \geq 0$, $0 \leq y \leq 8$, and $6x^2 + 10y^2 \leq 850$. 850 divided by 6 equals 141.67, and the square root of 141.67 is 11.9. Therefore, x can't be any larger than 11 or $6x^2 + 10y^2$ will be greater than 850; y is already restricted to at most 8. We present the program below:

```
INTEGER X,Y,PMAX,P
PMAX=0
DO 1 I=1,12
X=I-1
DO 1 J=1,9
Y=J-1
IF(6*X**2+10*Y**2.GT.850) GO TO 1
P=10*X+4*X*Y+9*Y**2
IF(P.GT.PMAX) GO TO 2
GO TO 1
```

```
2   IX=X
    IY=Y
    PMAX=P
1   CONTINUE
    WRITE(6,3)IX,IY,PMAX
3   FORMAT('0',3I10)
    STOP
    END


    THE PRINTOUT IS

    5      8      786
```

The solution is:

$x = 5, y = 8$, and maximum $P = 786$

As before, statement 1 declares the four variables to be integers. Statement 2 sets PMAX to be a value smaller than the true maximum (in this case zero, which is a good value to use in most practical maximization problems). Statements 3 through 14 comprise the outer loop which varies X from 0 to 1, to 2 through 11, while the inner loop (in statements 5 through 14) varies Y from 0 through 8 for each of the X values. Statement 7 checks to see if the constraint $6x^2 + 10y^2 \leq 850$ is satisfied. If it is not satisfied, the program jumps to the end of the loop (GO TO 1 takes the program to statement 14). If the constraint is satisfied (statement 7 is false), then the program proceeds to statement 8 where the P function is evaluated. Then statement 9 checks to see if the P value is the largest so far. If it is, the GO TO 2 orders the program to line 11 where the current optimum is stored. Then the program is at the bottom of the loop so it returns to the start for a new ordered pair. If the P value is less than or equal to the current PMAX value, then statement 9 is false and so the program proceeds to statement 10 where the program follows GO TO 1 and jumps over the storage area to the end of the loop. Then the program continues to the top of the loop and proceeds with the next ordered pair.

Notice that the FORTRAN variables X, Y, PMAX and P were selected just for convenience. P is perhaps short for profits, PMAX is short for maximum profit, and x and Y represent the two variables. However, any sequence of up to six letters, numbers, and dollar sign can be used as a variable as long as the variable doesn't start with a number. This is up to the person who writes the program. However, using variables that are somewhat descriptive of what the program is designed to do can be helpful.

Note, however, that the structure of these programs and the ones to follow for any integer programming problem are basically the same. They consist of:

Declaration statements—mainly to declare what variables are to be integers. In FORTRAN this means that any value (not already an integer) will be rounded down to the nearest whole number before being assigned to that integer variable. No fractions or decimals are allowed.

Initialization statements—usually just assigns a very small value to the eventual maximum P value (say PMAX) or a very large number to the eventual minimum cost value (or whatever is being minimized).

DO-loops—to check all of the possible points. One loop for each variable. Each loop is to be completely nested inside the loop outside of it. If loops end on the same statement line, this is considered nested as long as they started as nested loops with the same DO number (for example, DO 1 followed later by another DO 1).

Constraints—these should be reversed in FORTRAN so that if any one is not satisfied the program jumps to the end of the loop. This way if there are a series of constraints, only when they are all satisfied will the possible (feasible) points get to the function evaluation stage.

Objective function (profit or cost, etc.) to be optimized.

Comparison statement—checks to see if the current function value is the optimum so far.

Storage—for the current optimum solution. Stores both the coordinates and the current optimum value.

Printing statements—a statement or statements to output the answer.

Let's look at another example. Maximize $P = e^{(x + .25y)} + xy + x^2$ subject to $x \geq 0$, $y \geq 0$, $x^2 + y \leq 200$, and $x + 4y \leq 50$. The constraint $x^2 + y \leq 200$ also tells us ($\sqrt{200} = 14.14$) that x can be no larger than 14. The constraint $x + 4y \leq 50$ also tells us that x can be no larger than 50. Therefore, the smaller of the two is 14. So we shall set up the x loop so that x goes from 0 to 14. The program is presented below.

```
      INTEGER X,Y
      PMAX=0
      DO 1 I=1,15
      X=I-1
      DO 1 J=1,13
      Y=J-1
      IF(X**2+Y.GT.200) GO TO 1
      IF(X+4*Y.GT.50) GO TO 1
      P=EXP(X+.25*Y)+X*Y+X**2
      IF(P.GT.PMAX) GO TO 2
      GO TO 1
2     IX=X
      IY=Y
      PMAX=P
1     CONTINUE
      WRITE(6,3)IX,IY,PMAX
```

```
3   FORMAT('0',I10,I10,F15.7)
    STOP
    END


    THE PRINTOUT IS

    13   9   4197787
```

The solution is:

$x = 13$, $y = 9$, and maximum $P = 4,197,787$

Notice that the inner loop is run $15 \times 13 = 195$ times—one time each for each of the 195 possible solution ordered pairs from $(0,0)$, $(0,1), \ldots ,(14,12)$. Lines 7 and 8 form the bank of constraints. They are reversed so that if the constraint values exceed 200 or 50, respectively, the program jumps to the end of the loop skipping that ordered pair. However, if both constraints are satisfied, the computer proceeds sequentially from statement 7 to 8 to 9 and evaluates the function and proceeds. Remember that when a comparison statement is false the computer automatically proceeds to the next statement.

All the programs run so far have taken a very small fraction of a second to compute the optimum answer. Also, in the previous program the computer had no difficulty in handling a nonlinear objective function $e^{(x + .25y)} + xy + x^2$ with a nonlinear constraint, $x^2 + y \leq 200$. This would not be an easy job theoretically. The computer thinks all optimization problems are solvable—and the computer is right!

Let's try to maximize $P = 2x + 7y$ subject to $x \geq 0$, $y \geq 0$, $x + 4y \leq 32$, and $x \geq 2y$. The constraint $x + 4y \leq 32$ tells us that x can't be any larger than 32 and y can't be any larger than 8. Be sure to reverse the constraints in the bank of constraints section of the program. $x + 4y \leq 32$ is written as IF(X+4*Y.GT.32) GO TO 1. $x \geq 2y$ is written as IF(X.LT.2*Y) GO TO 1. (.GT. means greater than and .LT. means less than in FORTRAN.) The program is presented below:

```
    INTEGER X,Y,PMAX,P
    PMAX=0
    DO 1 I=1,33
    X=I-1
    DO 1 J=1,9
    Y=J-1
    IF(X+4*Y.GT.32) GO TO 1
    IF(X.LT.2*Y) GO TO 1
    P=2*X+7*Y
    IF(P.GT.PMAX) GO TO 2
    GO TO 1
2   IX=X
```

```
      IY=Y
      PMAX=P
1     CONTINUE
      WRITE(6,3)IX,IY,PMAX
3     FORMAT('0',3I10)
      STOP
      END
```

```
      THE PRINTOUT IS

      32    0    64
```

The solution is:

$x = 32, y = 0$, and maximum $P = 64$

Again, the structure of the program is the same as the others. Just the objective function and the constraints are different. Also, except for finding the limits for x and y, no analysis of the problem is necessary.

Let's maximize $P = 17x - y + y^2$ subject to $x \geq 0, y \geq 0, x + y \leq 30, 2x + 7y \leq 55$, and $13x + 2y + xy \leq 100$. X can't be any larger than 7 because of $13x + 2y + xy \leq 100$, as 13 into 100 equals 7.69. Y can't be any larger than 7 because of $2x + 7y \leq 55$, as 7 into 55 equals 7.86. These facts are reflected in the program. Also PMAX is assigned a number much less than zero because the minus sign in the P function leaves some doubt as to whether or not the optimum will be nonnegative.

```
      INTEGER X,Y,PMAX,P
      PMAX=-999999
      DO 1 I=1,8
      X=I-1
      DO 1 J=1,8
      Y=J-1
      IF(X+Y.GT.30) GO TO 1
      IF(2*X+7*Y.GT.55) GO TO 1
      IF(13*X+2*Y+X*Y.GT.100) GO TO 1
      P=17*X-Y+Y**2
      IF(P.GT.PMAX) GO TO 2
      GO TO 1
2     IX=X
      IY=Y
      PMAX=P
1     CONTINUE
      WRITE(6,3)IX,IY,PMAX
3     FORMAT('0',3I10)
      STOP
      END
```

```
THE PRINTOUT IS

7     0     119
```

The solution is:

$x = 7, y = 0$, and maximum $P = 119$

Again, the IF(P.GT.PMAX) GO TO 2 insures that the largest P value (and the coordinates that produced it) will be stored in the storage section and printed at the conclusion of the program as the true optimum solution.

EXERCISES

2.1. Maximize $P = 19x_1^2 + 3x_2$ subject to $x_1 \geq 0$, $x_2 \geq 0$, and $10x_1 + 3x_2 \leq 300$.

2.2. $P = 2x_1 + 5x_1x_2^3$ subject to $x_1 \geq 0$, $x_2 \geq 0$, $x_1 + x_2 \leq 100$, and $4x_1 + x_2 \leq 150$. Maximize P.

2.3. Maximize $C = 2x_1 + 7x_2 + 8x_3^4$ subject to $0 \leq x_1 \leq 50$, $0 \leq x_2 \leq 50$, $0 \leq x_3 \leq 50$, $x_1 + x_2 + x_3 \leq 120$, $2x_1 + 4x_2 + 7x_3 \leq 400$, and $x_1^2 + 5x_2 \leq 800$.

CHAPTER 3

Optimization Problems of Two through Eight Variables

The previous chapter presented a series of programs designed to solve integer programming problems of two variables. Let's now look at an example of a three-variable problem and realize that we still take the same approach except now we use three nested loops (one for each variable) to search all the possible solutions to find the optimum. Keeping this in mind, let's maximize $P = 14x + 5y + 2z$ subject to $x \geq 0$, $y \geq 0$, $z \geq 0$, $3x + 2y + 4z \leq 100$, $x + 7y + 28z \leq 200$, and $6x + y + 4z \leq 100$.

```
INTEGER X,Y,Z,PMAX,P
PMAX=0
DO 1 I=1,201
X=I-1
DO 1 J=1,101
Y=J-1
DO 1 K=1,26
Z=K-1
IF(3*X+2*Y+4*Z.GT.100) GO TO 1
IF(X+7*Y+28*Z.GT.200) GO TO 1
```

```
      IF(6*X+Y+4*Z.GT.100) GO TO 1
      P=14*X+5*Y+2*Z
      IF(P.GT.PMAX) GO TO 2
      GO TO 1
    2 IX=X
      IY=Y
      IZ=Z
      PMAX=P
    1 CONTINUE
      WRITE(6,3)IX,IY,IZ,PMAX
    3 FORMAT('0',4I10)
      STOP
      END


      THE PRINTOUT IS

    12    26    0    298
```

The solution is:

$x = 12$, $y = 26$, $z = 0$, and maximum $P = 298$

Notice that this time the author neglected to investigate the constraints to see that the upper limits on x, y, and z were 16, 28, and 7, respectively. Therefore, the computer was programmed to go to larger limits. However, it still threw out all of the irrelevant points and found the true optimum. In a larger problem (five or ten variables) this might have added a lot of computer time. But in this problem it really made no difference. The only real error to guard against is setting the limits on the variables to be too small so that some feasible solutions are left out. When in doubt, make the limits high. However, with a little thought, the limits on the variables can be determined quite accurately.

With the three nested loops (one for each variable), the outer loop value ascends the slowest. The middle loop value is next, and the inner loop value ascends the fastest. So, in this case, I is fixed at 1, J is fixed at 1, and K goes from 1 to 26. Then I is fixed at 1, J is upped to 2, and K goes from 1 to 26. Then I is fixed at 1, J is upped to 3, and K goes from 1 to 26. This continues until all combinations have been run through. Of course, X = I − 1, Y = J − 1, and Z = K − 1 because we want to consider the points with zeros in them, and in FORTRAN the DO-loops have to start with a positive whole number (not zero). That is just a rule of FORTRAN, so the subtracting of 1 is a device to get around it.

Next, let's minimize $C = 3x + 8y$ subject to $x \geq 0$, $y \geq 0$, $2x + 3y \geq 21$, $x + 3y \geq 16$, $x \leq 40$, and $y \leq 50$. The program and discussion are given below:

```
    INTEGER X,Y,CMIN,C
    CMIN=999999
    DO 1 I=1,41
    X=I-1
    DO 1 J=1,51
    Y=J-1
    IF(2*X+3*Y.LT.21) GO TO 1
    IF(X+3*Y.LT.16) GO TO 1
    C=3*X+8*Y
    IF(C.LT.CMIN) GO TO 2
    GO TO 1
  2 IX=X
    IY=Y
    CMIN=C
  1 CONTINUE
    WRITE(6,3)IX,IY,CMIN
  3 FORMAT('0',3I10)
    STOP
    END


    THE PRINTOUT IS

    7    3    45
```

The solution is:

$x = 7$, $y = 3$, and minimum $C = 45$

Line 1 declares x, y, CMIN, and c to be integer variables. Statement 2 sets CMIN (the variable which will eventually store the minimum cost value) to be a very large number. The loops consider the following ordered pairs: (0,0), (0,1), (0,2),..., (0,50), (1,0), (1,1), (1,2),..., (1,50), (2,0), (2,1), (2,2),..., (2,50),..., (40,50). The first of these pairs to satisfy the constraints of $2x + 3y \geq 21$ and $x + 3y \geq 16$ will get to line 9 and evaluate the C function. Then line 10 compares this C function value with the current value of CMIN which is 999,999. Therefore, C will be smaller so the program follows GO TO 2 and stores the C value in CMIN (along with the X,Y values that produced C) erasing 999,999. This process continues and each time a C value is less than the currently stored CMIN value (the minimum so far) the program jumps to the storage area and stores the new minimum. Finally, at the end of the program the current stored minimum is the true minimum because all possible solutions have been considered.

This approach is exactly like the procedure to maximize a function except that here we go through all the solutions and find the minimum, and in the maximize case we find the maximum.

Now, let's look at a three-variable integer programming maximization problem. Maximize $P = 2x + 2y + 5z$ subject to $x \geq 0$, $y \geq 0$, $z \geq 0$, $x + 2y + 3z \leq 25$, $x + y + z \leq 22$, $x + y \leq 15$, and $x + z \leq 20$. Because of $x + 2y + 3z \leq 25$, y cannot exceed 12. And because of $x + 2y + 3z \leq 25$, z can't exceed 8. Also, we use three nested loops (one for each variable) and we reverse all the constraints to greater than (.GT. in FORTRAN) to skip over ordered triples that don't meet the constraints. The program follows:

```
      INTEGER X,Y,Z,PMAX,P
      PMAX=0
      DO 1 I=1,16
      X=I-1
      DO 1 J=1,13
      Y=J-1
      DO 1 K=1,9
      Z=K-1
      IF(X+2*Y+3*Z.GT.25) GO TO 1
      IF(X+Y+Z.GT.22) GO TO 1
      IF(X+Y.GT.15) GO TO 1
      IF(X+Z.GT.20) GO TO 1
      P=2*X+2*Y+5*Z
      IF(P.GT.PMAX) GO TO 2
      GO TO 1
2     IX=X
      IY=Y
      IZ=Z
      PMAX=P
1     CONTINUE
      WRITE(6,3)IX,IY,IZ,PMAX
3     FORMAT('0',4I10)
      STOP
      END
```

THE PRINTOUT IS

13   0   4   46

The solution is:

$x = 13$, $y = 0$, $z = 4$, and maximum $P = 46$

The storage space is made a little larger to accommodate the extra variable. It is:

```
IX = X
IY = Y
IZ = Z
PMAX = P
```

The statements

```
WRITE(6,3)IX,IY,IZ,PMAX
3 FORMAT ('0', 4I10)
```

print the X,Y,Z and attendant maximum P solution in a horizontal pattern. This WRITE statement and its FORMAT statement (which controls the output) may vary slightly from computer to computer. So the reader should check his computer installation for the various printing options available and use the one that suits him best. The WRITE and FORMAT statements as presented here should work with very little or no modification on most computers.

Now, let's write a program to maximize $P = 3x + 4y - z$ subject to $x \geq 4$, $y \geq 10$, $z \geq 15$, $y + z \leq 100$, $x + z \leq 50$, $x + zy + z^2 \leq 1000$, $x \leq 50$, $y \leq 50$, and $z \leq 50$. Therefore, x goes from 4 to 50, y from 10 to 50, and z from 15 to 50. The structure is the same as before.

```
      INTEGER X,Y,Z,PMAX,P
      PMAX=-999999
      DO 1 I=4,50
      X=I
      DO 1 J=10,50
      Y=J
      DO 1 K=15,50
      Z=K
      IF(Y+Z.GT.100) GO TO 1
      IF(X+Z.GT.50) GO TO 1
      IF(X+Z*Y+Z**2.GT.1000) GO TO 1
      P=3*X+4*Y-Z
      IF(P.GT.PMAX) GO TO 2
      GO TO 1
    2 IX=X
      IY=Y
      IZ=Z
      PMAX=P
    1 CONTINUE
      WRITE(6,3)IX,IY,IZ,PMAX
    3 FORMAT('0',4I10)
      STOP
      END


      THE PRINTOUT IS

      35   49   15   286
```

The solution is:

$x = 35$, $y = 49$, $z = 15$, and maximum $P = 286$

This time the computer starts with the point (4,10,15) and continues to the point (50,50,50) checking $47 \times 41 \times 36 = 69,372$ ordered triples (throwing out the ones that violate any constraints) for the one that produces the largest P value. The winner was, of course, (35,49,15) with its corresponding P value of 286.

Next, write a program to minimize the preceding integer programming problem. Finally, minimize $C = 3x + 4y - z$ subject to $x \geq 4$, $y \geq 10$, $z \geq 15$, $y + z \leq 100$, $x + z \leq 50$, $x + zy + z^2 \leq 1000$, $x \leq 50$, $y \leq 50$, $z \leq 50$. Everything is the same as before except that we let CMIN be a very large number (to get the comparison going in the right direction) and we search the 69,372 ordered triples (throwing out the ones that violate any constraints) for the one that produces the smallest C value. Note that we label the equation C instead of P as before. But it is the same equation.

```
      INTEGER X,Y,Z,CMIN,C
      CMIN=999999
      DO 1 I=4,50
      X=I
      DO 1 J=10,50
      Y=J
      DO 1 K=15,50
      Z=K
      IF(Y+Z.GT.100) GO TO 1
      IF(X+Z.GT.50) GO TO 1
      IF(X+Z*Y+Z**2.GT.1000) GO TO 1
      C=3*X+4*Y-Z
      IF(C.LT.CMIN) GO TO 2
      GO TO 1
    2 IX=X
      IY=Y
      IZ=Z
      CMIN=C
    1 CONTINUE
      WRITE(6,3)IX,IY,IZ,CMIN
    3 FORMAT('0',4I10)
      STOP
      END


      THE PRINTOUT IS

      4  10  26    26
```

The solution is:

$x = 4$, $y = 10$, $z = 26$, and minimum $C = 26$

Now, let's look at a four-variable problem. Maximize $P = x + 2y + 3z + 6w$ subject to $x \geq 0$, $y \geq 0$, $z \geq 0$, $w \geq 0$, $x^2 + y^2 + z^2 + w^2 \leq 400$, $x + y + 2z \leq 50$, and $y + w \leq 50$.

Notice that $\sqrt{400} = 20$, so no variable can be larger than 20. This time we have four nested DO-loops (one for each variable) to check all the 194,481 possible combinations from (0,0,0,0) to (20,20,20,20).

```
INTEGER X,Y,Z,W,PMAX,P
PMAX=0
DO 1 I=1,21
X=I-1
DO 1 J=1,21
Y=J-1
DO 1 K=1,21
Z=K-1
DO 1 L=1,21
W=L-1
IF(X**2+Y**2+Z**2+W**2.GT.400) GO TO 1
IF(X+Y+2*Z.GT.50) GO TO 1
IF(Y+W.GT.50) GO TO 1
P=X+2*Y+3*Z+6*W
IF(P.GT.PMAX) GO TO 2
GO TO 1
2   IX=X
IY=Y
IZ=Z
IW=W
PMAX=P
1   CONTINUE
WRITE(6,3)IX,IY,IZ,IW,PMAX
3   FORMAT('0',5I10)
STOP
END


THE PRINTOUT IS

2   5   9   17   141
```

The solution is

$x = 2$, $y = 5$, $z = 9$, $w = 17$, and maximum $P = 141$

At this point the reader may wonder what we will do when we start looking at problems that have dozens of variables to consider. This is a valid question because the four variables, each able to take values from 0 to 20, gave us $21^4 = 194,481$ combinations for the computer to check. This still takes the computer less than a minute (an IBM 360-65). However, if we had 32 variables, each able to take the values 0 to 20, there would be $2.046526777 \times 10^{42}$ combinations to check. That would take years, to say the least. But Part Two of this text is devoted to showing how to handle problems of this type by taking a large random sample of the possible solutions and optimizing that. Much statistical evidence is presented to justify the technique by showing that those answers are for all practical purposes nearly optimum. In fact in many cases, considering cost of solution factors, our answer may be better than the true optimum. Chapter 7 presents a 2000-variable problem as an illustration; subsequent chapters offer dozens of other large-variable problems.

We will now write a program to maximize $P = 53x + 29y$ subject to $x \geq 0$, $y \geq 0$, $x + 6y \leq 20$, and $12x + 14y \leq 1200$. Because of $x + 6y \leq 20$, x can't be any larger than 20 and y can't be any larger than 3. The loops reflect this fact in the program below:

```
      INTEGER X,Y,PMAX
      PMAX=0
      DO 1 I=1,21
      X=I-1
      DO 1 J=1,4
      Y=J-1
      IF(X+6*Y.GT.20) GO TO 1
      IF(12*X+14*Y.GT.1200) GO TO 1
      P=53*X+29*Y
      IF(P.GT.PMAX) GO TO 2
      GO TO 1
    2 IX=X
      IY=Y
      PMAX=P
    1 CONTINUE
      WRITE(6,3)IX,IY,PMAX
    3 FORMAT('0',3I10)
      STOP
      END


      THE PRINTOUT IS

      20    0    1060
```

The solution is:

$x = 20$, $y = 0$, and maximum $P = 1060$

Additional examples comprise the rest of the chapter. All still use the same basic structure. They have one loop per variable, and loop lengths are adjusted to fit the constraints as before.

EXAMPLE 3.1

Maximize $15.8x + 27.3y + 16z$ subject to $x \geq 0$, $y \geq 0$, $z \geq 0$, $x + y + z \leq 150$, $x + 7y - z \leq 190$, $z \leq 15$, and $x^2 + y^3 \leq 180$. The constraint $x^2 + y^3 \leq 180$ guarantees that x can be no larger than 13 ($\sqrt{180} = 13.42$) and that y can be no larger than 5 ($\sqrt[3]{180} = 5.65$). The program is below:

```
INTEGER X,Y,Z
PMAX=0
DO 1 I=1,14
X=I-1
DO 1 J=1,6
Y=J-1
DO 1 K=1,16
Z=K-1
IF(X+Y+Z.GT.150) GO TO 1
IF(X+7*Y-Z.GT.190) GO TO 1
IF(X**2+Y**3.GT.180) GO TO 1
P=15.8*X+27.3*Y+16*Z
IF(P.GT.PMAX) GO TO 2
GO TO 1
2    IX=X
     IY=Y
     IZ=Z
     PMAX=P
1    CONTINUE
     WRITE(6,3)IX,IY,IZ,PMAX
3    FORMAT('0',3I10,F15.7)
     STOP
     END


     THE PRINTOUT IS

12   3   15      511.5
```

The solution is:

$x = 12$, $y = 3$, $z = 15$, and maximum $P = 511.5$

EXAMPLE 3.2

Maximize $P = 4x + 10y + 7z + 8w$ subject to $x \geq 0$, $y \geq 0$, $z \geq 0$, $w \geq 0$, $24x + 16y + 2z + 5w \leq 50$, $x + y \leq 20$, $x + z \leq 20$, $15x + 35y + 55z + 72w \leq 1200$, and $18x + 27y + 51z + 14w \leq 900$.

```
INTEGER X,Y,Z,W,PMAX
PMAX=0
DO 1 I=1,21
```

```
     X=I-1
     DO 1 J=1,21
     Y=J-1
     DO 1 K=1,21
     Z=K-1
     DO 1 L=1,17
     W=L-1
     IF(24*X+16*Y+2*Z+5*W.GT.50) GO TO 1
     IF(X+Y.GT.20) GO TO 1
     IF(X+Z.GT.20) GO TO 1
     IF(15*X+35*Y+55*Z+72*W.GT.1200) GO TO 1
     IF(18*X+27*Y+51*Z+14*W.GT.900) GO TO 1
     P=4*X+10*Y+7*Z+8*W
     IF(P.GT.PMAX) GO TO 2
     GO TO 1
2    IX=X
     IY=Y
     IZ=Z
     IW=W
     PMAX=P
1    CONTINUE
     WRITE(6,3)IX,IY,IZ,IW,PMAX
3    FORMAT('0',5I10)
     STOP
     END
```

```
        THE PRINTOUT IS

     0    0    15    4    137
```

The solution is:

$x = 0$, $y = 0$, $z = 15$, $w = 4$, and maximum $P = 137$

Notice that in this case the loop limits are larger (21,21,21, and 17) than they really have to be. No harm is done, though. The solution will be correct as long as you guess the limits too high. The program will just throw out the irrelevant ones.

EXAMPLE 3.3

Maximize $P = 3x + y$ subject to $x \geq 0$, $y \geq 0$, $y \leq -.5x + 10$, and $y \leq -2x + 20$. From $y \leq -2x + 20$ we can see that x has to be less than or equal to 10. From $y \leq -.5x + 10$ we can see that y has to be less than or equal to 10.

```
     INTEGER X,Y,PMAX
     PMAX=0
     DO 1 I=1,11
     X=I-1
     DO 1 J=1,11
```

```
      Y=J-1
      IF(Y.GT.-.5*X+10) GO TO 1
      IF(Y.GT.-2*X+20) GO TO 1
      P=3*X+Y
      IF(P.GT.PMAX) GO TO 2
      GO TO 1
2     IX=X
      IY=Y
      PMAX=P
1     CONTINUE
      WRITE(6,3)IX,IY,PMAX
3     FORMAT('0',3I10)
      STOP
      END


      THE PRINTOUT IS

      10    0    30
```

The solution is:

$x = 10$, $y = 0$, and maximum $P = 30$

Again, notice that the constraints are left in their same form but merely reversed as usual.

EXAMPLE 3.4

Maximize $P = 10x + 6y + 4z + 95w + 18u$ subject to $x \geq 0$, $y \geq 0$, $z \geq 0$, $w \geq 0$, $u \geq 0$, $x + y + w + u + z \leq 19$, $17x - 2y + 4z + 21w + 22u \leq 2000$, $18x + 11y + 14z + 12w + 104u \leq 3000$, and $x + y + z + 90w + 35u \leq 1500$.

Just observing the constraint $x + y + w + u + z \leq 19$ indicates that all the variables have to be less than or equal to 19. We use this fact in fixing the five loop limits. We could, of course, reduce some of these limits, but this approach will work fine. The computer just starts with $(0,0,0,0,0)$ and goes through all the possible combinations to $(19,19,19,19,19)$. There are $20^5 = 3,200,000$ combinations to check. The structure of the program is as before.

```
      INTEGER X,Y,Z,W,U,PMAX
      PMAX=0
      DO 1 I=1,20
      X=I-1
      DO 1 J=1,20
      Y=J-1
      DO 1 K=1,20
      Z=K-1
      DO 1 L=1,20
      W=L-1
```

```
      DO 1 M=1,20
      U=M-1
      IF(X+Y+Z+W+U.GT.19) GO TO 1
      IF(17*X-2*Y+4*Z+21*W+22*U.GT.2000) GO TO 1
      IF(18*X+11*Y+14*Z+12*W+104*U.GT.3000) GO TO 1
      IF(X+Y+Z+90*W+35*U.GT.1500) GO TO 1
      P=10*X+6*Y+4*Z+95*W+18*U
      IF(P.GT.PMAX) GO TO 2
      GO TO 1
2     IX=X
      IY=Y
      IZ=Z
      IW=W
      IU=U
      PMAX=P
1     CONTINUE
      WRITE(6,3)IX,IY,IZ,IW,IU,PMAX
3     FORMAT('0',6I10)
      STOP
      END


      THE PRINTOUT IS

2     0     0     16    1     1558
```

The solution is:

$x = 2, y = 0, z = 0, w = 16, u = 1$, and maximum $P = 1558$

EXAMPLE 3.5

Maximize $P = 6x + 14y + 17z + 8w + 41u + 9v$ subject to $x \geq 0, y \geq 0, z \geq 0, w \geq 0, u \geq 0, v \geq 0, x + y + z + w + u + v \leq 11, 12x + 11y + 18z + 66w + 4u + v \leq 9000, 18x + 72y + 16z + 41w + 39u + 10v \leq 10,000$, and $8x + 7y + 39z + 21w + u + 29v \leq 5000$.

Just observing the constraint $x + y + z + w + u + v \leq 11$ tells us that all the variables have to be less than or equal to 11. We use this fact in fixing the six loop limits. We can do this because even though various combinations might satisfy other constraints, they have to satisfy all constraints simultaneously. Therefore, x, y, z, w, u, and v can never be larger than 11 because of $x + y + z + w + u + v \leq 11$. Notice we use six loops (one for each variable) to check all combinations from $(0,0,0,0,0,0)$ to $(11,11,11,11,11,11)$. There are $12^6 = 2,985,984$ possibilities to check for the combination that maximizes P.

```
      INTEGER X,Y,Z,W,U,V,PMAX
      PMAX=0
      DO 1 I=1,12
      X=I-1
```

```
     DO 1 J=1,12
     Y=J-1
     DO 1 K=1,12
     Z=K-1
     DO 1 L=1,12
     W=L-1
     DO 1 M=1,12
     U=M-1
     DO 1 N=1,12
     V=N-1
     IF(X+Y+Z+W+U+V.GT.11) GO TO 1
     IF(12*X+11*Y+18*Z+66*W+4*U+V.GT.9000) GO TO 1
     IF(18*X+72*Y+16*Z+41*W+39*U+10*V.GT.10000) GO TO 1
     IF(8*X+7*Y+39*Z+21*W+U+29*V.GT.5000) GO TO 1
     P=6*X+14*Y+17*Z+8*W+41*U+9*V
     IF(P.GT.PMAX) GO TO 2
     GO TO 1
   2 IX=X
     IY=Y
     IZ=Z
     IW=W
     IU=U
     IV=V
     PMAX=P
   1 CONTINUE
     WRITE(6,3)IX,IY,IZ,IW,IU,IV,PMAX
   3 FORMAT('0',7I10)
     STOP
     END


         THE PRINTOUT IS

   0    0    0    0    11    0    451
```

The solution is:

$x = 0$, $y = 0$, $z = 0$, $w = 0$, $u = 11$, $v = 0$, and maximum $P = 451$

EXAMPLE 3.6

Maximize $P = 12x + 12y + 18z + 17w + 8u + 14v + 18s$ subject to $x \geq 0$, $y \geq 0$, $z \geq 0$, $w \geq 0$, $u \geq 0$, $v \geq 0$ $s \geq 0$, $x + y + z + w + u + v + s \leq 5$, $33x + 30y + 21z + 47w + 11u + 35v + 10s \leq 9,008$, $23x + 31y + 23z + 34w + 31u + 50v + 12s \leq 20,000$, and $18x + 109y + 31z + 19w + 36u + 10v + 11s \leq 1000$.

The constraint $x + y + z + w + u + v + s \leq 5$ guarantees that the variables must be less than or equal to five. We use seven loops (one for each variable) to go through the $6^7 = 279,936$ combinations from $(0,0,0,0,0,0,0)$ to $(5,5,5,5,5,5,5)$ to find the combination that optimizes P.

```
INTEGER X,Y,Z,W,U,V,S,PMAX
PMAX=0
DO 1 I=1,6
X=I-1
DO 1 J=1,6
Y=J-1
DO 1 K=1,6
Z=K-1
DO 1 L=1,6
W=L-1
DO 1 M=1,6
U=M-1
DO 1 N=1,6
V=N-1
DO 1 II=1,6
S=II-1
IF(X+Y+Z+W+U+V+S.GT.5) GO TO 1
IF(33*X+30*Y+21*Z+47*W+11*U+35*V+10*S.GT.9008) GO TO 1
IF(23*X+31*Y+23*Z+34*W+31*U+50*V+12*S.GT.20000) GO TO 1
IF(18*X+109*Y+31*Z+19*W+36*U+10*V+11*S.GT.1000) GO TO 1
P=12*X+12*Y+18*Z+17*W+8*U+14*V+18*S
IF(P.GT.PMAX) GO TO 2
GO TO 1
2   IX=X
IY=Y
IZ=Z
IW=W
IU=U
IV=V
IS=S
PMAX=P
1   CONTINUE
WRITE(6,3)IX,IY,IZ,IW,IU,IV,IS,PMAX
3   FORMAT('0',8I10)
STOP
END
```

```
       THE PRINTOUT IS

0   0   0   0   0   0   5    90
```

The solution is:

$x = 0$, $y = 0$, $z = 0$, $w = 0$, $u = 0$, $v = 0$, $s = 5$, and maximum $P = 90$

EXAMPLE 3.7

Maximize $P = 11x + 3y + 27z + 37w + 20u + 36v + 25s + 53t$ subject to $x \geq 0$, $y \geq 0$, $z \geq 0$, $w \geq 0$, $u \geq 0$, $v \geq 0$, $s \geq 0$, $t \geq 0$, $x + y + z + w + u + v$

$+ s + t \leq 4$, $46x + 32y + 33z + 6w + 18u + 22v + 16s + 20t \leq 10080$, and
$14x + 14y + 14z + 23w + 21u + 10v + 21s + 26t \leq 5000$.

We determine loop limits from $x + y + z + w + u + v + s + t \leq 4$. Notice we
use eight loops for the eight variables.

```
INTEGER X,Y,Z,W,U,V,S,T,PMAX
PMAX=0
DO 1 I=1,5
X=I-1
DO 1 J=1,5
Y=J-1
DO 1 K=1,5
Z=K-1
DO 1 L=1,5
W=L-1
DO 1 M=1,5
U=M-1
DO 1 N=1,5
V=N-1
DO 1 II=1,5
S=II-1
DO 1 JJ=1,5
T=JJ-1
IF(X+Y+Z+W+U+V+S+T.GT.4) GO TO 1
IF(46*X+32*Y+33*Z+6*W+18*U+22*V+16*S+20*T.GT.10080) GO TO 1
IF(14*X+14*Y+14*Z+23*W+21*U+10*V+21*S+26*T.GT.5000) GO TO 1
P=11*X+3*Y+27*Z+37*W+20*U+36*V+25*S+53*T
IF(P.GT.PMAX) GO TO 2
GO TO 1
2   IX=X
IY=Y
IZ=Z
IW=W
IU=U
IV=V
IS=S
IT=T
PMAX=P
1   CONTINUE
WRITE(6,3)IX,IY,IZ,IW,IU,IV,IS,IT,PMAX
3   FORMAT('0',9I10)
STOP
END
```

                    THE PRINTOUT IS

    0   0   0   0   0   0   0   4   212

The solution is:

$x = 0, y = 0, z = 0, w = 0, u = 0, v = 0, s = 0, t = 4$, and maximum
$P = 212$

EXAMPLE 3.8

Maximize $P = 2x + 4y$ subject to $x \geq 0$, $y \geq 0$, $x \leq 10$, and $y \leq 10$. We need just two loops to check the points $(0,0)$, $(0,1)$, ..., $(0,10)$, $(1,0)$, $(1,1)$, ..., $(1,10)$, $(2,0)$, $(2,1)$, ..., $(2,10)$, ..., $(10,10)$ for the optimum combination.

```
  INTEGER X,Y,PMAX
  PMAX=0
  DO 1 I=1,11
  X=I-1
  DO 1 J=1,11
  Y=J-1
  P=2*X+4*Y
  IF(P.GT.PMAX) GO TO 2
  GO TO 1
2 IX=X
  IY=Y
  PMAX=P
1 CONTINUE
  WRITE(6,3)IX,IY,PMAX
3 FORMAT('0',3I10)
  STOP
  END


  THE PRINTOUT IS

  10    10    60
```

The solution is:

$x = 10$, $y = 10$, and maximum $P = 60$

In this particular problem it can readily be seen that $P = 2x + 4y$ is maximized by putting in 10 units of x and 10 units of y. Notice that is the answer the computer produced. So the technique really does work.

EXAMPLE 3.9

Maximize $P = 2x - y$ subject to $x \geq 0$, $y \geq 0$, $x \leq 10$, and $y \leq 10$.

```
  INTEGER X,Y,PMAX
  PMAX=0
  DO 1 I=1,11
  X=I-1
  DO 1 J=1,11
  Y=J-1
  P=2*X-Y
  IF(P.GT.PMAX) GO TO 2
  GO TO 1
2 IX=X
```

```
      IY=Y
      PMAX=P
1     CONTINUE
      WRITE(6,3)IX,IY,PMAX
3     FORMAT('0',3I10)
      STOP
      END
```

```
      THE PRINTOUT IS

      10     0     20
```

The solution is:

$x = 10, y = 0$, and maximum $P = 20$ as expected

EXAMPLE 3.10

Maximize $P = 2x^2 + xy - 2y$ subject to $x \geq 0, y \geq 0, x \leq 10$, and $y \leq 10$.

```
      INTEGER X,Y,PMAX
      PMAX=0
      DO 1 I=1,11
      X=I-1
      DO 1 J=1,11
      Y=J-1
      P=2*X**2+X*Y-2*Y
      IF(P.GT.PMAX) GO TO 2
      GO TO 1
2     IX=X
      IY=Y
      PMAX=P
1     CONTINUE
      WRITE(6,3)IX,IY,PMAX
3     FORMAT('0',3I10)
      STOP
      END
```

```
      THE PRINTOUT IS

      10    10    280
```

The solution is:

$x = 10, y = 10$, and maximum $P = 280$

EXAMPLE 3.11

Maximize $P = 2x^2 + xy - 2y$ subject to $x \geq 0, y \geq 0, x \leq 1000$, and $y \leq 1000$.

```
      INTEGER X,Y,PMAX
      PMAX=0
      DO 1 I=1,1001
      X=I-1
      DO 1 J=1,1001
      Y=J-1
      P=2*X**2+X*Y-2*Y
      IF(P.GT.PMAX) GO TO 2
      GO TO 1
2     IX=X
      IY=Y
      PMAX=P
1     CONTINUE
      WRITE(6,3)IX,IY,PMAX
3     FORMAT('0',3I10)
      STOP
      END


          THE PRINTOUT IS

   1000    1000    2998000
```

The solution is:

$x = 1000, y = 1000$, and maximum $P = 2,998,000$

EXAMPLE 3.12
Maximize $P = 2x + 4y$ subject to $x \geq 0, y \geq 0, x + y \leq 100, x + 7y \leq 95$, and $3x + y \leq 38$.

```
      INTEGER X,Y,PMAX
      PMAX=0
      DO 1 I=1,13
      X=I-1
      DO 1 J=1,14
      Y=J-1
      IF(X+Y.GT.100) GO TO 1
      IF(X+7*Y.GT.95) GO TO 1
      IF(3*X+Y.GT.38) GO TO 1
      P=2*X+4*Y
      IF(P.GT.PMAX) GO TO 2
      GO TO 1
2     IX=X
      IY=Y
      PMAX=P
1     CONTINUE
      WRITE(6,3)IX,IY,PMAX
3     FORMAT('0',3I10)
```

```
STOP
END
```

```
THE PRINTOUT IS

   8    12    64
```

The solution is:

$x = 8$, $y = 12$, and maximum $P = 64$

Notice that from the constraint $3x + y \leq 38$, x can be no larger than 12 (3 into 38 equals 12.67). Also, from the constraint $x + 7y \leq 95$, y can be no larger than 13 (7 into 95 equals 13.57).

EXAMPLE 3.13

Maximize $P = 2x - y$ subject to $x \geq 0$, $y \geq 0$, $x + y \leq 100$, $x + 7y \leq 95$, and $3x + y \leq 38$. These constraints are the same as in the previous problem so only the P function has to be changed.

```
      INTEGER X,Y,PMAX
      PMAX=0
      DO 1 I=1,13
      X=I-1
      DO 1 J=1,14
      Y=J-1
      IF(X+Y.GT.100) GO TO 1
      IF(X+7*Y.GT.95) GO TO 1
      IF(3*X+Y.GT.38) GO TO 1
      P=2*X-Y
      IF(P.GT.PMAX) GO TO 2
      GO TO 1
2     IX=X
      IY=Y
      PMAX=P
1     CONTINUE
      WRITE(6,3)IX,IY,PMAX
3     FORMAT('0',3I10)
      STOP
      END
```

```
THE PRINTOUT IS

   12    0    24
```

The solution is:

$x = 12$, $y = 0$, and maximum $P = 24$

EXAMPLE 3.14

Maximize $P = 2x^2 + xy - 2y$ subject to $x \geq 0$, $y \geq 0$, $x + y \leq 100$, $x + 7y \leq 95$, and $3x + y \leq 38$. These constraints are the same as in the previous two problems so only the P function has to be changed. Notice, the P function here is nonlinear which normally makes the problem much more difficult. But by using our technique of examining all points it really makes no difference to the computer how complicated and theoretically unmanageable the objective function and constraints are. This makes solving virtually any optimization problem that can be written down, possible.

```
      INTEGER X,Y,PMAX,P
      PMAX=0
      DO 1 I=1,13
      X=I-1
      DO 1 J=1,14
      Y=J-1
      IF(X+Y.GT.100) GO TO 1
      IF(X+7*Y.GT.95) GO TO 1
      IF(3*X+Y.GT.38) GO TO 1
      P=2*X**2+X*Y-2*Y
      IF(P.GT.PMAX) GO TO 2
      GO TO 1
    2 IX=X
      IY=Y
      PMAX=P
    1 CONTINUE
      WRITE(6,3)IX,IY,PMAX
    3 FORMAT('0',3I10)
      STOP
      END


      THE PRINTOUT IS

      12    2    308
```

The solution is:

$x = 12$, $y = 2$, and maximum $P = 308$

EXAMPLE 3.15

Maximize $P = 2x^2 + xy - 2y$ subject to $x \geq 0$, $y \geq 0$, $x + y \leq 100$, $3x^2 + xy \leq 100$, $x + 7y \leq 95$, and $3x + y^2 \leq 38$. The constraints $3x + y^2 \leq 38$ and $x + 7y \leq 95$ were used to get the loop limits of 13 and 14 for x and y, respectively. However, a more careful analysis could have lowered them.

```
      INTEGER X,Y,PMAX,P
      PMAX=0
      DO 1 I=1,13
```

```
      X=I-1
      DO 1 J=1,14
      Y=J-1
      IF(X+Y.GT.100) GO TO 1
      IF(3*X**2+X*Y.GT.100) GO TO 1
      IF(X+7*Y.GT.95) GO TO 1
      IF(3*X+Y**2.GT.38) GO TO 1
      P=2*X**2+X*Y-2*Y
      IF(P.GT.PMAX) GO TO 2
      GO TO 1
2     IX=X
      IY=Y
      PMAX=P
1     CONTINUE
      WRITE(6,3)IX,IY,PMAX
3     FORMAT('0',3I10)
      STOP
      END


      THE PRINTOUT IS

        5     4     62
```

The solution is:

$x = 5$, $y = 4$, and maximum $P = 62$

EXAMPLE 3.16

Minimize $C = 2x^2 + xy - 2y$ subject to $x \geq 0, y \geq 0, x \leq 200, y \leq 200, x + 16xy + y \geq 55, x - y \geq 41$, and $x + y \geq 28$. First of all, x and y can go from 0 to 200. This fixes the loop limits. Statement 1 declares X, Y, CMIN and C to be integer variables. Then line 2 assigns CMIN an extremely large number so that the first C value to get to line 11 will be smaller than CMIN and hence be the first minimum stored. This gets the search for the minimum started in the right direction. Now, of all the ordered pairs $(0,0)$ $(0,1), \ldots,$ $(200,200)$ that could produce the minimum, we only want to really look at those ordered pairs that satisfy the constraints $x + 16xy + y \geq 55, x - y \geq 41$, and $x + y \geq 28$. So we set up a bank of constraints with the inequalities reversed in lines 7, 8, and 9 as follows:

```
IF(X+16*X*Y+Y.LT.55) GO TO 1
IF(X-Y.LT.41) GO TO 1
IF(X+Y.LT.28) GO TO 1
```

All three of the real constraints ($x + 16xy + y \geq 55, x - y \geq 41$, and $x + y \geq 28$) are satisfied only if lines 7, 8, and 9 are all false, and only if they are all false will the program get to line 10 to evaluate the C function and check it to see if it is a possible minimum. If it is, it is stored in the storage variables IX, IY and CMIN. Then the program continues through another loop. However, if any of the real constraints (x + 16xy + y ≥ 55, x − y ≥ 41, and x + y ≥ 28) are not satisfied, then the corresponding FORTRAN statement in line 7, 8, or 9 will be true and then the computer will GO TO 1 (the CONTINUE statement) and proceed to the next ordered pair, skipping over the current ordered pair which doesn't satisfy the constraints and is hence not a feasible (possible) solution.

```
    INTEGER X,Y,CMIN,C
    CMIN=9999999
    DO 1 I=1,201
    X=I-1
    DO 1 J=1,201
    Y=J-1
    IF(X+16*X*Y+Y.LT.55) GO TO 1
    IF(X-Y.LT.41) GO TO 1
    IF(X+Y.LT.28) GO TO 1
    C=2*X**2+X*Y-2*Y
    IF(C.LT.CMIN) GO TO 2
    GO TO 1
  2 IX=X
    IY=Y
    CMIN=C
  1 CONTINUE
    WRITE(6,3)IX,IY,CMIN
  3 FORMAT('0',3I10)
    STOP
    END


    THE PRINTOUT IS

    42    1    3568
```

The solution is:

x = 42, y = 1, and minimum C = 3568

EXAMPLE 3.17

Minimize C = $2x^2$ + xy − $2y$ subject to x ≥ 0, y ≥ 0, x ≤ 200, y ≤ 200, x^2 + 16xy^2 + y ≥ 105, y − x^2 ≥ 12, and x + y ≥ 32. Notice that here we are to minimize the same objective (C function) as in Example 3.16, except that the constraints have changed. The program is the same as the program for Example 3.16 except the bank of constraints has changed. This points up the fact that one can manipulate the function and change the constraints so easily that in a business decision or industrial production problem the decision maker can look at many models easily before making a decision. No new theory is ever needed. Just substitutions for the changed function and/or constraints are required. When the day of the super powerful desk-top minicomputer arrives (most experts think by 1982), enormously complicated modeling problems will be examined for dozens of different combinations of conditions and constraints to find not only the optimum solution, but the optimum model. The day of these computers is here already if you or your organization wants to pay for it. But, in a few years, these giant capacity computers should be reasonable enough for any decision maker to afford.

```
      INTEGER X,Y,CMIN,C
      CMIN=9999999
      DO 1 I=1,201
      X=I-1
      DO 1 J=1,201
      Y=J-1
      IF(X**2+16*X*Y**2+Y.LT.105) GO TO 1
      IF(Y-X**2.LT.12) GO TO 1
      IF(X+Y.LT.32) GO TO 1
      C=2*X**2+X*Y-2*Y
      IF(C.LT.CMIN) GO TO 2
      GO TO 1
2     IX=X
      IY=Y
      CMIN=C
1     CONTINUE
      WRITE(6,3)IX,IY,CMIN
3     FORMAT('0',3I10)
      STOP
      END


      THE PRINTOUT IS

      0    200    -400
```

The solution is:

$x = 0$, $y = 200$, and minimum $C = -400$

EXAMPLE 3.18

Maximize $P = x + y$ subject to $x \geq 0$, $y \geq 0$, $x \leq 10$, and $y \leq 10$.

```
      INTEGER X,Y,PMAX,P
      PMAX=0
      DO 1 I=1,11
      X=I-1
      DO 1 J=1,11
      Y=J-1
      P=X+Y
      IF(P.GT.PMAX) GO TO 2
      GO TO 1
```

```
2   IX=X
    IY=Y
    PMAX=P
1   CONTINUE
    WRITE(6,3)IX,IY,PMAX
3   FORMAT('0',3I10)
    STOP
    END
```

```
THE PRINTOUT IS

   10   10   20
```

The solution is:

$x = 10, y = 10,$ and maximum $P = 20$

EXAMPLE 3.19

Minimize $C = x + y$ subject to $x \geq 0, y \geq 0, x \leq 10,$ and $y \leq 10$.

```
INTEGER X,Y,CMIN,C
CMIN=9999999
DO 1 I=1,11
X=I-1
DO 1 J=1,11
Y=J-1
C=X+Y
IF(C.LT.CMIN) GO TO 2
GO TO 1
2   IX=X
    IY=Y
    CMIN=C
1   CONTINUE
    WRITE(6,3)IX,IY,CMIN
3   FORMAT('0',3I10)
    STOP
    END
```

```
THE PRINTOUT IS

    0    0    0
```

The solution is:

$x = 0, y = 0,$ and $C = 0$ as expected from inspection of the problem

EXAMPLE 3.20

A company produces three products, A, B, and C. Product A yields a profit of $30 per unit, while B and C yield profits of $20 and $15, respectively. The table below shows how much time is required in each of two departments to make one unit of each of the three products:

Department	Time required (hours)		
	Product A	Product B	Product C
1	7	7	3
2	3	1	2

Department 1 has no more than 100 man-hours available per day. Department 2 has no more than 50 man-hours per day available.

Find the number of A, B, and C that should be made to maximize the profit. The relevant information can be summarized as follows: Maximize $P = 30x + 20y + 15z$ subject to $x \geq 0$, $y \geq 0$, $z \geq 0$, $7x + 7y + 3z \leq 100$, and $3x + y + 2z \leq 50$. We have just written in equations and inequalities the information given in the story problem. The program follows below:

```
      INTEGER X,Y,Z,PMAX,P
      PMAX=0
      DO 1 I=1,15
      X=I-1
      DO 1 J=1,15
      Y=J-1
      DO 1 K=1,26
      Z=K-1
      IF(7*X+7*Y+3*Z.GT.100) GO TO 1
      IF(3*X+Y+2*Z.GT.50) GO TO 1
      P=30*X+20*Y+15*Z
      IF(P.GT.PMAX) GO TO 2
      GO TO 1
2     IX=X
      IY=Y
      IZ=Z
      PMAX=P
1     CONTINUE
      WRITE(6,3)IX,IY,IZ,PMAX
3     FORMAT('0',4I10)
      STOP
      END


      THE PRINTOUT IS

10     0    10    450
```

The solution is:

$x = 10, y = 0, z = 10$, and maximum $P = 450$

Therefore, the company should produce 10 units of A, no units of B, and 10 units of C to achieve a maximum profit of $450 per day on those products.

EXAMPLE 3.21
The K Company manufactures products A and B at a profit of $50 and $75, respectively. The table below shows how much time is required in each of two departments to make one unit of each of the two products:

| | Time required (hours) | |
Department	Product A	Product B
1	10	6
2	5	14

Department 1 has no more than 200 man-hours available per day. Department 2 has no more than 300 man-hours per day available.

Find the number of A and B that should be made to maximize the profit. The relevant information can be summarized as follows: Maximize $P = 50x + 75y$ subject to $x \geq 0, y \geq 0, 10x + 6y \leq 200$, and $5x + 14y \leq 300$. Again, we have just written in equations and inequalities the information given in the story problem. From the inequality $10x + 6y \leq 200$, we get that x can be no larger than 20 (because 200 divided by 10 equals 20). From the inequality $5x + 14y \leq 300$, we get that y can be no larger than 21 (because 300 divided by 14 equals 21.43). The program is given below:

```
INTEGER X,Y,PMAX,P
PMAX=0
DO 1 I=1,21
X=I-1
DO 1 J=1,22
Y=J-1
IF(10*X+6*Y.GT.200) GO TO 1
IF(5*X+14*Y.GT.300) GO TO 1
P=50*X+75*Y
IF(P.GT.PMAX) GO TO 2
GO TO 1
2   IX=X
IY=Y
PMAX=P
1   CONTINUE
WRITE(6,3)IX,IY,PMAX
3   FORMAT('0',3I10)
STOP
END
```

THE PRINTOUT IS

9   18   1800

The solution is:

$x = 9$, $y = 18$, and maximum $P = 1800$

Therefore, the company should produce 9 units of A and 18 units of B to achieve a maximum profit of $1800 per day on those products.

EXAMPLE 3.22

The R Company makes products A, B, C, and D at a profit of $100, $150, $200, and $250, respectively. The table below shows how much time is required in each of three departments to make one unit of each of the four products:

Department	Time required (hours)			
	Product A	Product B	Product C	Product D
1	10	4	8	9
2	6	5	3	9
3	3	9	7	12

Department 1 has no more than 300 man-hours available per day. Department 2 is limited to no more than 400 man-hours per day. Similarly, Department 3 is limited to 425 man-hours per day.

Find the number of units of A, B, C, and D that should be produced to maximize the profit. The relevant information can be summarized as follows: Maximize $P = 100x + 150y + 200z + 250w$ subject to $x \geq 0$, $y \geq 0$, $z \geq 0$, $w \geq 0$, $10x + 4y + 8z + 9w \leq 300$, $6x + 5y + 3z + 9w \leq 400$, and $3x + 9y + 7z + 12w \leq 425$. From $10x + 4y + 8z + 9w \leq 300$, we see that x must be less than or equal to 30 (300/10 = 30), z must be less than or equal to 37 (300/8 = 37.5), and w must be less than or equal to 33 (300/9 = 33.33). From $3x + 9y + 7z + 12w \leq 425$, we see that y must be less than or equal to 47 (425/9 = 47.2). The program follows with four loops (one for each variable) to examine the 31 × 48 × 38 × 34 = 1,922,496 points from (0,0,0,0) to (30,47,37,33) to find the best combination.

```
INTEGER X,Y,Z,W,PMAX,P
PMAX=0
DO 1 I=1,31
X=I-1
DO 1 J=1,48
Y=J-1
DO 1 K=1,38
Z=K-1
DO 1 L=1,34
```

```
    W=L-1
    IF(10*X+4*Y+8*Z+9*W.GT.300) GO TO 1
    IF(6*X+5*Y+3*Z+9*W.GT.400) GO TO 1
    IF(3*X+9*Y+7*Z+12*W.GT.425) GO TO 1
    P=100*X+150*Y+200*Z+250*W
    IF(P.GT.PMAX) GO TO 2
    GO TO 1
2   IX=X
    IY=Y
    IZ=Z
    IW=W
    PMAX=P
1   CONTINUE
    WRITE(6,3)IX,IY,IZ,IW,PMAX
3   FORMAT('0',5I10)
    STOP
    END
```

```
    THE PRINTOUT IS

0   29   23   0   8950
```

The solution is:

$$x = 0, y = 29, z = 23, w = 0, \text{ and maximum } P = 8950$$

Therefore, the company should produce none of products A and D, and 29 and 23 of products B and C, respectively, to achieve a maximum profit of $8950 per day on these products.

EXAMPLE 3.23
The L Company produces products A, B, C, D, and E at a profit of $40, $50, $70, $80, and $120, respectively. The table below shows how much time is required in each of six departments to make one unit of each of the five products:

Department	Time required (hours)				
	Product A	Product B	Product C	Product D	Product E
1	3	7	2	3	5
2	2	6	7	6	4
3	5	2	3	2	6
4	4	1	8	5	3
5	1	1	4	2	5
6	8	5	1	2	2

Each department has no more than 100 man-hours available per day.

Find the number of units of A, B, C, D, and E that should be produced to maximize the profit. The relevant information can be summarized as follows: Maximize $P = 40x + 50y + 70z + 80w + 120u$ subject to $x \geq 0$, $y \geq 0$, $z \geq 0$, $w \geq 0$, $u \geq 0$, $3x + 7y + 2z + 3w + 5u \leq 100$, $2x + 6y + 7z + 6w + 4u \leq 100$, $5x + 2y + 3z + 2w + 6u \leq 100$, $4x + y + 8z + 5w + 3u \leq 100$, $x + y + 4z + 2w + 5u \leq 100$, and $8x + 5y + z + 2w + 2u \leq 100$. From $8x + 5y + z + 2w + 2u \leq 100$, we get that x can be no larger than 12 ($100/8 = 12.5$). From $3x + 7y + 2z + 3w + 5u \leq 100$, we get that y can be no larger than 14 ($100/7 = 14.28$). From $4x + y + 8z + 5w + 3u \leq 100$, we get that z can be no larger than 12 ($100/8 = 12.5$). From $2x + 6y + 7z + 6w + 4u \leq 100$, we get that w can be no larger than 16 ($100/6 = 16.67$), and, finally, from $5x + 2y + 3z + 2w + 6u \leq 100$, we get that u must be less than 16 ($100/6 = 16.67$). The program follows with five loops (one for each variable) to examine the $13 \times 15 \times 13 \times 17 \times 17 = 732,615$ points from $(0,0,0,0,0)$ to $(12,14,12,16,16)$ to find the optimum combination.

```
      INTEGER X,Y,Z,W,U,PMAX,P
      PMAX=0
      DO 1 I=1,13
      X=I-1
      DO 1 J=1,15
      Y=J-1
      DO 1 K=1,13
      Z=K-1
      DO 1 L=1,17
      W=L-1'
      DO 1 M=1,17
      U=M-1
      IF(3*X+7*Y+2*Z+3*W+5*U.GT.100) GO TO 1
      IF(2*X+6*Y+7*Z+6*W+4*U.GT.100) GO TO 1
      IF(5*X+2*Y+3*Z+2*W+6*U.GT.100) GO TO 1
      IF(4*X+Y+8*Z+5*W+3*U.GT.100) GO TO 1
      IF(X+Y+4*Z+2*W+5*U.GT.100) GO TO 1
      IF(8*X+5*Y+Z+2*W+2*U.GT.100) GO TO 1
      P=40*X+50*Y+70*Z+80*W+120*U
      IF(P.GT.PMAX) GO TO 2
      GO TO 1
2     IX=X
      IY=Y
      IZ=Z
      IW=W
      IU=U
      PMAX=P
1     CONTINUE
      WRITE(6,3)IX,IY,IZ,IW,IU,PMAX
3     FORMAT('0',6I10)
```

STOP
END

        THE PRINTOUT IS

0   0   0   7   14   2240

The solution is:

  $x = 0, y = 0, z = 0, w = 7, u = 14$, and maximum $P = 2240$

Therefore, the company should produce none of products A, B, and C, and 7 and 14 of products D and E, respectively, to obtain a maximum profit of $2240 per day on these products.

EXAMPLE 3.24

The M Company produces products A, B, C, D, E, and F at a profit of $20, $30, $40, $45, $55, and $60, respectively. The table below shows how much time is required in each of three departments to make one unit of each of the six products:

Time required (hours)

Product	Department 1	Department 2	Department 3
A	8	2	3
B	8	4	1
C	3	10	4
D	12	4	2
E	8	2	4
F	4	6	10

Each department has no more than 150 man-hours available per day.

Find the number of units of A, B, C, D, E, and F that should be produced to maximize the profit. The relevant information can be summarized as follows: Maximize $P = 20x + 30y + 40z + 45w + 55u + 60v$ subject to $x \geq 0, y \geq 0, z \geq 0, w \geq 0, u \geq 0, v \geq 0, 8x + 8y + 3z + 12w + 8u + 4v \leq 150, 2x + 4y + 10z + 4w + 2u + 6v \leq 150$, and $3x + y + 4z + 2w + 4u + 10v \leq 150$. From $8x + 8y + 3z + 12w + 8u + 4v \leq 150$, we get that $x, y,$ and u must be less than or equal to 18 ($150/8 = 18.75$). From $2x + 4y + 10z + 4w + 2u + 6v \leq 150$, we get that z must be less than or equal to 15 ($150/10 = 15$). From $8x + 8y + 3z + 12w + 8u + 4v \leq 150$, we get that w must be less than or equal to 12 ($150/12 = 12.5$), and from $3x + y + 4z + 2w + 4u + 10v \leq 150$, we get that v must be less than or equal to 15 ($150/10 = 15$). Notice again that we are trying to set the loop limits so that all feasible solutions (ones that satisfy the constraints) are considered while keeping the loop limits as small as possible. We use six loops (one for each variable) to examine the $19 \times 19 \times 16 \times 13 \times 19 \times 16 = 22,826,752$ points from $(0,0,0,0,0,0)$ to $(18,18,15,12,18,15)$ to find the optimum combination. As before, many of those points don't meet the constraints and are removed from consideration by the GO TO 1 statements. The program follows:

```
      INTEGER X,Y,Z,W,U,V,PMAX,P
      PMAX=0
      DO 1 I=1,19
      X=I-1
      DO 1 J=1,19
      Y=J-1
      DO 1 K=1,16
      Z=K-1
      DO 1 L=1,13
      W=L-1
      DO 1 M=1,19
      U=M-1
      DO 1 N=1,16
      V=N-1
      IF(8*X+8*Y+3*Z+12*W+8*U+4*V.GT.150) GO TO 1
      IF(2*X+4*Y+10*Z+4*W+2*U+6*V.GT.150) GO TO 1
      IF(3*X+Y+4*Z+2*W+4*U+10*V.GT.150) GO TO 1
      P=20*X+30*Y+40*Z+45*W+55*U+60*V
      IF(P.GT.PMAX) GO TO 2
      GO TO 1
2     IX=X
      IY=Y
      IZ=Z
      IW=W
      IU=U
      IV=V
      PMAX=P
1     CONTINUE
      WRITE(6,3)IX,IY,IZ,IW,IU,IV,PMAX
3     FORMAT('0',7I10)
      STOP
      END
```

                    THE PRINTOUT IS

  0   0   8   0   12   7   1400

The solution is:

$x = 0$, $y = 0$, $z = 8$, $w = 0$, $u = 12$, $v = 7$, and maximum $P = 1400$

Therefore, the company should produce none of products A, B, and D, and 8, 12, and 7 of products C, E, and F, respectively, to obtain a maximum profit of $1400 per day on these products.

EXAMPLE 3.25
Company J has two warehouses stocking Product P and three customers (A, B, and C) that need supplies of Product P. A needs 10 units per week, B needs 8 units per week, and C needs 30 units per week. This totals 48 units per week demanded. Warehouse 1 has 30 units per week to deliver and warehouse 2 has 18 units per week to deliver. The cost of delivering one unit from warehouse i to customer k is given in the following table:

	Delivery Cost		
From Warehouse	To Customer A	To Customer B	To Customer C
1	$1.20	$ .66	$ .72
2	$ .58	$1.32	$1.04

How should the 48 units per week be delivered in order to minimize the cost of delivery?

The problem can be summarized as follows: Minimize $C = 120A1 + 66B1 + 72C1 + 58A2 + 132B2 + 104C2$ subject to $A1 \geq 0, B1 \geq 0, C1 \geq 0, A2 \geq 0, B2 \geq 0, C2 \geq 0, A1 + B1 + C1 = 30, A2 + B2 + C2 = 18, A1 + A2 = 10, B1 + B2 = 8$, and $C1 + C2 = 30$. From the constraints we can see that $A1$ must be less than or equal to 10 ($A1 + A2 = 10$), and $B1$ must be less than or equal to 8. Also, $C1$ must equal $30 - A1 - B1$. These facts are reflected in the first two loops. From the constraints we can also see that $A2$ must be less than or equal to 10 ($A1 + A2 = 10$), and $B2$ must be less than or equal to 8 ($B1 + B2 = 8$). Also, $C2$ must equal $18 - A2 - B2$ ($A2 + B2 + C2 = 18$). These facts are reflected in the next two loops. The loops essentially guarantee that $A1 \geq 0, B1 \geq 0, C1 \geq 0, A2 \geq 0, B2 \geq 0, C2 \geq 0, A1 + B1 + C1 = 30$, and $A2 + B2 + C2 = 18$. Therefore, the only remaining constraints to be checked are $A1 + A2 = 10, B1 + B2 = 8$, and $C1 + C2 = 30$. These are checked in the constraint bank (lines 13, 14, and 15), again arranging to skip to 1 (GO TO 1) if any of the three equalities are not satisfied. Therefore, lines 3 through 15 enumerate all possible solutions, and the rest of the program finds and stores the optimum one as in the previous programs. The program is given below:

```
INTEGER A1,B1,C1,A2,B2,C2,CMIN,C
CMIN=9999999
DO 1 I=1,11
A1=I-1
DO 1 J=1,9
B1=J-1
```

```
      C1=30-A1-B1
      DO 1 L=1,11
      A2=L-1
      DO 1 M=1,9
      B2=M-1
      C2=18-A2-B2
      IF(A1+A2.NE.10) GO TO 1
      IF(B1+B2.NE.8) GO TO 1
      IF(C1+C2.NE.30) GO TO 1
      C=120*A1+66*B1+72*C1+58*A2+132*B2+104*C2
      IF(C.LT.CMIN) GO TO 2
      GO TO 1
2     IA1=A1
      IB1=B1
      IC1=C1
      IA2=A2
      IB2=B2
      IC2=C2
      CMIN=C
1     CONTINUE
      WRITE(6,3)IA1,IB1,IC1,IA2,IB2,IC2,CMIN
3     FORMAT('0',7I10)
      STOP
      END
```

THE PRINTOUT IS

 0   8   22   10   0   8   3524

The solution is:

$A1 = 0$, $B1 = 8$, $C1 = 22$, $A2 = 10$, $B2 = 0$, $C2 = 8$, and minimum $C = 3524$

Therefore, the company should ship 8 units from Warehouse 1 to Customer B; 22 units from Warehouse 1 to Customer C; 10 units from Warehouse 2 to Customer A, and 8 units from Warehouse 2 to Customer C to minimize their shipping costs. Notice that this is a transportation problem. We will have more to say about these later. It will be possible to solve transportation problems that are much larger than this example, whether the objective function is linear or nonlinear.

EXAMPLE 3.26
The T Furniture Company makes three types of tables—A, B, and C—for its customers. It earns a profit of $100, $200, and $300, respectively, on each type of table sold. The time (in hours) required in each of the four departments used to make the tables is summarized as follows:

| | Time required (hours) | | | |
Table	Department 1	Department 2	Department 3	Department 4
A	3	1	3	1
B	4	1	3	2
C	7	3	4	2

The number of man-hours available per day in each department is 200, 100, 200, and 100, respectively.

Find the number of tables A, B, and C that should be produced to maximize the profit. The relevant information can be summarized as follows: Maximize $P = 100x + 200y + 300z$ subject to $x \geq 0$, $y \geq 0$, $z \geq 0$, $3x + 4y + 7z \leq 200$, $x + y + 3z \leq 100$, $3x + 3y + 4z \leq 200$, and $x + 2y + 2z \leq 100$. From $3x + 4y + 7z \leq 200$, we see that x can be no larger than 66 ($200/3 = 66.67$), y can be no larger than 50 ($200/4 = 50$), and z can be no larger than 28 ($200/7 = 28.57$). The program is given below with three loops (one for each variable) to examine the $67 \times 51 \times 29 = 99{,}093$ points from $(0,0,0)$ to $(66,50,28)$ to find the optimum combination. Of those 99,093 combinations, as before, the ones that don't meet the constraints are removed from consideration by the GO TO 1 commands.

```
      INTEGER X,Y,Z,PMAX,P
      PMAX=0
      DO 1 I=1,67
      X=I-1
      DO 1 J=1,51
      Y=J-1
      DO 1 K=1,29
      Z=K-1
      IF(3*X+4*Y+7*Z.GT.200) GO TO 1
      IF(X+Y+3*Z.GT.100) GO TO 1
      IF(3*X+3*Y+4*Z.GT.200) GO TO 1
      IF(X+2*Y+2*Z.GT.100) GO TO 1
      P=100*X+200*Y+300*Z
      IF(P.GT.PMAX) GO TO 2
      GO TO 1
2     IX=X
      IY=Y
      IZ=Z
      PMAX=P
1     CONTINUE
      WRITE(6,3)IX,IY,IZ,PMAX
3     FORMAT('0',4I10)
      STOP
      END
```

THE PRINTOUT IS

    0   50   0   10000

The solution is:

$x = 0$, $y = 50$, $z = 0$, and maximum $P = 10,000$

Therefore, the company should produce no units of products A and C, and 50 units of Product B to obtain a maximum profit of $10,000 per day on this process.

EXAMPLE 3.27

The HJ Car Company can put a standard, deluxe, or sport paint job on Car K. It earns a profit on the paint job of $50, $75, and $100, respectively, on each type of paint job sold. The time (in minutes) required in each of the three departments to do each paint job is summarized below:

Paint job	Time required (minutes)		
	Department 1	Department 2	Department 3
Standard	30	30	20
Deluxe	45	30	30
Sport	70	30	50

The number of man-minutes available per day in each department is 10,000, 3,000, and 5,000, respectively.

Find the number of units of each type of paint job that should be done to maximize the profit. The relevant information can be summarized as follows: Maximize $P = 50x + 75y + 100z$ subject to $x \geq 0$, $y \geq 0$, $z \geq 0$, $30x + 45y + 70z \leq 10,000$, $30x + 30y + 30z \leq 3000$, and $20x + 30y + 50z \leq 5000$. From the constraint $30x + 30y + 30z \leq 3000$, we can see that x, y, and z can never be larger than 100 ($3000/30 = 100$). The program below examines the $101 \times 101 \times 101 = 1,030,301$ combinations from $(0,0,0)$ to $(100,100,100)$. Again, the combinations that don't meet the constraints are removed from consideration by the GO TO 1 statements, and the optimum combination is found, stored, and eventually printed at the end of the program.

```
INTEGER X,Y,Z,PMAX,P
PMAX=0
DO 1 I=1,101
X=I-1
DO 1 J=1,101
Y=J-1
```

```
    DO 1 K=1,101
    Z=K-1
    IF(30*X+45*Y+70*Z.GT.10000) GO TO 1
    IF(30*X+30*Y+30*Z.GT.3000) GO TO 1
    IF(20*X+30*Y+50*Z.GT.5000) GO TO 1
    P=50*X+75*Y+100*Z
    IF(P.GT.PMAX) GO TO 2
    GO TO 1
2   IX=X
    IY=Y
    IZ=Z
    PMAX=P
1   CONTINUE
    WRITE(6,3)IX,IY,IZ,PMAX
3   FORMAT('0',4I10)
    STOP
    END


    THE PRINTOUT IS

0   0   100    10000
```

The solution is:

$x = 0$, $y = 0$, $z = 100$, and maximum $P = 10,000$

Therefore, the company should paint 0 cars with the standard paint job, 0 cars with the deluxe paint job, and 100 cars with the sport paint job to maximize profit.

EXAMPLE 3.28

Minimize $C = x^3 + 2x^2y - 4xy^2 + 6y^3 - e^{.02xy}$ subject to $x \geq 0$, $y \geq 0$, $x \leq 100$, $y \leq 100$, $x + y \leq 150$, and $y \geq 2x$.

```
    INTEGER X,Y
    CMIN=+1.0 E67
    DO 1 I=1,101
    X=I-1
    DO 1 J=1,101
    Y=J-1
    IF(X+Y.GT.150) GO TO 1
    IF(Y.LT.2*X) GO TO 1
    C=X**3+2*X**2*Y-4*X*Y**2+6*Y**3-EXP(1./50.*X*Y)
    IF(C.LT.CMIN) GO TO 2
    GO TO 1
2   IX=X
    IY=Y
    CMIN=C
1   CONTINUE
    WRITE(6,3)IX,IY,CMIN
```

```
3   FORMAT('0',2I10,E15.7)
    STOP
    END
```

```
        THE PRINTOUT IS

50      100      -.2688117x10^44
```

The solution is:

$x = 50$, $y = 100$, and minimum $C = -.2688117 \times 10^{44}$

EXAMPLE 3.29

Maximize $P = x^3 + 2x^2y - 4xy^2 + 6y^3 - e^{.02xy}$ subject to $x \geq 0$, $y \geq 0$, $x \leq 100$, $y \leq 100$, $x + y \leq 150$, and $y \leq 2x$. Notice that this is exactly the same as the problem in Example 3.28, except that here we are to find the maximum and there we found the minimum.

```
    INTEGER X,Y
    PMAX=-1.0 E67
    DO 1 I=1,101
    X=I-1
    DO 1 J=1,101
    Y=J-1
    IF(X+Y.GT.150) GO TO 1
    IF(Y.GT.2*X) GO TO 1
    P=X**3+2*X**2*Y-4*X*Y**2+6*Y**3-EXP(1./50.*X*Y)
    IF(P.GT.PMAX) GO TO 2
    GO TO 1
2   IX=X
    IY=Y
    PMAX=P
1   CONTINUE
    WRITE(6,3)IX,IY,PMAX
3   FORMAT('0',2I10,F15.7)
    STOP
    END
```

```
        THE PRINTOUT IS

100     4      1071003.0000000
```

The solution is:

$x = 100$, $y = 4$, and maximum $P = 1,071,003$

EXAMPLE 3.30

Minimize $C = .1xy^2 - .5x - .33y + 16x^2 - x^3 - 3yx^2 + 6x^2y^2$ subject to $x \geq 0$, $y \geq 0$, $x \leq 200$, $y \leq 600$, $x + 3y \leq 400$, and $5x + 2y \leq 1000$. X can't be larger than 200. From the constraint $x + 3y \leq 400$, we see that y can't be larger than 133 (400/3 = 133.33).

```
      INTEGER X,Y
      CMIN=1.0 E67
      DO 1 I=1,201
      X=I-1
      DO 1 J=1,134
      Y=J-1
      IF(X+3*Y.GT.400) GO TO 1
      IF(5*X+2*Y.GT.1000) GO TO 1
      C=.1*X*Y**2-.5*X-1./3.*Y+16.*X**2-X**3-3.*Y*X**2+6.*X**2*Y**2
      IF(C.LT.CMIN) GO TO 2
      GO TO 1
2     IX=X
      IY=Y
      CMIN=C
1     CONTINUE
      WRITE(6,3)IX,IY,CMIN
3     FORMAT('0',2I10,E15.7)
      STOP
      END
```

```
      THE PRINTOUT IS

    200    0    -7359900
```

The solution is:

$x = 200$, $y = 0$, and minimum $C = -7,359,900$

EXAMPLE 3.31

Maximize $C = .1xy^2 - .5x - .33y + 16x^2 - x^3 - 3yx^2 + 6x^2y^2$ subject to $x \geq 0$, $y \geq 0$, $x \leq 200$, $y \leq 600$, $x + 3y \leq 400$, and $5x + 2y \leq 1000$. This is the same problem as presented in Example 3.30, except that here we are looking for the maximum combination.

```
      INTEGER X,Y
      PMAX=-1.0 E67
      DO 1 I=1,201
      X=I-1
      DO 1 J=1,134
      Y=J-1
      IF(X+3*Y.GT.400) GO TO 1
```

```
      IF(5.*X+2*Y.GT.1000) GO TO 1
      P=.1*X*Y**2-.5*X-1./3.*Y+16*X**2-X**3-3*Y*X**2+6*X**2*Y**2
      IF(P.GT.PMAX) GO TO 2
      GO TO 1
2     IX=X
      IY=Y
      PMAX=P
1     CONTINUE
      WRITE(6,3)IX,IY,PMAX
3     FORMAT('0',2I10,E15.7)
      STOP
      END
```

```
      THE PRINTOUT IS
```

169   77   .1005162x10^{10}

The solution is:

$x = 169$, $y = 77$, and maximum $P = 1,005,162,000$

EXAMPLE 3.32

Minimize $C = -4x - xy + x^2 + 2y^2$ subject to $x \geq 0$, $y \geq 0$, $10x + 4y \leq 300$, and $x + 8y \leq 500$. From the constraint $10x + 4y \leq 300$, we see that x can be no larger than 30 ($300/10 = 30$). From the constraint $x + 8y \leq 500$, we see that y can be no larger than 62 ($500/8 = 62.5$). The program below searches the $31 \times 63 = 1953$ ordered pairs from $(0,0)$ to $(30,62)$, throwing out the ones that don't satisfy the constraints, and finds the combination that produces the minimum.

```
      INTEGER X,Y,CMIN,C
      CMIN=9999999
      DO 1 I=1,31
      X=I-1
      DO 1 J=1,63
      Y=J-1
      IF(10*X+4*Y.GT.300) GO TO 1
      IF(X+8*Y.GT.500) GO TO 1
      C=-4*X-X*Y+X**2+2*Y**2
      IF(C.LT.CMIN) GO TO 2
      GO TO 1
2     IX=X
      IY=Y
      CMIN=C
1     CONTINUE
      WRITE(6,3)IX,IY,CMIN
3     FORMAT('0',3I10)
```

```
STOP
END
```

```
THE PRINTOUT IS
```

```
2     0     -4
```

The solution is:

$x = 2, y = 0$, and minimum $C = -4$

EXAMPLE 3.33

Maximize $P = -4x - xy + x^2 + 2y^2$ subject to $x \geq 0, y \geq 0, x \leq 10, y \leq 10, 10x + 4y \leq 30, x + 8y \leq 50$, and x and y are in increments of .1. Therefore, x and y can take the values 0, .1, .2, .3,...,1.1, 1.2, 1.3, 1.4,..., 9.8, 9.9, 10.

The statements DO 1 I = 1,101, X = (I − 1)/10., DO 1 J = 1,101, and Y = (J − 1)/10 allow the 101 × 101 = 10,201 pairs (ordered by increments of .1) from (0,0) to (10,10) to be considered in looking for the optimum pair.

```
     PMAX=-1.0 E67
     DO 1 I=1,101
     X=(I-1)/10.
     DO 1 J=1,101
     Y=(J-1)/10.
     IF(10*X+4*Y.GT.30) GO TO 1
     IF(X+8*Y.GT.50) GO TO 1
     P=-4*X-X*Y+X**2+2*Y**2
     IF(P.GT.PMAX) GO TO 2
     GO TO 1
2    XIX=X
     XIY=Y
     PMAX=P
1    CONTINUE
     WRITE(6,3)XIX,XIY,PMAX
3    FORMAT('0',3E15.7)
     STOP
     END
```

```
          THE PRINTOUT IS
```

```
0.0000000E 00   0.6200000E 01   0.7687997E 02
```

The solution is:

$x = 0, y = 6.2$, and maximum $P = 76.88$

EXAMPLE 3.34

Minimize $C = x - y + z - w + xy - xw + w^2 - x^2$ subject to $x \geq 0, y \geq 0, z \geq 0,$
$w \geq 0, x + y + 3z \leq 55, y + w \leq 52, x + 3w \leq 38,$ and $x^2 + xw \leq 45.$ The
constraint $x^2 + xw \leq 45$ guarantees that x can be no larger than 6 ($\sqrt{45} = 6.708$), and
$y + w \leq 52$ limits y to, at most, 52. The constraint $x + y + 3z \leq 55$ limits z to 18
($55/3 = 18.33$), while $x + 3w \leq 38$ limits w to 12 ($38/3 = 12.67$).

```
      INTEGER X,Y,Z,W,CMIN,C
      CMIN=9999999
      DO 1 I=1,7
      X=I-1
      DO 1 J=1,53
      Y=J-1
      DO 1 K=1,19
      Z=K-1
      DO 1 L=1,13
      W=L-1
      IF(X+Y+3*Z.GT.55) GO TO 1
      IF(Y+W.GT.52) GO TO 1
      IF(X+3*W.GT.38) GO TO 1
      IF(X**2+X*W.GT.45) GO TO 1
      C=X-Y+Z-W+X*Y-X*W+W**2-X**2
      IF(C.LT.CMIN) GO TO 2
      GO TO 1
  2   IX=X
      IY=Y
      IZ=Z
      IW=W
      CMIN=C
  1   CONTINUE
      WRITE(6,3)IX,IY,IZ,IW,CMIN
  3   FORMAT('0',5I10)
      STOP
      END


      THE PRINTOUT IS

  0   52   0   0   -52
```

The solution is:

$x = 0, y = 52, z = 0, w = 0,$ and minimum $C = -52$

EXAMPLE 3.35

Maximize $P = x - y + z - w + xy - xw + w^2 - x^2$ subject to $x \geq 0, y \geq 0, z \geq 0,$
$w \geq 0, x \leq 30, y \leq 30, z \leq 30, w \leq 30, x + y + 3z \leq 55, y + w \leq 52, x + 3w$

≤ 38, and $x^2 + xw \leq 45$. All the loop limits are determined as in Example 3.34 except that y must be less than or equal to 30.

```
INTEGER X,Y,Z,W,PMAX,P
PMAX=9999999
DO 1 I=1,7
X=I-1
DO 1 J=1,31
Y=J-1
DO 1 K=1,19
Z=K-1
DO 1 L=1,13
W=L-1
IF(X+Y+3*Z.GT.55) GO TO 1
IF(Y+W.GT.52) GO TO 1
IF(X+3*W.GT.38) GO TO 1
IF(X**2+X*W.GT.45) GO TO 1
P=X-Y+Z-W+X*Y-X*W+W**2-X**2
IF(P.GT.PMAX) GO TO 2
GO TO 1
2   IX=X
    IY=Y
    IZ=Z
    IW=W
    PMAX=P
1   CONTINUE
    WRITE(6,3)IX,IY,IZ,IW,PMAX
3   FORMAT('0',5I10)
    STOP
    END
```

```
    THE PRINTOUT IS

0   0   18   12    150
```

The solution is:

$x = 0, y = 0, z = 18, w = 12$, and maximum $P = 150$

EXAMPLE 3.36
Minimize $C = 2xy^2 - 4xy + x^2 + y^2 - 27x^2y^2$ subject to $x \geq 0$, $y \geq 0$, $x \leq 500$, $y \leq 100$, $x^2 + 2xy + y^2 \leq 500$, and $x + 2y^2 \leq 400$. The constraint $x^2 + 2xy + y^2 \leq 500$ forces x to be 22 or less ($\sqrt{500} = 22.36$). The constraint $x + 2y^2 \leq 400$ forces y to be 14 or less ($\sqrt{400/2} = \sqrt{200} = 14.142$).

```
INTEGER X,Y,CMIN,C
CMIN=9999999
DO 1 I=1,23
```

```
      X=I-1
      DO 1 J=1,15
      Y=J-1
      IF(X**2+2*X*Y+Y**2.GT.500) GO TO 1
      IF(X+2*Y**2.GT.400) GO TO 1
      C=2*X*Y**2-4*X*Y+X**2+Y**2-27*X**2*Y**2
      IF(C.LT.CMIN) GO TO 2
      GO TO 1
    2 IX=X
      IY=Y
      CMIN=C
    1 CONTINUE
      WRITE(6,3)IX,IY,CMIN
    3 FORMAT('0',3I10)
      STOP
      END


      THE PRINTOUT IS

      11    11    -392887
```

The solution is:

$x = 11, y = 11$, and minimum $C = -392,887$

EXAMPLE 3.37

The Great Shot Golf Club Company makes three sets of golf clubs: a beginners set, a standard set, and a professional set. It earns a profit of $20, $50, and $100, respectively, on each type of set sold. The time (in hours) required in each of the five departments used to make the golf clubs is summarized below:

| Set | Time required (hours) | | | | |
	Depart- ment 1	Depart- ment 2	Depart- ment 3	Depart- ment 4	Depart- ment 5
Beginners	1	1/2	1	2	1
Standard	2	1/2	1	2	2
Professional	2	1/2	1.5	3	2

The number of man-hours available per day in each of the five departments is 200, 100, 150, 250, and 200, respectively.

Find the number of sets of each type that should be made to maximize the profit. The relevant information can be summarized as follows: Maximize $P = 20x + 50y + 100z$ subject to $x \geq 0, y \geq 0, z \geq 0, x + 2y + 2z \leq 200, .5x + .5y + .5z \leq 100$, $x + y + 1.5z \leq 150, 2x + 2y + 3z \leq 250$, and $x + 2y + 2z \leq 200$. The constraint

$2x + 2y + 3z \leq 250$ establishes that x can be no larger than 125 ($250/2 = 125$), and that z can be no larger than 83 ($250/3 = 83.33$). The constraint $x + 2y + 2z \leq 200$ assures that y can be no larger than 100 ($200/2 = 100$).

```
      INTEGER X,Y,Z,PMAX,P
      PMAX=0
      DO 1 I=1,126
      X=I-1
      DO 1 J=1,101
      Y=J-1
      DO 1 K=1,84
      Z=K-1
      IF(X+2*Y+2*Z.GT.200) GO TO 1
      IF(.5*X+.5*Y+.5*Z.GT.100) GO TO 1
      IF(X+Y+1.5*Z.GT.150) GO TO 1
      IF(2*X+2*Y+3*Z.GT.250) GO TO 1
      IF(X+2*Y+2*Z.GT.200) GO TO 1
      P=20*X+50*Y+100*Z
      IF(P.GT.PMAX) GO TO 2
      GO TO 1
    2 IX=X
      IY=Y
      IZ=Z
      PMAX=P
    1 CONTINUE
      WRITE(6,3)IX,IY,IZ,PMAX
    3 FORMAT('0',4I10)
      STOP
```

```
      THE PRINTOUT IS

   0    0    83       8300
```

The solution is:

$x = 0$, $y = 0$, $z = 83$, and maximum $P = 8300$

Therefore, the company should produce no beginners or standard sets and 83 professional sets to realize a maximum profit of $8300 per day.

EXAMPLE 3.38
The Great Shot Golf Club Company also makes golf balls. They make a standard ball with a profit of 20¢ per ball, and they make a deluxe ball with a profit of 50¢ per ball. The time (in minutes) required in each of the three departments to make one of each golf ball is summarized below:

Golf ball	Time required (minutes)		
	Department 1	Department 2	Department 3
Standard	1/3	1/2	1⅓
Deluxe	1/2	1	1⅓

The number of man-minutes available per day in each of the three departments is 1,000, 2,000, and 3,000, respectively.

Find the number of each type of ball that should be made to maximize the profit. The relevant information can be summarized as follows: Maximize $P = 20x + 50y$ subject to $x \geq 0$, $y \geq 0$, $.333x + .5y \leq 1000$, $.5x + y \leq 2000$, $1.333x + 1.333y \leq 3000$. The constraint $1.333x + 1.333y \leq 3000$ guarantees that x can be no larger than 2250 (3000/1.33 = 2250). The constraint $.5x + y \leq 2000$ guarantees that y can be no larger than 2000.

```
      INTEGER X,Y,PMAX,P
      PMAX=0
      DO 1 I=1,2251
      X=I-1
      DO 1 J=1,2001
      Y=J-1
      IF(1./3.*X+1./2.*Y.GT.1000.) GO TO 1
      IF(1./2.*X+Y.GT.2000.) GO TO 1
      IF(4./3.*X+4./3.*Y.GT.3000.) GO TO 1
      P=20*X+50*Y
      IF(P.GT.PMAX) GO TO 2
      GO TO 1
2     IX=X
      IY=Y
      PMAX=P
1     CONTINUE
      WRITE(6,3)IX,IY,PMAX
3     FORMAT('0',3I10)
      STOP
      END



      THE PRINTOUT IS

0     2000       100000
```

The solution is:

$x = 0$, $y = 2000$, and maximum $P = 100,000$ cents

Therefore, the company should make no standard golf balls and 2000 deluxe golf balls per day to realize a maximum profit of $1000.00 each day.

EXAMPLE 3.39

The Easy Add Calculator Company makes two types of calculators: household Model A and student Model B. They make a profit of $12 per calculator with the household model and $21 per calculator with the student model. The time in minutes required in each of the four departments to make one of each type of calculator is summarized below:

| | Time required (minutes) | | | |
Model	Department 1	Department 2	Department 3	Department 4
A	1	3	2	5
B	2	3	3	8

The number of man-minutes available per hour in each department is 2,000, 2,000, 5,000, and 9,000, respectively.

Find the number of each type of calculator that should be made to maximize the profit. The relevant information can be summarized as follows: Maximize $P = 12x + 21y$ subject to $x \geq 0$, $y \geq 0$, $x + 2y \leq 2000$, $3x + 3y \leq 2000$, $2x + 3y \leq 5000$, and $5x + 8y \leq 9000$. The constraint $3x + 3y \leq 2000$ guarantees that both x and y can be no larger than 666 (2000/3 = 666.67). The program has two loops for the two variables.

```
      INTEGER X,Y,PMAX,P
      PMAX=0
      DO 1 I=1,667
      X=I-1
      DO 1 J=1,667
      Y=J-1
      IF(X+2*Y.GT.2000) GO TO 1
      IF(3*X+3*Y.GT.2000) GO TO 1
      IF(2*X+3*Y.GT.5000) GO TO 1
      IF(5*X+8*Y.GT.9000) GO TO 1
      P=12*X+21*Y
      IF(P.GT.PMAX) GO TO 2
      GO TO 1
2     IX=X
      IY=Y
      PMAX=P
1     CONTINUE
      WRITE(6,3)IX,IY,PMAX
3     FORMAT('0',3I10)
      STOP
      END


      THE PRINTOUT IS

   0     666      13986
```

The solution is:

$x = 0$, $y = 666$, and maximum $P = 13,986$

Therefore, the company should produce no household Model A calculators and 666 student Model B calculators to realize a maximum profit of $13,986 per hour on these units.

EXAMPLE 3.40
The Very Beautiful Upholstering Company re-covers hassocks, chairs, and couches. They make a profit of $40 per hassock, $80 per chair, and $130 per couch. The time required in hours in each of the three departments used to re-cover the various pieces of furniture is summarized below:

	Time required (hours)		
Furniture	Department 1	Department 2	Department 3
Hassock	1	1	1
Chair	1	3	2
Couch	2	4	5

There are 120 man-hours per week available in each of the three departments.

Find the number of each type of furniture that should be re-covered to maximize the profit. The relevant information can be summarized as follows: Maximize $P = 40x + 80y + 130z$ subject to $x \geq 0$, $y \geq 0$, $z \geq 0$, $x + y + 2z \leq 120$, $x + 3y + 4z \leq 120$, and $x + 2y + 5z \leq 120$. The constraint $x + 3y + 4z \leq 120$ guarantees that x will be no larger than 120 and that y will be no larger than 40 ($120/3 = 40$). The constraint $x + 2y + 5z \leq 120$ guarantees that z will be no larger than 24 ($120/5 = 24$). There are three loops (one for each variable) in the program.

```
INTEGER X,Y,Z,PMAX,P
PMAX=0
DO 1 I=1,121
X=I-1
DO 1 J=1,41
Y=J-1
DO 1 K=1,25
Z=K-1
IF(X+Y+2*Z.GT.120) GO TO 1
IF(X+3*Y+4*Z.GT.120) GO TO 1
IF(X+2*Y+5*Z.GT.120) GO TO 1
P=40*X+80*Y+130*Z
IF(P.GT.PMAX) GO TO 2
GO TO 1
2    IX=X
IY=Y
IZ=Z
```

```
        PMAX=P
1 CONTINUE
        WRITE(6,3)IX,IY,IZ,PMAX
3 FORMAT('0',4I10)
        STOP
        END


        THE PRINTOUT IS

        120   0   0   4800
```

The solution is:

$x = 120$, $y = 0$, $z = 0$, and maximum $P = 4800$

Therefore, the company should re-cover 120 hassocks, no chairs, and no couches to realize a profit of $4800 per week.

EXAMPLE 3.41

The Very Beautiful Upholstering Company is considering hiring an additional employee and putting him in Department 2. They plan to have 2 employees in Department 1, 4 employees in Department 2, and 4 employees in Department 3. The additional cost of hiring the extra employee is $200 per week. Should they hire the new employee? Will the profit be greater this way?

Now, 80, 160, and 160 hours will be available in departments 1, 2, and 3, respectively. The time requirements in each department for each of the three furniture pieces is summarized below:

	Time required (hours)		
Furniture	Department 1	Department 2	Department 3
Hassock	1	1	1
Chair	1	3	2
Couch	2	4	5

We wish to find the number of each type of furniture that should be re-covered to maximize the profit. The relevant information can be summarized as follows: Maximize $P = 40x + 80y + 130z$ subject to $x \geq 0$, $y \geq 0$, $z \geq 0$, $x + y + 2z \leq 80$, $x + 3y + 4z \leq 160$, and $x + 2y + 5z \leq 160$. The constraint $x + y + 2z \leq 80$ assures that x will be less than or equal to 80. The constraint $x + 3y + 4z \leq 160$ determines that y will be less than or equal to 53 ($160/3 = 53.33$). The inequality $x + 2y + 5z \leq 160$ assures that z will be less than or equal to 32 ($160/5 = 32$). The program follows with three loops to examine the $81 \times 54 \times 33 = 144,342$ combinations from (0,0,0) to (80,53,32), throwing out the ones that violate one or more constraints, to find the combination that maximizes P.

```
INTEGER X,Y,Z,PMAX,P
PMAX=0
DO 1 I=1,81
X=I-1
DO 1 J=1,54
Y=J-1
DO 1 K=1,33
Z=K-1
IF(X+Y+2*Z.GT.80) GO TO 1
IF(X+3*Y+4*Z.GT.160) GO TO 1
IF(X+2*Y+5*Z.GT.160) GO TO 1
P=40*X+80*Y+130*Z
IF(P.GT.PMAX) GO TO 2
GO TO 1
2    IX=X
     IY=Y
     IZ=Z
     PMAX=P
1    CONTINUE
     WRITE(6,3)IX,IY,IZ,PMAX
3    FORMAT('0',4I10)
     STOP
     END


     THE PRINTOUT IS

20      20      20      5000
```

The solution is:

$x = 20$, $y = 20$, $z = 20$, and maximum $P = 5000 - 200 = 4800$

(The $200 is the weekly cost of adding the extra man.) Therefore, the company can re-cover 20 hassocks, 20 chairs, and 20 couches to realize a profit of $4800 per week.

EXAMPLE 3.42

In addition, the Very Beautiful Upholstering Company is considering hiring an additional employee for each of the three departments at a weekly cost of $200 per employee. Should they hire the new employees? Will the profit be greater this way?

Therefore, 120, 200, and 200 hours will be available in departments 1, 2, and 3, respectively (representing 3, 5, and 5 employees in the departments). The time requirements in each department for each of the three furniture pieces is summarized below:

	Time required (hours)		
Furniture	Department 1	Department 2	Department 3
Hassock	1	1	1
Chair	1	3	2
Couch	2	4	5

We wish to find the number of each type of furniture that should be re-covered to maximize the profit. The relevant information can be summarized as follows: Maximize $P = 40x + 80y + 130z$ subject to $x \geq 0, y \geq 0, z \geq 0, x + y + 2z \leq 120$, $x + 3y + 4z \leq 200$, and $x + 2y + 5z \leq 200$. The constraint $x + y + 2z \leq 120$ restricts x to less than or equal to 120. The constraint $x + 3y + 4z \leq 200$ restricts y to less than or equal to 66 ($200/3 = 66.67$). The constraint $x + 2y + 5z \leq 200$ restricts z to less than or equal to 40 ($200/5 = 40$).

```
      INTEGER X,Y,Z,PMAX,P
      PMAX=0
      DO 1 I=1,121
      X=I-1
      DO 1 J=1,67
      Y=J-1
      DO 1 K=1,41
      Z=K-1
      IF(X+Y+2*Z.GT.120) GO TO 1
      IF(X+3*Y+4*Z.GT.200) GO TO 1
      IF(X+2*Y+5*Z.GT.200) GO TO 1
      P=40*X+80*Y+130*Z
      IF(P.GT.PMAX) GO TO 2
      GO TO 1
2     IX=X
      IY=Y
      IZ=Z
      PMAX=P
1     CONTINUE
      WRITE(6,3)IX,IY,IZ,PMAX
3     FORMAT('0',4I10)
      STOP
      END


      THE PRINTOUT IS

60    20    20    6600
```

The solution is:

$x = 60, y = 20, z = 20$, and maximum $P = 6600 - 800 = 5{,}800$

($800 because there are now four new employees, three from this change and one from the previous one.) Thus, the company can re-cover 60 hassocks, 20 chairs, and 20 couches to realize a profit of $5,800. This is greater than the other ways of operating and therefore this approach should be adopted.

EXAMPLE 3.43
The Very Beautiful Upholstering Company is considering hiring an additional employee for departments 2 and 3 at a weekly cost of $200 per employee. Therefore, 3, 6, and 6 employees representing 120, 240, and 240 hours per week would be available in departments 1, 2, and 3, respectively. Should they hire the new employees? Will the profit be greater this way? The time requirements are the same as before:

	Time required (hours)		
Furniture	Department 1	Department 2	Department 3
Hassock	1	1	1
Chair	1	3	2
Couch	2	4	5

We wish to find the number of each type of furniture that should be re-covered to maximize the profit. The relevant information can be summarized as follows: Maximize $P = 40x + 80y + 130z$ subject to $x \geq 0, y \geq 0, z \geq 0, x + y + 2z \leq 120$, $x + 3y + 4z \leq 240$, and $x + 2y + 5z \leq 240$. The constraint $x + y + 2z \leq 120$ restricts x to less than or equal to 120. The constraint $x + 3y + 4z \leq 240$ restricts y to less than or equal to 80 ($240/3 = 80$). The inequality $x + 2y + 5z \leq 240$ restricts z to 48 ($240/5 = 48$). The program uses three loops to consider all possible points from (0,0,0) to (120,80,48), throwing out the ones that don't satisfy a constraint, and to find the combination of the three variables that maximizes P.

```
      INTEGER X,Y,Z,PMAX,P
      PMAX=0
      DO 1 I=1,121
      X=I-1
      DO 1 J=1,81
      Y=J-1
      DO 1 K=1,49
      Z=K-1
      IF(X+Y+2*Z.GT.120) GO TO 1
      IF(X+3*Y+4*Z.GT.240) GO TO 1
      IF(X+2*Y+5*Z.GT.240) GO TO 1
      P=40*X+80*Y+130*Z
      IF(P.GT.PMAX) GO TO 2
      GO TO 1
2     IX=X
```

```
      IY=Y
      IZ=Z
      PMAX=P
1     CONTINUE
      WRITE(6,3)IX,IY,IZ,PMAX
3     FORMAT('0',4I10)
      STOP
      END
```

```
          THE PRINTOUT IS

   30    30    30      7500
```

The solution is:

$x = 30$, $y = 30$, $z = 30$, and maximum $P = 7500 - 1200 = 6300$

($1200 is due to six new employees, at $200 each, having been added since the original problem was stated.) Therefore, the company can re-cover 30 hassocks, 30 chairs, and 30 couches to realize a profit of $6300. This is greater than the other ways of operating and therefore should be adopted.

Notice that with a desk-top minicomputer a manager or planner could consider dozens of worker combinations in a short time to see which deployment of workers could increase profit.

The previous discussion assumed that regardless of the output, all units could be sold at the same price. This is often the case. However, it also frequently happens that sales are a function of price. When this is the case, we frequently encounter a downward sloping demand curve (as the price is reduced the sales increase). This puts squared terms in the profit function, which produces nonlinear integer programming problems. These are generally unsolvable. Actually, we should say "were" unsolvable because the computer doesn't know the difference, as long as we use our technique. A few examples of this are now presented.

EXAMPLE 3.44

Suppose that the price of a product is related to the quantity sold in the sense that as the price is decreased the quantity sold increases. Specifically, the A Company produces and markets products B and C. The daily price-quantity curve for Product B is $y = -.5x_1 + 20$ where x_1 is the quantity sold and y is the price. The daily price-quantity curve for Product C is $y = -.333x_2 + 25$ where x_2 is the quantity sold and y is the price. Product B costs $2 per unit to make; Product C costs $3 per unit to make.

The profit equation for Product B is:

$$P_b = x_1 y - 2x_1$$
$$P_b = x_1 (-.5x_1 + 20) - 2x_1$$

$$P_b = -.5x_1^2 + 20x_1 - 2x_1$$
$$P_b = -.5x_1^2 + 18x_1 \quad \text{for } 0 \le x_1 \le 36$$

The profit equation for Product C is:

$$P_c = x_2 y - 3x_2$$
$$P_c = x_2 (-.333x_2 + 25) - 3x_2$$
$$P_c = -.333x_2^2 + 25x_2 - 3x_2$$
$$P_c = -.333x_2^2 + 22x_2 \quad \text{for } 0 \le x_2 \le 66$$

Therefore, the profit equation for producing and selling products B and C is:

$$P = Pb + Pc$$
$$P = -.5x_1^2 + 18x_1 - .333x_2^2 + 22x_2$$

Let us maximize P subject to $x_1 \ge 0$, $x_2 \ge 0$, $x_1 \le 36$, and $x_2 \le 66$. Set $-.5x_1^2 + 18x_1$ equal to zero and solve for x:

$$-.5x_1^2 + 18x_1 = 0$$
$$x_1(-.5x_1 + 18) = 0$$

Therefore

$$x_1 = 0 \quad \text{or} \quad -.5x_1 + 18 = 0$$
$$.5x_1 = 18$$
$$x_1 = 36$$

When $x_1 = 36$, the profit from Product B is zero. So a sales of more than 36 will make the profit on B negative. Therefore, $x_1 \le 36$. Similarly with

$$-.33x_2^2 + 22x_2 = 0$$
$$x_2 (-.33x_2 + 22) = 0$$

Therefore

$$x_2 = 0 \quad \text{or} \quad -.33x_2 + 22 = 0$$
$$.33x_2 = 22$$
$$x_2 = 66$$

When $x_2 = 66$, the profit from Product C is zero. So a sales of more than 66 will make the profit on C negative. Therefore, $x_2 \le 66$.

```
INTEGER X1,X2
PMAX=0
DO 1 I=1,37
X1=I-1
DO 1 J=1,66
```

```
     X2=J-1
     P=-.5*X1*X1+18.*X1-1./3.*X2*X2+22.*X2
     IF(P.GT.PMAX) GO TO 2
     GO TO 1
2    IX1=X1
     IX2=X2
     PMAX=P
1    CONTINUE
     WRITE(6,3)IX1,IX2,PMAX
3    FORMAT('0',2I10,F15.7)
     STOP
     END


          THE PRINTOUT IS

     18       33       525.0002000
```

The solution is:

$x_1 = 18$, $x_2 = 33$, and maximum $P = 525.0002$

Therefore, the company should make and sell 18 units of A and 33 units of B to realize a maximum profit of $525 per day on these two products.

EXAMPLE 3.45
Suppose that the price of a product is related to the quantity sold in the sense that as the price is decreased the quantity sold increases. Specifically, the AA Company produces and markets products D and E. The daily price-quantity curve for Product D is $y = -.25x_3 + 40$ where x_3 is the quantity sold and y is the price. The daily price-quantity curve for Product E is $y = -.5x_4 + 60$ where x_4 is the quantity sold and y is the price. Product D costs $1.50 per unit to make; Product E costs $3.00 per unit to make.

The profit equation for Product D is:

$$P_D = x_3y - 1.5x_3$$
$$P_D = x_3(-.25x_3 + 40) - 1.5x_3$$
$$P_D = -.25x_3^2 + 40x_3 - 1.5x_3$$
$$P_D = -.25x_3^2 + 38.5x_3 \quad \text{for the } 0 \le x_3 \le 154$$

The profit equation for Product E is:

$$P_E = x_4y - 3x_4$$
$$P_E - x_4(-.5x_4 + 60) - 3x_4$$
$$P_E = -.5x_4^2 + 60x_4 - 3x_4$$
$$P_E = -.5x_4^2 + 57x_4$$

Therefore, the profit equation for producing and selling products D and E is:

$$P = P_D + P_E$$

$P = -.25x_3^2 + 38.5x_3 - .5x_4^2 + 57x_4$. Let us maximize P subject to $x_3 \geq 0$, $x_4 \geq 0$, $x_3 \leq 154$, and $x_4 \leq 114$. The upper bounds of $x_3 \leq 154$ and $x_4 \leq 114$ came from solving $-.25x_3^2 + 38.5x_3 = 0$, and $-.5x_4^2 + 57x_4 = 0$ as in Example 3.44.

```
   INTEGER X3,X4
   PMAX=0
   DO 1 I=1,155
   X3=I-1
   DO 1 J=1,115
   X4=J-1
   P=-.25*X3*X3+38.5*X3-.5*X4*X4+57.*X4
   IF(P.GT.PMAX) GO TO 2
   GO TO 1
 2 IX3=X3
   IX4=X4
   PMAX=P
 1 CONTINUE
   WRITE(6,3)IX3,IX4,PMAX
 3 FORMAT('0',2I10,F15.7)
   STOP
   END


         THE PRINTOUT IS

   77      57      3106.7500000
```

The solution is:

$x_3 = 77$, $x_4 = 57$, and maximum $P = 3106.75$

Therefore, the company should make and sell $x_3 = 77$ units of D and $x_4 = 57$ units of E to realize a maximum profit of $3,106.75 a day on these two products.

EXAMPLE 3.46

Suppose that the price of a product is related to the quantity sold in the sense that as the price is decreased the quantity sold increases. Specifically, the ABCD Company produces and markets products F and G. The daily price-quantity curve for Product F is $y = -.4x_5 + 15$ where x is the quantity sold and y is the price. The daily price-quantity curve for Product G is $Y = -.3x_6 + 22$ where x is the quantity sold and y is the price. Product F costs $2 per unit to make; Product G costs $1 per unit to make.

The profit equation for Product F is:

$$P_F = x_5 y - 2x_5$$

$$P_F = x_5 (-.4x_5 + 15) - 2x_5$$

$$P_F = -.4x_5^2 + 13x_5 \text{ for } 0 \le x_5 \le 32$$

The profit equation for Product G is:

$$P_G = x_6 y - x_6$$

$$P_G = x_6 (-.3x_6 + 22) - x_6$$

$$P_G = -.3x_6^2 + 21x_6 \quad \text{for} \quad 0 \le x_6 \le 70$$

Again, the limits $x_5 \le 32$ and $x_6 \le 70$ are derived by solving $-.4x_5^2 + 13x_5 = 0$ and $-.3x_6^2 + 21x_6 = 0$. Any x_5 value larger than 32 will make the profit contribution of Product F negative. Any x_6 value larger than 70 will make the profit contribution of Product G negative.

```
INTEGER X5,X6
PMAX=0.
DO 1 I=1,33
X5=I-1
DO 1 J=1,71
X6=J-1
P=-.4*X5*X5+13.*X5-.3*X6*X6+21.*X6
IF(P.GT.PMAX) GO TO 2
GO TO 1
2   IX5=X5
    IX6=X6
    PMAX=P
1   CONTINUE
    WRITE(6,3)IX5,IX6,PMAX
3   FORMAT('0',2I10,F15.7)
    STOP
    END
```

```
        THE PRINTOUT IS

   16      35      473.1000000
```

The solution is:

$x_5 = 16$, $x_6 = 35$, and maximum $P = 473.10$

Therefore, the company should make and sell 16 units of F and 35 units of G to realize a maximum profit of $473.10 per day on these products.

EXAMPLE 3.47

The ABCD Company decides to produce Product H along with products F and G described earlier in Example 3.46. Product H has a daily price-quantity curve of $y =$

$- .45x_7 + 32$ where x_7 is the quantity sold and y is the price. Product H costs $\$.80$ to make.

The profit equation for Product H is:

$$P_H = x_7y - .8x_7$$
$$P_H = x_7(-.45x_7 + 32) - .8x_7$$
$$P = -.45x_7^2 + 32x_7 - .8x_7$$
$$P = -.45x_7^2 + 31.2x_7 \quad \text{for } 0 \le x_7 \le 69.33$$

Therefore, the profit equation for products F, G, and H is:

$$P = P_F + P_G + P_H$$

$P = -.4x_5^2 + 13x_5 - .3x_6^2 + 21x_6 - .45x_7^2 + 31.2x_7$. Let us maximize P subject to $x_5 \ge 0$, $x_6 \ge 0$, $x_7 \ge 0$, $x_5 \le 32$, $x_6 \le 70$, and $x_7 \le 69$. Again, the limit $x_7 \le 69$ was derived from solving $-.45x_7^2 + 31.2x_7 = 0$.

```
      INTEGER X5,X6,X7
      PMAX=0
      DO 1 I=1,33
      X5=I-1
      DO 1 J=1, 71
      X6=J-1
      DO 1 K=1,70
      X7=K-1
      P=-.4*X5*X5+13.*X5-.3*X6*X6+21.*X6-.45*X7*X7+31.2*X7
      IF(P.GT.PMAX) GO TO 2
      GO TO 1
2     IX5=X5
      IX6=X6
      IX7=X7
      PMAX=P
1     CONTINUE
      WRITE(6,3)IX5,IX6,IX7,PMAX
3     FORMAT('0',3I10,F15.7)
      STOP
      END
```

```
           THE PRINTOUT IS

16      35      35      1013.8500000
```

The solution is:

$x_5 = 16$, $x_6 = 35$, $x_7 = 35$, and maximum $P = 1013.85$

Therefore, the company should make and sell 16 units of F, 35 units of G, and 35 units of H to realize a maximum profit of $\$1,013.85$ per day.

EXAMPLE 3.48

The K Company produces and markets products R, S, and T. Product R has a daily price-quantity curve described as $y = -.6x_1 + 60$ where x_1 is the quantity sold and y is the price. Product R costs \$1 to make. The profit equation then for Product R is:

$$P_R = x_1 y - x_1$$
$$P_R = x_1(-.6x_1 + 60) - x_1$$
$$P_R = -.6x_1^2 + 60x_1 - x_1$$
$$P_R = -.6x_1^2 + 59x_1 \quad \text{for } 0 \le x_1 \le 98.33$$

Product S has a daily price-quantity curve described as $y = -.3x_2 + 25$ where x_2 is the quantity sold and y is the price. Product S costs \$1.50 per unit to make. Therefore the profit equation for Product S is:

$$P_S = x_2 y - 1.5x_2$$
$$P_S = x_2(-.3x_2 + 25) - 1.5x_2$$
$$P_S = -.3x_2^2 + 25x_2 - 1.5x_2$$
$$P_S = -.3x_2^2 + 23.5x_2 \quad \text{for } 0 \le x_2 \le 75$$

Product T has a daily price quantity curve of $y = -.2x_3 + 30$ where x_3 is the quantity sold and y is the price. Product T costs \$1.50 per unit to make and its profit equation is:

$$P_T = x_3 y - 1.5x_3$$
$$P_T = x_3(-.2x_3 + 30) - 1.5x_3$$
$$P_T = .2x_3^2 + 30x_3 - 1.5x_3$$
$$P_T = -.2x_3^2 + 28.5x \quad \text{for } 0 \le x_3 \le 142.5$$

Therefore the profit equation for producing and selling products R, S, and T is:

$$P = P_R + P_S + P_T$$

$P = -.6x_1^2 + 59x_1 - .3x_2^2 + 23.5x_2 - .2x_3^2 + 28.5x_3$. Let us maximize P subject to $x_1 \ge 0$, $x_2 \ge 0$, $x_3 \ge 0$, $x_1 \le 98.33$, $x_2 \le 75$, and $x_3 \le 142.5$.

```
      INTEGER X1,X2,X3
      PMAX=-9999999
      DO 1 I=1,99
      X1=I-1
      DO 1 J=1,76
      X2=J-1
      DO 1 K=1,143
      X3=K-1
      P=-.6*X1*X1+59.*X1-.3*X2*X2+23.5*X2-.2*X3*X3+28.5*X3
      IF(P.GT.PMAX) GO TO 2
      GO TO 1
2     IX1=X1
```

```
      IX2=X2
      IX3=X3
      PMAX=P
  1   CONTINUE
      WRITE(6,3)IX1,IX2,IX3,PMAX
  3   FORMAT('0',3I10,F15.7)
      STOP
      END
```

THE PRINTOUT IS

49   39   71   2925.9000000

The solution is:

$x_1 = 49$, $x_2 = 39$, $x_3 = 71$, and maximum $P = 2925.90$

Therefore, the company should make and sell 49 units of R, 39 units of S, and 71 units of T to realize a maximum profit of $2,925.90 per day.

EXAMPLE 3.49

The A Company (from Example 3.44) merges with the AA Company (from Example 3.45), and as a result the new conglomerate decides to continue to make and market products B, C, D, and E together. Therefore, the new resultant profit equation is:

$$P = P_B + P_C + P_D + P_E$$

$P = -.5x_1^2 + 18x_1 - .33x_2^2 + 22x_2 - .25x_3^2 + 38.5x_3 - .5x_4^2 + 57x_4$. We wish to maximize this subject to $x_1 \geq 0$, $x_2 \geq 0$, $x_3 \geq 0$, $x_4 \geq 0$, $x_1 \leq 36$, $x_2 \leq 66$, $x_3 \leq 154$, and $x_4 \leq 114$.

The profit equation of products B and C is functionally independent of the profit equation of products D and E and therefore the maximum of their sum is just the sum of their maximums. In other words, the solutions from examples 3.44 and 3.45, $x_1 = 18$, $x_2 = 33$, $x_3 = 77$, $x_4 = 57$, produce the maximum $P = \$525 + \$3,106.75 = \$3,631.75$ of their combination. This is so because there are no cross-product terms (like x_2x_3) or constraints ($x_2 + x_4 \leq 50$) which would make the two systems dependent. Also, it should be pointed out that in examples 3.44 through 3.48 each variable could have been maximized individually because the variables were not competing for the same resources. In other words, there were no constraints involving more than one variable. Also, a failure to notice these things made no difference in our computer approach. The computer just had to search many more points than necessary.

This is not to advocate lack of care in doing optimization problems, but merely to point out the flexibility of the approach. No conditions have to be met. The functions and/or constraints don't have to be written in a certain form. One merely does the problem by putting in the loops, the constraints, the function to be optimized, the storage space, and the "print" statement. Any simplifications are appreciated but they aren't really necessary.

Now, as stated, each of the preceding profit equations derived from the price quantity curves could be maximized separately and then, for example, $P = P_A + P_B + P_C$ would yield max P at x_1, x_2, x_3 such that $P_A(x_1) = $ max, $P_B(x_2) = $ max, and $P_C(x_3) = $ max. However, perhaps, as discussed earlier, certain time or labor or other constraints interrelate with various variables causing max P to not necessarily be the point which maximizes the individual variable profit equations. When this is the case, our 2-dimensional, 3-dimensional, 4-dimensional, etc., search becomes necessary to find the optimum solution.

For example, let's do a few examples like the preceding nonlinear equations subject to some interrelating constraints.

EXAMPLE 3.50

Maximize $P = -.5x_1^2 + 18x_1 - .33x_2^2 + 22x_2 - .25x_3^2 + 38.5x_3 - .5x_4^2 + 57x_4$ subject to $x_1 \geq 0, x_2 \geq 0, x_3 \geq 0, x_4 \geq 0, x_1 \leq 36, x_2 \leq 66, x_3 \leq 154, x_4 \leq 114, x_1 + x_2 + 2x_3 + x_4 \leq 200$, and $x_1 + 2x_2 + 3x_3 + 7x_4 \leq 310$.

```
      INTEGER X1,X2,X3,X4
      PMAX=0
      DO 1 I=1,37
      X1=I-1
      DO 1 J=1,67
      X2=J-1
      DO 1 K=1,104
      X3=K-1
      DO 1 L=1,45
      X4=L-1
      IF(X1+X2+2*X3+X4.GT.200) GO TO 1
      IF(X1+2*X2+3*X3+7*X4.GT.310) GO TO 1
      P=-.5*X1*X1+18.*X1-1./3.*X2*X2+22*X2
     A-.25*X3*X3+38.5*X3-.5*X4*X4+57.*X4
      IF(P.GT.PMAX) GO TO 2
      GO TO 1
    2 IX1=X1
      IX2=X2
      IX3=X3
      IX4=X4
      PMAX=P
    1 CONTINUE
      WRITE(6,3)IX1,IX2,IX3,IX4,PMAX
    3 FORMAT('0',4I10,F15.7)
      STOP
      END
```

```
                THE PRINTOUT IS
```

13   16   44   19   2528.6660000

The solution is:

$x_1 = 13$, $x_2 = 16$, $x_3 = 44$, $x_4 = 19$, and maximum $P = 2528.67$

EXAMPLE 3.51
Maximize $P = -.6x_1^2 + 59x_1 - .3x_2^2 + 23.5x_2 - .2x_3^2 + 28.5x_3$ subject to $x_1 \geq 0, x_2 \geq 0, x_3 \geq 0, x_1 \leq 98.33, x_2 \leq 75, x_3 \leq 142.5, x_1 + x_2 + x_3 \leq 200$, and $x_1 + 3x_2 + x_3 \leq 220$.

```
      INTEGER X1,X2,X3
      PMAX=-9999999
      DO 1 I=1,99
      X1=I-1
      DO 1 J=1,74
      X2=J-1
      DO 1 K=1,143
      X3=K-1
      IF(X1+X2+X3.GT.200) GO TO 1
      IF(X1+3*X2+X3.GT.220) GO TO 1
      P=-.6*X1*X1+59.*X1-.3*X2*X2+23.5*X2-.2*X3*X3+28.5*X3
      IF(P.GT.PMAX) GO TO 2
      GO TO 1
  2   IX1=X1
      IX2=X2
      IX3=X3
      PMAX=P
  1   CONTINUE
      WRITE(6,3)IX1,IX2,IX3,PMAX
  3   FORMAT('0',3I10,F15.7)
      STOP
      END
```

```
                THE PRINTOUT IS
```

49   34   69   2916.9000000

The solution is:

$x_1 = 49$, $x_2 = 34$, $x_3 = 69$, and maximum $P = 2916.90$

EXAMPLE 3.52
Suppose that the price of Product A is related to the quantity sold in the sense that as

the price is decreased the quantity sold increases. The daily price-quantity curve for Product A is $y = -.1x_1 + 100$ where x_1 is the quantity sold and y is the price.

Suppose also that the price of product B is related to the quantity sold in the sense that as the price is increased the quantity sold increases (as with some fad items). The daily price-quantity curve for Product B is $y = .05x_2 + 110$.

However, products A and B are made in departments 1 and 2. There are 1000 minutes per day available in Department 1 and 2000 minutes per day available in Department 2. The time requirements for each product are shown below:

Time required (minutes)

Product	Department 1	Department 2
A	1	2
B	1	3

Product A costs $.25 per unit to make and Product B costs $.10 per unit to make. Therefore:

$$P_A = x_1y - .25x_1$$
$$P_A = x_1(-.1x_1 + 100) - .25x_1$$
$$P_A = -.1x_1^2 + 100x_1 - .25x_1$$
$$P_A = -.1x_1^2 + 99.75x_1$$

and
$$P_B = x_2y - .10x_2$$
$$P_B = x_2(.05x_2 + 110) - .10x_2$$
$$P_B = .05x_2^2 + 110x_2 - .10x_2$$
$$P_B = .05x_2^2 + 109.9x_2$$

Therefore

$$P = P_A + P_B$$

$P = -.1x_1^2 + 99.75x_1 + .05x_2^2 + 109.9x_2$. We seek to maximize P subject to $x_1 \geq 0$, $x_2 \geq 0$, $x_1 \leq 1000$, $x_1 + x_2 \leq 1000$, $2x_1 + 3x_2 \leq 2000$. From the constraint $2x_1 + 3x_2 \leq 2000$, we see that x_2 can be no larger than 666 (2000/3 = 666.67).

```
INTEGER X1,X2
PMAX=-9999999
DO 1 I=1,1001
X1=I-1
DO 1 J=1,667
X2=J-1
IF(X1+X2.GT.1000) GO TO 1
IF(2*X1+3*X2.GT.2000) GO TO 1
P=-.1*X1*X1+99.75*X1+.05*X2*X2+109.9*X2
IF(P.GT.PMAX) GO TO 2
```

```
    GO TO 1
2   IX1=X1
    IX2=X2
    PMAX=P
1   CONTINUE
    WRITE(6,3)IX1,IX2,PMAX
3   FORMAT('0',2I10,F15.7)
    STOP
    END
```

THE PRINTOUT IS

1   666   95470.81

Therefore, Product B is the better product.

EXAMPLE 3.53
Suppose that the prices of products A and B are related to the quantity sold in the sense that as the price is decreased the quantity sold increases. The daily price-quantity curve for Product A is $y = -.15x_1 + 92$ where x_1 is the quantity sold and y is the price. Product A costs $.22 to produce and Product B costs $.14 to make. Product B's price-quantity curve is $y = -.08x_2 + 80$.

However, products A and B are made in departments 1, 2, and 3. There are 800 man-minutes available per day in each of the three departments. The time requirements for each product are shown below:

	Time required (minutes)		
Product	Department 1	Department 2	Department 3
A	1	2	3
B	2	3	1

We can calculate P_A and P_B as below:

$$P_A = x_1 y - .22x_1$$
$$P_A = x_1(-.15x_1 + 92) - .22x_1$$
$$P_A = -.15x_1^2 + 92x_1 - .22x_1$$
$$P_A = -.15x_1^2 + 91.78x_1$$
$$P_B = x_2 y - .14x_2$$
$$P_B = x_2(-.08x_2 + 80) - .14x_2$$
$$P_B = -.08x_2^2 + 79.86x_2$$

Therefore,

$$P = P_A + P_B$$

$P = -.15x_1^2 + 91.78x_1 - .08x_2^2 + 79.86x_2$. We seek to maximize P subject to $x_1 \geq 0$, $x_2 \geq 0$, $x_1 \leq 614$, $x_2 \leq 1000$, $x_1 + 2x_2 \leq 800$, $2x_1 + 3x_2 \leq 800$, and $3x_1 + x_2 \leq 800$. The constraint $3x_1 + x_2 \leq 800$ determines that x_1 can be no larger than 266 (800/3 = 266.67). The constraint $2x_1 + 3x_2 \leq 800$ assures that x_2 can be no larger than 266 also (800/3 = 266.67).

```
      INTEGER X1,X2
      PMAX=-9999999
      DO 1 I=1,267
      X1=I-1
      DO 1 J=1,267
      X2=J-1
      IF(X1+2*X2.GT.800) GO TO 1
      IF(2*X1+3*X2.GT.800) GO TO 1
      IF(3*X1+X2.GT.800) GO TO 1
      P=-.15*X1*X1+91.78*X1-.08*X2*X2+79.86*X2
      IF(P.GT.PMAX) GO TO 2
      GO TO 1
2     IX1=X1
      IX2=X2
      PMAX=P
1     CONTINUE
      WRITE(6,3)IX1,IX2,PMAX
3     FORMAT('0',2I10,F15.7)
      STOP
      END


      THE PRINTOUT IS

181    146    21652.300
```

The solution is:

$x_1 = 181$, $x_2 = 146$, and maximum $P = 21,652.30$

Therefore, the company should make and sell 181 units of A and 146 units of B to achieve a maximum profit of $21,652.30 each day on these two products.

The rest of the book will deal with optimization problems with a large number of variables. A technique for solving these problems, which is virtually identical to the approach we have taken so far, is presented. A considerable amount of effort is taken to justify this approach statistically. The reader who doesn't wish to take the time (or who has no background in statistics) is reminded that it is not necessary to understand the statistical justification to do the problems. One only has to believe it. The statistical justification is presented, then, for those who like to have their beliefs based on a few facts.

EXAMPLE 3.54

Maximize $P = -.5x_1^2 + 18x_1 - .33x_2^2 + 22x_2$ subject to $x_1 \geq 0$, $x_2 \geq 0$, $x_1 + x_2 \leq 50$, and $x_1 + 3x_2 \leq 60$. The P equation reveals that x_1 can be no larger than 36; x_2 can be no larger than 20.

```
      INTEGER X1,X2
      PMAX=-9999999
      DO 1 I=1,37
      X1=I-1
      DO 1 J=1,21
      X2=J-1
      IF(X1+X2.GT.50) GO TO 1
      IF(X1+3*X2.GT.60) GO TO 1
      P=-.5*X1*X1+18.*X1-1./3.*X2*X2+22.*X2
      IF(P.GT.PMAX) GO TO 2
      GO TO 1
2     IX1=X1
      IX2=X2
      PMAX=P
1     CONTINUE
      WRITE(6,3)IX1,IX2,PMAX
3     FORMAT('0',2I10,F15.7)
      STOP
      END
```

```
      THE PRINTOUT IS

15      15      412.5000000
```

The solution is:

$x_1 = 15$, $x_2 = 15$, and maximum $P = 412.50$

EXAMPLE 3.55

Maximize $P = -.25x_3^2 + 38.5x_3 - .5x_4^2 + 57x_4$ subject to $x_3 \geq 0$, $x_4 \geq 0$, $x_3 + x_4 \leq 100$, and $4x_3 + x_4 \leq 100$. The constraint $4x_3 + x_4 \leq 100$ forces x_3 to be no larger than 25 and x_4 no larger than 100.

```
      INTEGER X3,X4
      PMAX=0
      DO 1 I=1,26
      X3=I-1
      DO 1 J=1,101
      X4=J-1
```

```
      IF(X3+X4.GT.100) GO TO 1
      IF(4*X3+X4.GT.100) GO TO 1
      P=-.25*X3*X3+38.5*X3-.5*X4*X4+57.*X4
      IF(P.GT.PMAX) GO TO 2
      GO TO 1
    2 IX3=X3
      IX4=X4
      PMAX=P
    1 CONTINUE
      WRITE(6,3)IX3,IX4,PMAX
    3 FORMAT('0',2I10,F15.7)
      STOP
      END
```

```
      THE PRINTOUT IS

   13    48     2042.2500000
```

The solution is:

$x_3 = 13, x_4 = 48$, and maximum $P = 2042.25$

EXAMPLE 3.56

Maximize $P = -.4x_5^2 + 13x_5 - .3x_6^2 + 21x_6$ subject to $x_5 \geq 0, x_6 \geq 0, x_5 + x_6 \leq 40$, and $2x_5 + x_6 \leq 50$. From the constraints $2x_5 + x_6 \leq 50$ and $x_5 + x_6 \leq 40$, we can see that x_5 must be less than or equal to 25 and x_6 must be less than or equal to 40.

```
      INTEGER X5,X6
      PMAX=0
      DO 1 I=1,26
      X5=I-1
      DO 1 J=1,41
      X6=J-1
      IF(X5+X6.GT.40) GO TO 1
      IF(2*X5+X6.GT.50) GO TO 1
      P=-.4*X5*X5+13.*X5-.3*X6*X6+21.*X6
      IF(P.GT.PMAX) GO TO 2
      GO TO 1
    2 IX5=X5
      IX6=X6
      PMAX=P
    1 CONTINUE
      WRITE(6,3)IX5,IX6,PMAX
    3 FORMAT('0',2I10,F15.7)
      STOP
      END
```

```
      THE PRINTOUT IS

   10    30     450.0000000
```

The solution is:

$x_5 = 10$, $x_6 = 30$, and maximum $P = 450$.

EXAMPLE 3.57
A preliminary statistical study of the yield of a particular chemical process has given experimenters the following yield equation:

$$y = 2.9 + 7x_1 + 9x_2 + 14x_3 + 12.2x_1x_2 + 6x_2x_3 + 2.6x_1x_2x_3 - 7.6x_3^2 - 2.5x_3^3$$

where x_1 is the temperature in units that must be between 50 and 100, x_2 is the pressure in units that must be between 40 and 100, and x_3 is the reaction time in units that must be no larger than 120.

The chemists seek to maximize P subject to $50 \le x_1 \le 100$, $40 \le x_2 \le 100$, and $0 \le x_3 \le 120$.

```
      INTEGER X1,X2,X3
      YMAX=0
      DO 1 I=50,100
      X1=I
      DO 1 J=40,100
      X2=J
      DO 1 K=1,121
      X3=K-1
      Y=2.9+7*X1+9*X2+14*X3+12.2*X1*X2+
      A6*X2*X3+2.6*X1*X2*X3-7.6*X3**2-2.5*X3**3
      IF(Y.GT.YMAX) GO TO 2
      GOTO  1
  2   IX1=X1
      IX2=X2
      IX3=X3
      YMAX=Y
  1   CONTINUE
      WRITE(6,3)IX1,IX2,IX3
  3   FORMAT('0',3I10)
      WRITE(6,4)YMAX
  4   FORMAT('0',F14.2)
      STOP
      END
```

```
      THE PRINTOUT IS

  100      100       59

           1153922.00
```

The solution is:

$x_1 = 100$, $x_2 = 100$, $x_3 = 59$, and maximum $P = 1,153,922$

Therefore, the temperature and pressure should be set at 100 and the reaction time should be 59 units in order to maximize the yield of the chemical process.

EXAMPLE 3.58

A preliminary statistical study of the yield of a new chemical process has given the experimenter the following yield equation:

$$Y = 18 + 2.6x_1 + 9.3x_2 + 12x_3^{1.4} + 6.5x_1x_2 + 6x_2x_3 + 5x_1x_3 - 6.5x_1x_2x_3$$

where x_1 is the temperature in units that must be between 20 and 50, x_2 is the amount of the first catalyst in units that must be between 25 and 60, and x_3 is the amount of the experimental catalyst in units that must be no larger than 95.

The chemist seeks to maximize P subject to $20 \le x_1 \le 50$, $25 \le x_2 \le 60$, and $0 \le x_3 \le 95$.

```
      INTEGER X1,X2,X3
      YMAX=0
      DO 1 I=20,50
      X1=I
      DO 1 J=25,60
      X2=J
      DO 1 K=1,96
      X3=K-1
      Y=18+2.6*X1+9.3*X2+12*X3**1.4+6.5*X1*X2
     A+6*X2*X3+5*X1*X3-6.5*X1*X2*X3
      IF(Y.GT.YMAX) GO TO 2
      GO TO 1
    2 IX1=X1
      IX2=X2
      IX3=X3
      YMAX=Y
    1 CONTINUE
      WRITE(6,3)IX1,IX2,IX3
    3 FORMAT('0',3I10)
      WRITE(6,4)YMAX
    4 FORMAT('0',F14.7)
      STOP
      END
```

```
THE PRINTOUT IS

50      60      0

  20205.9960938
```

The solution is:

$x_1 = 50$, $x_2 = 60$, $x_3 = 0$, and maximum $P = 20205.996$

Therefore, the temperature should be set at 50 and 60 units of the first catalyst, and none of the second should be added to maximize the yield of this chemical process.

The problems with demand curves presented in this chapter could have just as easily had nonlinear demand curves (with squared or cubed terms, etc.) or demand curves that were a function of two or more variables (price, competitor's price, real income available, interest rate, etc.). The problems could have also had fixed costs and the cost of capital put in them.

The constraints could have been nonlinear if, for instance, the worker's productivity increased as they got better at their departmental jobs. This is frequently the case, especially when making a product for the first time.

Our solution approach would be just as easy with these additional nonlinearities in the problem. Also, in a practical problem, the number of units of production of each product could run into the hundreds of thousands or millions. These problems would still be solvable by searching by increments of 100 or 1,000 units, for example.

Using these techniques, we can optimize any econometric model, any inventory model, and any chemical yield equation under any possible set of constraints. This gives us complete freedom to develop more accurate models.

EXERCISES

3.1 Maximize $P = 12x_1 + x_2 + 3x_3 + 5x_4$ subject to $x_1 \geq 0, x_2 \geq 0, x_3 \geq 0, x_4 \geq 0, x_1 + x_2 \leq 20, x_3 + x_4 \leq 25$, and $x_1 + x_2 + x_3 + x_4 \leq 55$.

3.2 Maximize $P = .8x_1 + 19.2x_2^2 + 16.3x_3 + 12x_4^3 + x_5$ subject to $0 \leq x_1 \leq 5, 0 \leq x_2 \leq 10, 0 \leq x_3 \leq 14, 0 \leq x_4 \leq 18, 0 \leq x_5 \leq 12, x_1 + x_2 + x_3 \leq 10, x_1 + x_2 + x_3 + x_4 \leq 35$, and $.5x_1 + 2x_5 \leq 16$.

3.3 Minimize $C = 92x_1 + 18x_2 + 75x_3 + 6x_4 + 8x_5 + x_6$ subject to $0 \leq x_i \leq 10$ for $i = 1,6, 2x_1 + 7x_2 + 9x_5 \geq 50, 18x_1 + x_4 + 2x_6 \geq 100$, and $x_1 + x_2 + x_3 + x_4 + x_5 + x_6 \geq 40$.

3.4 Maximize $P = .5x_1^2 + 18x_1 - .33x_2^2 + 22x_2$ subject to $x_1 \geq 0, x_2 \geq 0, x_1 \leq 36, x_2 \leq 66, x_1 + x_2 \leq 50$, and $x_1 + 3x_2 \leq 60$.

3.5 Maximize $P = -.4x_5^2 + 13x_5 - 3x_6^2 + 21x_6$ subject to $x_5 \geq 0, x_6 \geq 0, x_5 \leq 32, x_6 \leq 63, x_5 + x_6 \leq 40$, and $2x_5 + x_6 \leq 50$.

3.6 Maximize $P = -.4x_5^2 + 13x_5 - .3x_6^2 + 21x_6 - .45x_7^2 + 31.2x_7$ subject to $x_5 \geq 0, x_6 \geq 0, x_7 \geq 0, x_5 \leq 32, x_6 \leq 63, x_7 \leq 69, x_5 + x_6 + x_7 \leq 72$, and $2x_5 + 7x_6 + x_7 \leq 100$.

3.7 Maximize $P = e^{-2x} - xy + e^{4x}$ subject to $x \geq 0, y \geq 0, x \leq 500, y \leq 100, x + 4y \leq 700$, and $6x + y \leq 600$.

3.8   Minimize $C = e^{-2x} - xy + e^{4x}$ subject to $x \geq 0$, $y \geq 0$, $x \leq 500$, $y \leq 100$, $x + 4y \leq 700$, and $6x + y \leq 600$.

3.9   Maximize $P = 2xy^2 - 4xy + x^2 + y^2 - 27x^2y$ subject to $x \geq 0$, $y \geq 0$, $x^2 + 2xy + y^2 \leq 500$, and $x + 2y^2 \leq 400$.

3.10   Maximize $P = 40x + 80y + 130z$ subject to $x \geq 0$, $y \geq 0$, $z \geq 0$, $x + y + 2z \leq 85$, $x + 3y + 4z \leq 150$, and $x + 2y + 5z \leq 160$.

3.11   Refer to Example 3.40:

The Very Beautiful Upholstering Company is considering moving one employee out of Department 1 and into Department 3. This will reduce the number of man-hours per week by 40 in Department 1 and increase it by 40 in Department 3. Is this a good idea? Will the profit be greater after this change? The time requirements in each department for each of the three furniture pieces is summarized below:

	Time required (hours)		
Furniture	Department 1	Department 2	Department 3
Hassock	1	1	1
Chair	1	3	2
Couch	2	4	5

We wish to find the number of each type of furniture that should be re-covered to maximize the profit. The relevant information can be summarized as follows: Maximize $P = 40x + 80y + 130z$ subject to $x \geq 0$, $y \geq 0$, $z \geq 0$, $x + y + 2z \leq 80$, $x + 3y + 4z \leq 120$, and $x + 2y + 5z \leq 160$.

3.12   Minimize $C = 21x^3 - 14xy + 17y$ subject to $x \leq 14$, $y \leq 22$, and $x + 2y \leq 100$ ($x \geq 0$, $y \geq 0$, of course).

3.13   Refer to Example 3.38:

The Great Shot Golf Club Company finds that if they cut the time in Department 3 to $\frac{1}{3}$ of a minute (from $\frac{2}{3}$ of a minute) for both golf balls, they will have a 25% defective rate with the standard ball and a 35% defective rate with the deluxe ball. They can sell these balls as "rejects" for a profit of 14¢ and 35¢ per ball, respectively. With this in mind, find the number of each type of the standard and the deluxe ball that they should attempt to make to maximize the profit. Do you recommend that they adopt this time-saving step?

The relevant information can be summarized as follows:

Golf Ball	Time required (minutes)		
	Department 1	Department 2	Department 3
Standard	1/3	1/2	1/3
Deluxe	1/2	1	1/3
Time available	1000	2000	3000

Maximize $P = 20(.75x) + 14(.25x) + 50(.65y) + 35(.35y)$ subject to $x \geq 0, y \geq 0$, $.333x + .5y \leq 1000$, $.5x + y \leq 2000$, and $.333x + .333y \leq 3000$.

3.14 A school cafeteria is planning to serve a meal consisting of meat, a vegetable, and dessert. It has five different meat dishes to choose from, four vegetables, and three selections for dessert. However, the selections must contain at least a total of 100 units of Nutrient A, 200 units of Nutrient B, and 150 units of Nutrient C. The following chart lists each food selection with the amount of each nutrient it contains. It also tells the price per serving.

	Units			
	Nutrient A	Nutrient B	Nutrient C	Cost per serving (¢)
Meat 1	32	85	62	68
Meat 2	48	92	73	75
Meat 3	52	104	58	84
Meat 4	47	68	100	92
Meat 5	35	95	29	82
Vegetable 1	29	60	60	49
Vegetable 2	22	25	60	52
Vegetable 3	28	15	58	40
Vegetable 4	42	55	40	35
Dessert 1	22	48	55	46
Dessert 2	29	47	65	38
Dessert 3	50	40	38	28

Which combination of one meat item, one vegetable item, and one dessert item will fulfill the nutrient requirements and minimize the cost to the school cafeteria?

Hint: The nutrition problem can be summarized as follows: Minimize $C = 68x_1 + 75x_2 + 84x_3 + 92x_4 + 82x_5 + 49x_6 + 52x_7 + 40x_8 + 35x_9 + 46x_{10} + 38x_{11} + 28x_{12}$ subject to all x_i are either 0 or 1, and

$$x_1 + x_2 + x_3 + x_4 + x_5 = 1$$

$$x_6 + x_7 + x_8 + x_9 = 1$$

$$x_{10} + x_{11} + x_{12} = 1$$

and

$32x_1 + 48x_2 + 52x_3 + 47x_4 + 35x_5 + 29x_6 + 22x_7 + 28x_8 + 42x_9 + 22x_{10} + 29x_{11} + 50x_{12} \geq 100$

$85x_1 + 92x_2 + 104x_3 + 68x_4 + 95x_5 + 60x_6 + 25x_7 + 15x_8 + 55x_9 + 48x_{10} + 47x_{11} + 40x_{12} \geq 200$

and

$62x_1 + 73x_2 + 58x_3 + 100x_4 + 29x_5 + 60x_6 + 60x_7 + 58x_8 + 40x_9 + 55x_{10} + 65x_{11} + 38x_{12} \geq 150.$

```
INTEGER X1,X2,X3,X4,X5,X6,X7,X8,X9,X10,X11,X12
MINC=9999999
DO 1 I=1,2
X1=I-1
DO 1 J=1,2
X2=J-1
DO 1 K=1,2
X3=K-1
DO 1 L=1,2
X4=L-1
DO 1 M=1,2
X5=M-1
DO 1 N=1,2
X6=N-1
DO 1 IA=1,2
X7=IA-1
DO 1 JA=1,2
X8=JA-1
DO 1 KA=1,2
X9=KA-1
DO 1 LA=1,2
X10=LA-1
DO 1 MA=1,2
X11=MA-1
DO 1 NA=1,2
X12=NA-1
IF(X1+X2+X3+X4+X5.NE.1) GO TO 1
IF(X6+X7+X8+X9.NE.1) GO TO 1
IF(X10+X11+X12.NE.1) GO TO 1
IF(32*X1+48*X2+52*X3+47*X4+35*X5
A+29*X6+22*X7+28*X8+42*X9
A+22*X10+29*X11+50*X12.LT.100) GO TO 1
IF(85*X1+92*X2+104*X3+68*X4+95*X5
A+60*X6+25*X7+15*X8+55*X9
A+48*X10+47*X11+40*X12.LT.200) GO TO 1
IF(62*X1+73*X2+58*X3+100*X4+29*X5
A+60*X6+60*X7+58*X8+40*X9
A+55*X10+65*X11+38*X12.LT.150) GO TO 1
C=68*X1+75*X2+84*X3+92*X4+82*X5+49*X6
A+52*X7+40*X8+35*X9+46*X10+38*X11+28*X12
IF(C.LT.MINC) GO TO 2
GO TO 1
```

```
2   IX1=X1
    IX2=X2
    IX3=X3
    IX4=X4
    IX5=X5
    IX6=X6
    IX7=X7
    IX8=X8
    IX9=X9
    IX10=X10
    IX11=X11
    IX12=X12
    MINC=C
1   CONTINUE
    WRITE(6,3)IX1,IX2,IX3,IX4,IX5,IX6,IX7,IX8,IX9,IX10,IX11,IX12
3   FORMAT('0',12I10)
    WRITE(6,4)MINC
4   FORMAT('0',I12)
    STOP
    END
```

Fill out the following after running the program.

The solution is:

$x_1 =$ $x_2 =$ $x_3 =$ $x_4 =$ $x_5 =$ $x_6 =$

$x_7 =$ $x_8 =$ $x_9 =$ $x_{10} =$ $x_{11} =$ $x_{12} =$

and the minimum $C =$

Therefore, the cafeteria should serve

Meat _____ Vegetable _____ and Dessert _____ to meet the nutrition requirements and have a minimum cost of _____.

Part Two

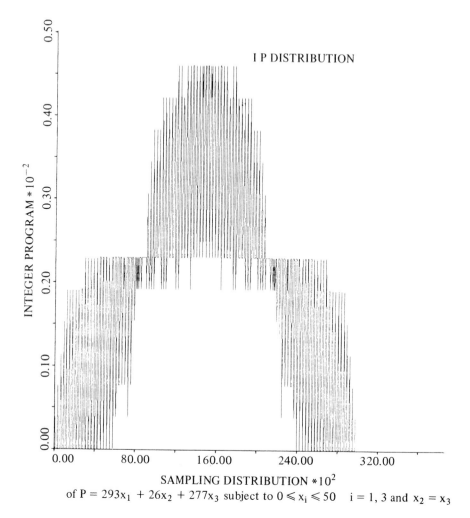

I P DISTRIBUTION

INTEGER PROGRAM $*10^{-2}$

SAMPLING DISTRIBUTION $*10^2$

of $P = 293x_1 + 26x_2 + 277x_3$ subject to $0 \leqslant x_i \leqslant 50$ $i = 1, 3$ and $x_2 = x_3$

CHAPTER 4

Monte Carlo Integer Programming

The technique presented in the first part of the book "appears" to have a serious drawback. The limitation is that we are restricted to integer programming problems that have few enough variables, that take on few enough values, so that there are only about one million or less feasible solutions. If we start getting more solutions than that, with the type of computer available to most people, it would be hard to evaluate all possible solutions in a reasonable time.

We will solve this problem by taking random samples of feasible solutions and using our program approach to find the best solution (maximum or minimum) of these random samples. We will take as large a sample as our computer and computer time permits. Sometimes a sample as large as a million is obtainable.

Many computer experts believe that in a few years (possibly by 1982) desk-top minicomputers with the power and capacity of an IBM 370 will be available and affordable to most computer users. This is already almost true, if you can afford the current price. But these or comparable machines should be available soon. When this happens, taking a random sample of one million, ten million, or one hundred million feasible solutions and finding the optimum of that sample will be as easy as pushing a few buttons on a desk. Therefore, the author believes that the Monte Carlo, or exhaustive search approach to integer programming in particular and optimization in general, is an idea whose time has come. This approach certainly didn't used to be practical, but it is now and will increase in importance and practicality as computer science advances.

Assuming we can write and run Monte Carlo integer programs as easily as we could our "search all points programs" of Part One (and we *can* do them as easily), the big question remains, How good is the answer obtained by this method? It is the author's contention that in virtually any practical integer programming problem the answer is nearly optimum. Much of the remaining text will devote itself to making this point statistically. However, even if it were not true, one would still have the best course of action out of one million decisions. That wouldn't be too bad. Let's work out a Monte Carlo integer programming problem example and then we will return to the justification and take a more scientific approach.

EXAMPLE 4.1

We seek to maximize $P = x_1^2 + x_1 x_2 - x_2^2 + x_3 x_1 - x_3^2 + 8x_4^2 - 17x_5^2 + 6x_6^3 + x_6 x_5 x_4 x_7 + x_8^3 + x_9^4 - x_{10}^5 - x_{10} x_5 + 18x_3 x_7 x_6$ subject to $x_i \geq 0$, $i = 1,10$ and $x_i \leq 99$, $i = 1,10$.

There are 100^{10} points to check. This is too many points so we will use the Monte Carlo integer programming technique to check a random sample of the 100^{10} points for a good feasible solution, namely, the point from the sample that produces the maximum P. We will look at a random sample of 1,000,000 possible solutions. We present the program, then a discussion and explanation follows.

```
       DIMENSION Y(10)
       INTEGER X(10)
       PMAX=-1.0 E 67
       CALL RSTART(1684727,8643219)
       DO 1 I=1,1000000
       DO 10 J=1,10
       Y(J)=UNI(0)
10     X(J)=Y(J)*100.
       P=X(1)*X(1)+X(1)*X(2)-X(2)*X(2)+X(3)*X(1)
       A-X(3)*X(3)+8*X(4)*X(4)-17*X(5)*X(5)
       A+6*X(6)**3+X(6)*X(5)*X(4)*X(7)+X(8)**3
       A+X(9)**4-X(10)**5-X(10)*X(5)+18*X(3)*X(7)*X(6)
       IF(P.GT.PMAX) GO TO 2
       GO TO 1
2      IX1=X(1)
       IX2=X(2)
       IX3=X(3)
       IX4=X(4)
       IX5=X(5)
       IX6=X(6)
       IX7=X(7)
```

```
      IX8=X(8)
      IX9=X(9)
      IX10=X(10)
      PMAX=P
1     CONTINUE
      WRITE(6,3)IX1,IX2,IX3,IX4,IX5,IX6,IX7,IX8,IX9,IX10,PMAX
3     FORMAT('0',10I10,F15.2)
      STOP
      END
```

THE PRINTOUT IS

70 66 66 98 97 95 95 9 99 9   197580315

The solution is:

$x_1 = 70$, $x_2 = 66$, $x_3 = 66$, $x_4 = 98$, $x_5 = 97$, $x_6 = 95$,

$x_7 = 95$, $x_8 = 9$, $x_9 = 99$, $x_{10} = 9$, and maximum $P = 197,580,315$

First of all, keep in mind that nothing has changed as far as the structure of the programs from Part One. We still check feasible solutions in the function and store the current best one in the storage space and print the best answer at the end.

This is a ten-variable problem so in statement 1 we write DIMENSION Y(10) which gives 10 variables Y(1), Y(2), ... , Y(10) to use in the program. INTEGER X(10) gives ten integer variables (only whole number values are assigned to them) X(1), X(2),..., X(10) to use in the program. PMAX = − 1.0E67 declares PMAX to be a very small number so that in the initial comparison in statement 10 (IF (P.GT.PMAX) GO TO 2), P will be larger than PMAX. Statement 4, CALL RSTART (1684727,8643219), tells the computer to bring the random number generator subroutine into the program so that a random number between 0 and .9999999 will be produced every time the expression UNI(0) is written to the right of an equals sign. This random number will be assigned to the variable on the left of the equals sign. For example, in our program Y(J) = UNI (0) assigns a random number to Y(1) or Y(2),... , Y(10) (depending on the value of J) every time that statement is encountered. As an illustration, the first ten random numbers assigned might be

```
Y(1) = .8251634
Y(2) = .6283351
Y(3) = .7944183
Y(4) = .2215664
Y(5) = .1824536
Y(6) = .0024381
Y(7) = .9438625
Y(8) = .5836941
Y(9) = .7285311
Y(10) = .1845621
```

So the numbers the random number generator has to choose from are 0, .0000001, .0000002, .0000003, .0000004, .0000005, .0000006, .0000007, .0000008, .0000009, .0000010, .0000011, .0000012,...,.9999999. There are ten million of them in all, and the random number generator accessed by the statement CALL RSTART (large positive odd integer, large positive odd integer different from the first one) assigns them in no particular order to the variable on the left of = UNI(0) whenever this expression is encountered. Each random number from 0 to .9999999 has one chance in ten million of being assigned each time.

It must be pointed out that this CALL RSTART (,) and = UNI(0) subprogram and expression might or might not exist on the reader's computer. However, most any computer and/or computer center have subprograms that generate uniformly distributed (equally likely chance of each number occurring) random numbers. So if your center has a different subprogram and expression, insert yours in place of CALL RSTART (,) and = UNI(0).

Once we have the ability to generate these random numbers, the question becomes, What can be done with them to solve our integer programming problem? Notice that our constraints say that x_1, x_2, x_3, x_4, x_5, x_6, x_7, x_8, x_9, and x_{10} have to take integer values from 0 through 99. Therefore, statement 8, X(J) = Y(J)*100., effectively moves the decimal point over two places to the right on the seven-digit decimal random numbers and drops the five last digits (the ones to the right of the new decimal point). This leaves us a random number of 0 through 99. Let's illustrate this. Recalling our previous list of ten random numbers, Y(J)*100 would change them as follows:

Y(1) = 82.51634
Y(2) = 62.83351
Y(3) = 79.44183
Y(4) = 22.15664
Y(5) = 18.24536
Y(6) = 00.24381
Y(7) = 94.38625
Y(8) = 58.36941
Y(9) = 72.85311
Y(10) = 18.45621

And X(J) = Y(J)*100 would truncate the decimal part, leaving the following values stored in the X(J)'s:

X(1) = 82
X(2) = 62
X(3) = 79
X(4) = 22
X(5) = 18
X(6) = 0
X(7) = 94
X(8) = 58
X(9) = 72
X(10) = 18

In our program, the DO 1 I = 1,1000000 repeats the above process one million times, each time generating a new feasible solution (at random) which is evaluated for the corresponding P value (statement 9). The P value is checked, as before, in statement 10 to see if it is the largest P value so far. If it is, the program follows GO TO 2 and stores this solution in the IX storage variables as follows:

```
IX1 = X(1)
IX2 = X(2)
IX3 = X(3)
IX4 = X(4)
IX5 = X(5)
IX6 = X(6)
IX7 = X(7)
IX8 = X(8)
IX9 = X(9)
IX10 = X(10)
PMAX = P
```

After one million such combinations have been checked, the optimum combination along with its corresponding maximum value are printed in the output. So the solution programs take the same form as the programs we wrote in Part One of the text. The only difference is that we look at a random sample (of a million or so) of feasible solutions and take the best one. At the worst, that gives us the best course of action out of a million possibilities. And at its best, it provides a nearly optimum solution and definitely the ability to look for the optimum. But the question remains, how good is the answer? If the true maximum P value were 1000, could we be fairly certain of getting a combination that produced a P value of at least 990, for example? Two answers to this question are appropriate. The first answer is for readers who have no background in probability and statistics and who don't have the time to go into the details of the statistical justification of the technique. These people merely want useful answers quickly. Therefore, in most any conceivable practical integer programming problem you can get an answer quickly and easily that is very near the true optimum. The answer is obtained in a short time and with very modest effort. This cuts the cost of solution so much that the random sample solution may be better than the true optimum solution when the costs of solution are taken into consideration. And, of course, our technique works on so-called theoretically unsolvable problems, too.

Readers who are interested in a fairly scientific justification of the Monte Carlo approach are asked to pay close attention to the statistical and probabilistic justification given throughout the rest of the book. These justifications are interspersed among the problems and examples. Also, sampling distributions of feasible solutions of various integer programming problems are graphed throughout the remaining chapters and Appendix A. Appendix B gives an explanation (complete with sample programs) of how they are generated. The statistical justification explains why they are useful. If the reader is familiar with statistics, a sampling distribution is just the distribution of a particular statistic in a particular sampling

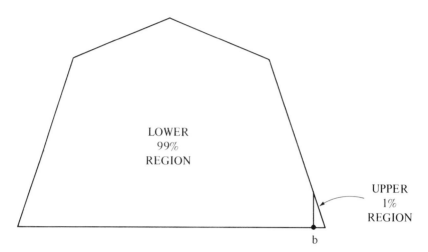

Figure 4.1

situation. The author proposes to treat the objective function of an integer programming problem as a statistic and assume each feasible solution (the X values) is a random sample. Then all samples are looked at (this only works in cases where there are, say, one million or less feasible solutions) to determine the distribution. A Calcomp plotter then draws the graph of the solution. The explanation of the details are in Appendix B.

Let's suppose that the sampling distribution of an arbitrary integer programming problem took the shape illustrated in Figure 4.1. The true optimum P value is at the extreme right. 99% of the P values (calculated from all feasible solutions) are to the left of point *b*. Only the 1% largest P values are to the right of *b*. If the distribution doesn't have a tail that is too thin (no isolated extreme P value), then any value in the upper .01 region will be reasonably close to the true optimum value of P. What is the probability that of one million feasible solutions, the largest P value will be in the upper .01 region, giving us a good answer if the tails aren't too thin? That probability is:

$1 - .99^{1,000,000}$ (where $.99^{1,000,000}$ is the probability that none of the one million P values will be in the upper .01 region)

$1 - .99^{1,000,000} = 1$ (accurate to one hundred or more decimal places). So we will get a P value in the upper .01 region near P

What is the probability of getting a P value in the upper .0001 region? It is:

$1 - .9999^{1,000,000} = 1$ (accurate to 43 decimal places)

   or

   $= .999999999\ldots9$ (43 nines)

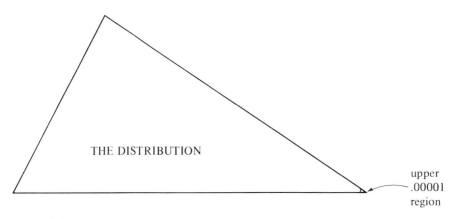

THE DISTRIBUTION

upper
.00001
region

Figure 4.2

What is the probability of getting a P value in the upper .00001 region? It is:

$$1 - .99999^{1,000,000} = .9999546023$$

or approximately 1.

Now a value in the upper .00001 region (Figure 4.2) should be almost on top of the true optimum if the integer program distribution (I.P. distribution) is reasonably well behaved (no isolated extreme points). So for all practical purposes we will have obtained a very good (nearly optimum) answer through our random sampling approach. We would only be in trouble if there were an isolated maximum point as in Figure 4.3. If this happened, the best answer might be a long way from the true optimum. However, it is the author's contention that this does not and will not ever happen in any practical problem. To reassure the reader, this chapter, the remaining chapters, and Appendix A display sampling distributions of 26 integer programming

Figure 4.3

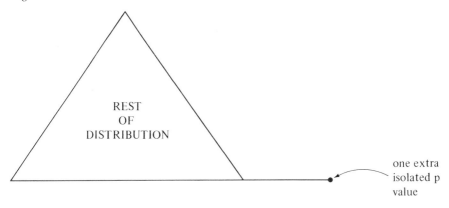

REST
OF
DISTRIBUTION

one extra
isolated p
value

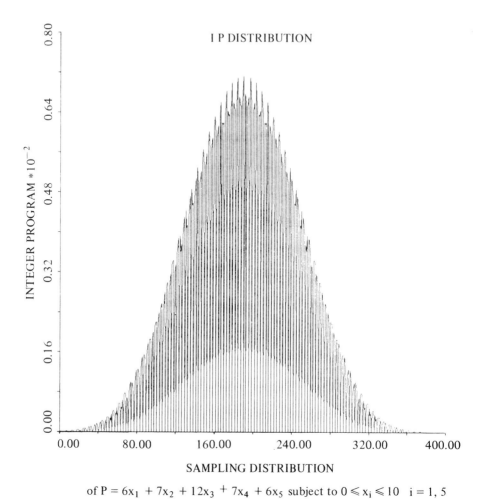

Figure 4.4 (Reprinted by permission of the National Bureau of Standards, Special Publication 503, p. 365)

problems. Note that they are all connected with thick tails. Also, this is just a fraction of the integer programming distributions that the author has generated. And there never was a problem with any of them. This does not constitute a mathematical proof, but it is very strong evidence to support the contention, and of course the longer the program runs the better the answer will get.

Also, in relation to our first example, we can easily find the true optimum. After doing a few more simulations and studying the function, it became apparent that in the optimum solution $x_1 = 99, x_4 = 99, x_6 = 99, x_7 = 99, x_8 = 99, x_9 = 99$, and $x_{10} = 0$. A few more simulations were run with these variables fixed and the true

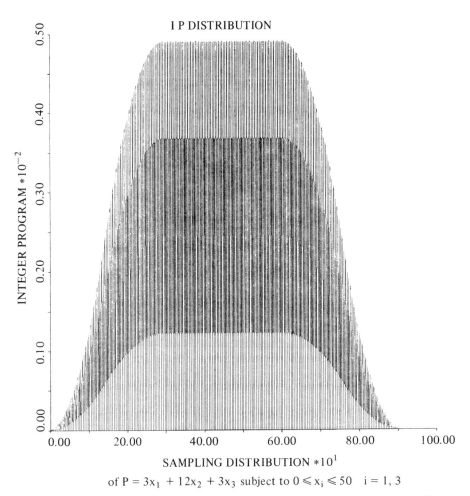

of $P = 3x_1 + 12x_2 + 3x_3$ subject to $0 \leqslant x_i \leqslant 50$ $i = 1, 3$

Figure 4.5 (Reprinted by permission of the National Bureau of Standards, Special Publication 503, p. 365)

optimum of $x_1 = 99$, $x_2 = 49.5$, $x_3 = 99$, $x_4 = 99$, $x_5 = 99$, $x_6 = 99$, $x_7 = 99$, $x_8 = 99$, $x_9 = 99$, and $x_{10} = 0$ was produced.

Figures 4.4 and 4.5* present graphs of sampling distributions of selected integer programming problems. Notice how well connected they are (no isolated extreme points). You can notice this in the other distributions in the remaining parts of the book, also.

Now we will return to our problems.

*These two graphs first appeared in National Bureau of Standards Publication 503.

EXAMPLE 4.2

We seek to maximize $P = x_1^2 + x_2^2 + 3x_3^2 + 4x_4^2 + 2x_5^2 - 8x_1 - 2x_2 - 3x_3 - x_4 - 2x_5$ subject to

$$x_1 \geq 0, x_2 \geq 0, x_3 \geq 0, x_4 \geq 0, x_5 \geq 0,$$

$$x_1 \leq 99, x_2 \leq 99, x_3 \leq 99, x_4 \leq 99, x_5 \leq 99,$$

$$x_1 + x_2 + x_3 + x_4 + x_5 \leq 400$$

$$x_1 + 2x_2 + 2x_3 + x_4 + 6x_5 \leq 800$$

$$2x_1 + x_2 + 6x_3 \leq 200$$

$$x_3 + x_4 + 5x_5 \leq 200$$

We have 100^5 points to check. Not all of these satisfy the constraints. However, 100^5 = 10,000,000,000 points will burden some computers so we will use the Monte Carlo integer programming technique to check a random sample of the 100^5 points for a good feasible solution, namely, the point from the sample that produces the maximum P. We will look at a sample of 1,500,000 points and take the one that gives a maximum P.

```
      DIMENSION IX(5),Y(5)
      INTEGER X(5),PMAX,P
      PMAX=-9999999
      CALL RSTART(17171717,15151515)
      DO 1 I=1,1500000
      DO 10 J=1,5
      Y(J)=UNI(0)
      X(J)=Y(J)*100.
   10 X(J)=X(J)
      IF(X(1)+X(2)+X(3)+X(4)+X(5).GT.400) GO TO 1
      IF(X(1)+2*X(2)+2*X(3)+X(4)+6*X(5).GT.800) GO TO 1
      IF(2*X(1)+X(2)+6*X(3).GT.200) GO TO 1
      IF(X(3)+X(4)+5*X(5).GT.200) GO TO 1
      P=X(1)*X(1)+X(2)*X(2)+3*X(3)*X(3)+4*X(4)*X(4)
      A+2*X(5)*X(5)-8*X(1)-2*X(2)-3*X(3)-X(4)-2*X(5)
      IF(P.GT.PMAX) GO TO 2
      GO TO 1
    2 CONTINUE
      DO 6 L=1,5
    6 IX(L)=X(L)
      PMAX=P
    1 CONTINUE
      WRITE(6,3)IX(1),IX(2),IX(3),IX(4),IX(5)
    3 FORMAT('0',5I10)
      WRITE(6,4)PMAX
    4 FORMAT('0',I10)
      STOP
      END
```

THE PRINTOUT IS

48   92   0   98   17   49062

The solution is:

$x_1 = 48$, $x_2 = 92$, $x_3 = 0$, $x_4 = 98$, $x_5 = 17$, and maximum $P = 49,062$.

Assuming the reader understood the ten-variable program presented earlier in this chapter, this explanation is just more of the same. However, it might be good to explain the five-variable program as a vehicle for going back over the Monte Carlo approach. We still check feasible solutions in the function and store the current best one in the storage space and print the best answer at the end.

This is a five-variable problem so in statement 1, we write DIMENSION IX(5), Y(5) which gives five variables, Y(1), Y(2), Y(3), Y(4), and Y(5), to use in the program. We could get by with just Y if we wished. The IX(1), IX(2), IX(3), IX(4), and IX(5) are the five storage variables which we subscripted this time to save space. INTEGER X(5), PMAX, P gives us five integer variables, X(1), X(2), X(3), X(4), and X(5), to use in our function evaluation. PMAX = –9999999 declares PMAX to be a very small number so that in the initial comparison in statement 15 (IF (P.GT.PMAX) GO TO 2) P will be larger than PMAX.

Statement 4, CALL RSTART (17171717,15151515), tells the computer to bring the random number generator subroutine into the program so that a random number between 0 and .9999999 will be produced every time the expression UNI(0) is written to the right of an equals sign. This random number will be assigned to the variable on the left of the equals sign. For example, in our program Y(J) = UNI(0) assigns a random number to Y(1), Y(2), Y(3), Y(4), or Y(5) (depending on the value of J) every time that statement is encountered. As an illustration, the first five random numbers assigned might be

Y(1) = .5432876
Y(2) = .8193582
Y(3) = .7621228
Y(4) = .3146218
Y(5) = .0153216

So the numbers the random number generator has to choose from are 0, .0000001, .0000002, .0000003, .0000004, .0000005, .0000006, .0000007, .0000008, .0000009, .0000010, .0000011, .0000012, ..., .9999999. There are ten million of them in all and the random number generator accessed by the statement CALL RSTART (large positive odd integer, large positive odd integer different from the first one) assigns them in no particular order to the variable on the left of = UNI(0) whenever this expression is encountered. Each random number from 0 to .9999999 has one chance in ten million of being assigned each time.

Again, it should be pointed out that the CALL RSTART(,) and = UNI(0) subprogram and expression may or may not exist on the reader's computer. However, most any computer and/or computer center have subprograms that generate uniformly distributed (equally likely chance of each number occurring) random numbers. So if your center has a different subprogram and expression, insert yours in place of CALL RSTART(,) and = UNI(0).

The five variables, x_1, x_2, x_3, x_4, and x_5 must take values from 0 to 99 inclusive. Therefore, statement 8, X(J) = Y(J)*100, effectively moves the decimal point over two places to the right on the seven-digit decimal random numbers and drops the five last digits (the ones to the right of the new decimal point). This leaves us with a random number of 0 through 99. Let's illustrate this. Recalling our previous list of five random numbers, Y(J)*100. would change them as follows:

Y(1) = 54.32876
Y(2) = 81.93582
Y(3) = 76.21228
Y(4) = 31.46218
Y(5) = 1.53216

and X(J) = Y(J)*100 would truncate the decimal part leaving the following values stored in the X(J)'s:

X(1) = 54
X(2) = 81
X(3) = 76
X(4) = 31
X(5) = 1

In the program, the DO 1 I = 1,1500000 repeats the above process one million five hundred thousand times, each time generating a new possible solution which must be checked in the bank of constraints (statements 10 through 13) to see if it is a feasible (possible) solution. If it is, the X values yield a P value in statement 14. The P value is checked in statement 15 to see if it is the largest P value so far. If it is, the program follows GO TO 2 and stores this solution in the IX storage variables as follows in

DO 6 L = 1,5
IX(L) = X(L)
PMAX = P

After one million five hundred thousand groups of five random numbers (from 0 to 99 inclusive) have tried to make it through the constraints and the rest of the program, the optimum combination along with its corresponding maximum value are printed in the output. So the solution programs take the same form as the programs we wrote in Part One of the text.

Note, if you wish to know how many of the groups of five numbers actually satisfied the constraints, put a statement N = 0 between statements 4 and 5 and a statement N = N + 1 after statement 13. Then arrange to print N. Also, in chapter 8 we will demonstrate a way of constructing the program so that every group of random numbers read in is adjusted so that it fits the constraints. This will waste no random numbers. This could be important in, say, a one hundred-variable problem where the one hundred random numbers almost never satisfy the constraints. We postpone the explanation of how to get around this until chapter 8, but it can be done easily in every problem.

EXAMPLE 4.3

We seek to minimize $P = x_1^2 + x_2^2 + 3x_3^2 + 4x_4^2 + 2x_5^2 - 8x_1 - 2x_2 - 3x_3 - x_4 - 2x_5$ subject to

$$x_1 \geq 0, x_2 \geq 0, x_3 \geq 0, x_4 \geq 0, x_5 \geq 0$$

$$x_1 \leq 99, x_2 \leq 99, x_3 \leq 99, x_4 \leq 99, x_5 \leq 99$$

$$x_1 + x_2 + x_3 + x_4 + x_5 \leq 400$$

$$x_1 + 2x_2 + 2x_3 + x_4 + 6x_5 \leq 800$$

$$2x_1 + x_2 + 6x_3 \leq 200$$

$$x_3 + x_4 + 5x_5 \leq 200$$

$$x_1 + x_2 + x_3 + x_4 + x_5 \geq 55$$

$$x_1 + x_2 + x_3 + x_4 \geq 48$$

$$x_2 + x_4 + x_5 \geq 34$$

$$6x_1 + 7x_5 \geq 104$$

We have 100^5 points to check. Not all of these satisfy the constraints. However, 100^5 = 10,000,000,000 points will burden some computers so we will use the Monte Carlo integer programming technique to check a random sample of the 100^5 points for a good feasible solution, namely, the point from the sample that produces the minimum P. We will look at a sample of 1,200,000 points and take the one that gives us a minimum P.

```
      DIMENSION IX(5),Y(5)
      INTEGER X(5),PMIN,P
      PMIN=9999999
      CALL RSTART(1111111,22212127)
      DO 1 I=1,1200000
      DO 10 J=1,5
      Y(J)=UNI(0)
      X(J)=Y(J)*100.
10    X(J)=X(J)
      IF(X(1)+X(2)+X(3)+X(4)+X(5).GT.400) GO TO 1
      IF(X(1)+2*X(2)+2*X(3)+X(4)+6*X(5).GT.800) GO TO 1
      IF(2*X(1)+X(2)+6*X(3).GT.200) GO TO 1
      IF(X(3)+X(4)+5*X(5).GT.200) GO TO 1
      IF(X(1)+X(2)+X(3)+X(4)+X(5).LT.55) GO TO 1
      IF(X(1)+X(2)+X(3)+X(4).LT.48) GO TO 1
      IF(X(2)+X(4)+X(5).LT.34) GO TO 1
```

```
      IF(6*X(1)+7*X(5).LT.104) GO TO 1
      P=X(1)*X(1)+X(2)*X(2)+3*X(3)*X(3)+4*X(4)*X(4)
      A+2*X(5)*X(5)-8*X(1)-2*X(2)-3*X(3)-X(4)-2*X(5)
      IF(P.LT.PMIN) GO TO 2
      GO TO 1
  2   CONTINUE
      DO 6 L=1,5
  6   IX(L)=X(L)
      PMIN=P
  1   CONTINUE
      WRITE(6,3)IX(1),IX(2),IX(3),IX(4),IX(5)
  3   FORMAT('0',5I10)
      WRITE(6,4)PMIN
  4   FORMAT('0',I10)
      STOP
      END

          THE PRINTOUT IS

  17   18   7   7   9        900
```

The solution is:

$x_1 = 17$, $x_2 = 18$, $x_3 = 7$, $x_4 = 7$, $x_5 = 9$ and minimum $P = 900$

Everything is the same in form as the two previously explained Monte Carlo integer programming problems, except that in this problem we are looking for the minimum of P. Therefore, PMIN = 9999999 declares PMIN to be so large that in statement 19 (IF(P.LT.PMIN) GO TO 2) P will surely be less than PMIN the first time in order to get the first real P value stored and the program under way. Statements 22, 23, and 24 are the storage space.

EXERCISES

4.1 Maximize $P = 12x_1 + 25x_2$ subject to $0 \le x_1 \le 9999$, $0 \le x_2 \le 9999$, $x_1 + x_2 \le 15000$, and $x_1 + 2x_2 \le 18000$.

4.2 Maximize $P = 4.8x_1 + 12.6x_2 + 22x_3$ subject to $0 \le x_1 \le 999$, $0 \le x_2 \le 999$, $0 \le x_3 \le 999$, $x_1 + x_2 + 5x_3 \le 4000$, and $12x_1 + 20x_2 \le 22000$.

4.3 Maximize $P = 6x_1^2 + 9x_1x_2^2 + x_3^3$ subject to $0 \le x_1 \le 999$, $0 \le x_2 \le 999$, $0 \le x_3 \le 999$, $x_1 + x_2 + x_3 \le 2000$, and $x_1 + 6x_2 + 2x_3 \le 5000$.

4.4 Maximize the output equation of a chemical process described by $P = x^2 + xyz - yz + y^2 - x^2y^2$ subject to $x \ge 0$, $y \ge 0$, $z \ge 0$, $x \le 99$, $y \le 99$, and $z \le 999$ where x is the number of units of the catalyst added to the process, y is the temperature, and z is the time in minutes that the temperature is maintained.

CHAPTER 5

Integer Programming Problems with a Few Variables

This chapter begins by presenting three graphs which show the sampling distributions of the feasible solutions of three more integer programming problems. Notice that their tails are thick. Also, remember that as access to computers increases (through having one's own minicomputer) and as they increase in speed, the random sample approach will be able to produce a value that will be extremely close to the very end (true optimum) of the distribution.

Following the graphs are additional Monte Carlo programming examples.

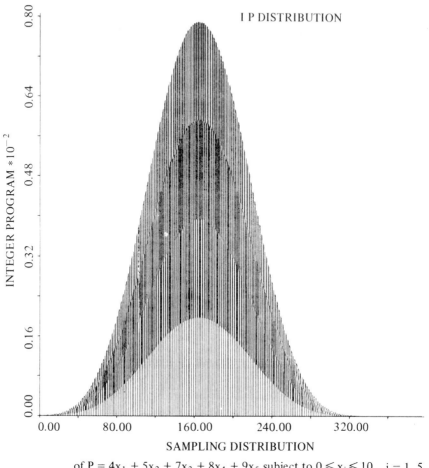

Figure 5.1

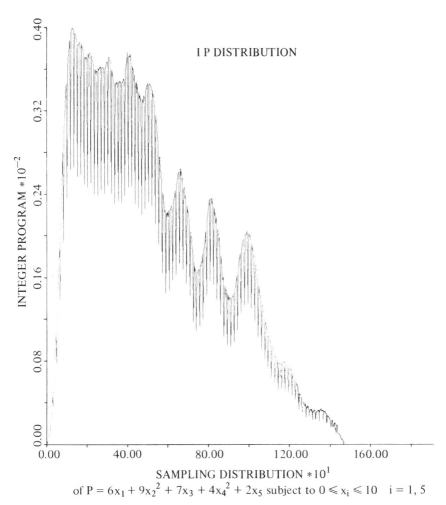

Figure 5.2 *(Reprinted by permission of the National Bureau of Standards, Special*
Publication 503, p. 364)

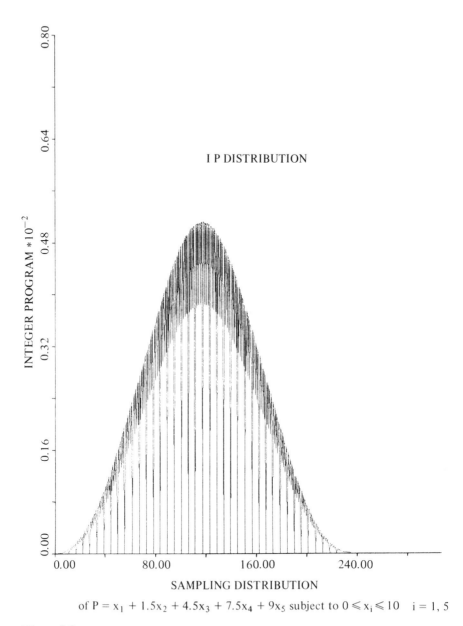

Figure 5.3

of $P = x_1 + 1.5x_2 + 4.5x_3 + 7.5x_4 + 9x_5$ subject to $0 \leqslant x_i \leqslant 10$ $i = 1, 5$

EXAMPLE 5.1

We seek to minimize $P = 6x_1^2 + 18x_2^2 + 7x_3^2 - 2x_1 - 16x_2 - 31x_3 - 12x_1x_2x_3$ subject to

$$x_1 \geq 0, \; x_2 \geq 0, \; x_3 \geq 0, \; x_1 \leq 999, \; x_2 \leq 999, \; x_3 \leq 999,$$

$$x_1 + x_2 + 2x_3 \leq 2000$$

$$x_1 + 17x_2 \leq 8000$$

$$x_2 + 5x_3 \leq 4000$$

$$x_1 + 7x_2 + 2x_3 \geq 200$$

$$x_1 + x_2 + x_3 \geq 200$$

$$x_1^2 + x_2x_3 \geq 900$$

We have 1000^3 points to check. Not all of these satisfy the constraints. However, $1000^3 = 1{,}000{,}000{,}000$ points will burden some computers, so we will use the Monte Carlo integer programming technique to check a random sample of the 1000^3 points for a good feasible solution, namely, the point from the sample that produces the minimum P. We will look at a sample of 800,000 points and take the one that gives a minimum P.

```
      DIMENSION IX(3),Y(3)
      INTEGER X(3),P
      PMIN=9999999
      CALL RSTART(2222221,7775577)
      DO 1 I=1,800000
      DO 10 J=1,3
      Y(J)=UNI(0)
  10  X(J)=Y(J)*1000.
      IF(X(1)+X(2)+2*X(3).GT.2000) GO TO 1
      IF(X(1)+17*X(2).GT.8000) GO TO 1
      IF(X(2)+5*X(3).GT.4000) GO TO 1
      IF(X(1)+7*X(2)+2*X(3).LT.200) GO TO 1
      IF(X(1)+X(2)+X(3).LT.200) GO TO 1
      IF(X(1)*X(1)+X(2)*X(3).LT.900) GO TO 1
      P=6*X(1)*X(1)+18*X(2)*X(2)+7*X(3)*X(3)-2*X(1)
     A-16*X(2)-31*X(3)-12*X(1)*X(2)*X(3)
      IF(P.LT.PMIN) GO TO 2
      GO TO 1
   2  CONTINUE
      DO 6 L=1,3
   6  IX(L)=X(L)
      PMIN=P
   1  CONTINUE
      WRITE(6,3)IX(1),IX(2),IX(3)
   3  FORMAT('0',3I10)
      WRITE(6,4)PMIN
   4  FORMAT('0',F16.1)
```

```
STOP
END
```

```
THE PRINTOUT IS
```

```
720   424   428   -1560310784.0
```

The solution is:

$x_1 = 720$, $x_2 = 424$, $x_3 = 428$, and minimum $P = -1560310784$

Again, the idea is to read in three random numbers at a time (one for each variable) and then shift the decimal over and truncate it. However, this time random numbers can take values from 0 through 999, so we multiply by 1000. For example, if Y(J) = UNI(0) made the following assignments of random numbers

```
Y(1) = .2853216
Y(2) = .6253771
Y(3) = .1854971
```

then Y(J)*1000. would yield

```
Y(1) = 285.3216
Y(2) = 625.3771
Y(3) = 185.4971
```

and X(J) = Y(J)*1000 would truncate them to

```
X(1) = 285
X(2) = 625
X(3) = 185
```

Then this possible solution is checked to see if it satisfies the constraints. If it doesn't, then the program follows GO TO 1 and repeats itself with a new sequence of three random numbers. However, if they satisfy the constraints, then P is evaluated with these current X values. Then P is checked to see if it is less than the current PMIN VALUE (the current minimum). If it is, then the X's and the PMIN VALUE are stored. If not, the program continues as before.

Notice that many random numbers may be read in and not used, because they don't meet the constraints. Chapter 8 will demonstrate a way of forcing all random number groups to meet the constraints, thereby not wasting any.

Also, when X was restricted to 0 through 99, we multiplied by 100. When X was restricted to 0 through 999, we multiplied by 1000. If X was restricted to 0 through 450, we would multiply by 451. In general, multiply by one more than the upper limit and the random number will be in the range.

In addition, in the CALL RSTART (,) statement each different pair of odd integers produces a different random number sequence. Therefore, to avoid getting the same sequence each time, we keep changing these numbers. Check your local computer or computer center to see how your random numbers are produced.

EXAMPLE 5.2

Maximize the function $P = 16x_1^2 + 18x_1 + 7x_2^2 - 12x_2$ subject to the constraints $x_1 \geq 0$, $x_2 \geq 0$, $x_1 \leq 99999$, $x_2 \leq 99999$, $6x_1 - x_2 \leq 100$, and $x_1 + 2x_2 \leq 150000$.

Let's use the Monte Carlo approach to examine 1,110,000 points and take the one that produces the maximum P.

```
      DIMENSION IX(2),Y(2)
      INTEGER X(2)
      PMAX=-9999999
      CALL RSTART(7772221,5555519)
      DO 1 I=1,1100000
      DO 10 J=1,2
      Y(J)=UNI(0)
   10 X(J)=Y(J)*100000.
      IF(6*X(1)-X(2).GT.100) GO TO 1
      IF(X(1)+2*X(2).GT.150000) GO TO 1
      P=16*X(1)*X(1)+18*X(1)+7*X(2)*X(2)-12*X(2)
      IF(P.GT.PMAX) GO TO 2
      GO TO 1
    2 CONTINUE
      DO 6 L=1,2
    6 IX(L)=X(L)
      PMAX=P
    1 CONTINUE
      WRITE(6,3)IX(1),IX(2)
    3 FORMAT('0',2I10)
      WRITE(6,4)PMAX
    4 FORMAT('0',F15.2)
      STOP
      END
```

```
          THE PRINTOUT IS

123    74790      39154155498
```

The solution is:

$x_1 = 0$, $x_2 = 75000$, and maximum $P = 39,374,100,000$

This time, the X's range from 0 through 99,999 so we multiply the random numbers by 100,000. Otherwise, it is just a standard maximization problem.

EXAMPLE 5.3

Maximize the function $P = 15x_1^2 + 2x_1 + 3x_2^2 + 4x_2$ subject to the constraints $x_1 \geq 0$, $x_2 \geq 0$, $x_1 \leq 9999$, $x_2 \leq 9999$, $x_1 + x_2 \leq 15000$, $2x_1 + 7x_2 \leq 20000$, and $7x_1 + 2x_2 \leq 20000$.

Let's use the Monte Carlo approach to examine 1,000,000 points and take the one that produces the maximum P.

```
DIMENSION IX(2),Y(2)
INTEGER X(2),PMAX
PMAX=-9999999
CALL RSTART(5553333,1111177)
DO 1 I=1,1000000
DO 10 J=1,2
Y(J)=UNI(0)
10 X(J)=Y(J)*10000.
IF(X(1)+X(2).GT.15000) GO TO 1
IF(2*X(1)+7*X(2).GT.20000) GO TO 1
IF(7*X(1)+2*X(2).GT.20000) GO TO 1
P=15*X(1)*X(1)+2*X(1)+3*X(2)*X(2)+4*X(2)
IF(P.GT.PMAX) GO TO 2
GO TO 1
2 CONTINUE
DO 6 L=1,2
6 IX(L)=X(L)
PMAX=P
1 CONTINUE
WRITE(6,3)IX(1),IX(2)
3 FORMAT('0',2I10)
WRITE(6,4)PMAX
4 FORMAT('0',I10)
STOP
END
```

```
THE PRINTOUT IS

2842    7    121160319
```

The solution is:

$x_1 = 2857$, $x_2 = 0$, and maximum $P = 122,442,449$

This time the X's run from 0 through 9,999 so we multiply the random numbers by 10,000. Keep in mind that in all the Monte Carlo integer programming problems we are just instructing the computer to do a haphazard random search of as many solutions as possible and take the best one. This is a difficult approach if only ten solutions are looked at. But the computer can look at 10,000,000 feasible solutions, making it a very worthwhile technique for producing good answers. Also, once an answer is obtained, a search near that answer can be conducted by the computer to see if there are any better answers close by. The random sample answer may have put us right next to the true optimum. For example, in the last problem we obtained $x_1 = 2842$ and $x_2 = 7$ with a resulting P of 121,160,319. So x_1 could be checked from 2800 through 2900, while x_2 was checked from 0 through 10, to see if any of these $101 \times 11 = 1111$ ordered pairs produced a better answer than $x_1 = 2842$, $x_2 = 7$, and maximum $P = 121,160,319$. Once a statistically "good" answer is obtained, there is no harm in trying to improve on it.

EXAMPLE 5.4

Maximize the function $P = 6x_1 + x_2$ subject to the constraints $x_1 \geq 0$, $x_2 \geq 0$, $x_1 \leq 99999$, $x_2 \leq 99999$, $x_1 + x_2 \leq 150000$, $x_1 - x_2 \leq 50$, and $x_1 + 2x_2 \leq 180000$.

Let's use the Monte Carlo approach to examine 1,500,000 points and take the one that produces the maximum P.

```
       DIMENSION IX(2),Y(2)
       INTEGER X(2),PMAX,P
       PMAX=-9999999
       CALL RSTART(5577113,1188861)
       DO 1 I=1,1500000
       DO 10 J=1,2
       Y(J)=UNI(0)
10     X(J)=Y(J)*100000.
       IF(X(1)+X(2).GT.150000) GO TO 1
       IF(X(1)-X(2).GT.50) GO TO 1
       IF(X(1)+2*X(2).GT.180000) GO TO 1
       P=6*X(1)+X(2)
       IF(P.GT.PMAX) GO TO 2
       GO TO 1
 2     CONTINUE
       DO 6 L=1,2
 6     IX(L)=X(L)
       PMAX=P
 1     CONTINUE
       WRITE(6,3)IX(1),IX(2)
 3     FORMAT('0',2I10)
       WRITE(6,4)PMAX
 4     FORMAT('0',I10)
       STOP
       END


       THE PRINTOUT IS

 59948    59973    419661
```

The solution is:

$x_1 = 59948$, $x_2 = 59973$, and maximum $P = 419661$

EXAMPLE 5.5

Maximize the function $P = -12x_1^2 + 18x_2^2 + 21x_3^2 - 4x_4^2$ subject to $x_1 \geq 0$, $x_2 \geq 0$, $x_3 \geq 0$, $x_4 \geq 0$, $x_1 \leq 99999$, $x_2 \leq 99999$, $x_3 \leq 99999$, $x_4 \leq 99999$, $4x_1 + 2x_2 + x_3 + 3x_4 \leq 600,000$, and $x_1 + 6x_2 + 6x_3 + 2x_4 \leq 700,000$.

Use the Monte Carlo approach to examine 1,000,000 points and take the one that produces the maximum P.

```
      DIMENSION IX(4),Y(4)
      INTEGER X(4)
      PMAX=-9999999
      CALL RSTART(7773331,6666669)
      DO 1 I=1,1000000
      DO 10 J=1,4
      Y(J)=UNI(0)
10    X(J)=Y(J)*100000.
      IF(4*X(1)+2*X(2)+X(3)+3*X(4).GT.600000) GO TO 1
      IF(X(1)+6*X(2)+6*X(3)+2*X(4).GT.700000) GO TO 1
      P=-12*X(1)*X(1)+18*X(2)*X(2)+21*X(3)*X(3)-4*X(4)*X(4)
      IF(P.GT.PMAX) GO TO 2
      GO TO 1
2     CONTINUE
      DO 6 L=1,4
6     IX(L)=X(L)
      PMAX=P
1     CONTINUE
      WRITE(6,3)IX(1),IX(2),IX(3),IX(4)
3     FORMAT('0',F15.2)
      WRITE(6,4)PMAX
4     FORMAT('0',I10)
      STOP
      END
```

```
        THE PRINTOUT IS

  2150    16051    99106    2503

       210818876700
```

The solution is:

$x_1 = 0$, $x_2 = 16667$, $x_3 = 99999$, $x_4 = 0$, and maximum $P = 214,996,000,000$

EXAMPLE 5.6

Minimize $P = 3x_1 + 7x_2 - 20x_3$ subject to $x_1 \geq 0$, $x_2 \geq 0$, $x_3 \geq 0$, $x_1 \leq 99999$, $x_2 \leq 99999$, $x_3 \leq 99999$, $x_1 + x_2 + x_3 \leq 250,000$, $7x_1 + 9x_3 \leq 390,000$, and $x_1 \leq 2x_2$.

There are $100,000^3 = 1,000,000,000,000,000$ points to check so we will use the Monte Carlo approach on 1,600,000 points from a random sample and take the point that produces the minimum from the sample.

```
      DIMENSION IX(3)
      INTEGER X(3)
      PMIN=1.0 E50
      CALL RSTART(5577561,8732541)
      DO 1 I=1,1600000
      DO 10 J=1,3
      Y=UNI(0)
10    X(J)=Y*100000.
      IF(X(1)+X(2)+X(3).GT.250000) GO TO 1
      IF(7*X(1)+9*X(3).GT.390000) GO TO 1
      IF(X(1).GT.2*X(2)) GO TO 1
      P=3*X(1)+7*X(2)-20*X(3)
      IF(P.LT.PMIN) GO TO 2
      GO TO 1
 2    CONTINUE
      DO 6 L=1,3
 6    IX(L)=X(L)
      PMIN=P
 1    CONTINUE
      WRITE(6,3)IX
 3    FORMAT('0',3I10)
      WRITE(6,4)PMIN
 4    FORMAT('0',F15.7)
      STOP
      END


      THE PRINTOUT IS

      539    1161     42228

      -834816.0000000
```

The solution is:

$$x_1 = 0, x_2 = 0, x_3 = 43333, \text{ and minimum } P = -866,660$$

EXAMPLE 5.7

Maximize $P = 3x_1 + 4x_2 + 7x_3 + 9x_4 + 31x_5$ subject to $x_1 \geq 0, x_2 \geq 0, x_3 \geq 0, x_4 \geq 0, x_5 \geq 0$, and $x_i \leq 99,999$ for $i = 1,5, x_1 + x_2 + x_3 + x_4 + x_5 \leq 300,000$, and $x_1 + 2x_2 + 6x_3 + 7x_4 + 8x_5 \leq 1,000,000$.

We will use the Monte Carlo approach to examine 1,500,000 points, taking the one that produces the maximum P.

```
      DIMENSION IX(5),Y(5)
      INTEGER X(5),PMAX,P
      PMAX=-9999999
      CALL RSTART(2222229,9999993)
      DO 1 I=1,1500000
      DO 10 J=1,5
      Y(J)=UNI(0)
10    X(J)=Y(J)*100000
      IF(X(1)+X(2)+X(3)+X(4)+X(5).GT.300000) GO TO 1
      IF(X(1)+2*X(2)+6*X(3)+7*X(4)+8*X(5).GT.1000000) GO TO 1
      P=3*X(1)+4*X(2)+7*X(3)+9*X(4)+31*X(5)
      IF(P.GT.PMAX) GO TO 2
      GO TO 1
2     CONTINUE
      DO 6 L=1,5
6     IX(L)=X(L)
      PMAX=P
1     CONTINUE
      WRITE(6,3)IX(1),IX(2),IX(3),IX(4),IX(5)
3     FORMAT('0',5I10)
      WRITE(6,4)PMAX
4     FORMAT('0',I10)
      STOP
      END
```

```
            THE PRINTOUT IS

92403    37498    4142    21    99644

            3545348
```

The solution is:

$x_1 = 92403$, $x_2 = 37498$, $x_3 = 4142$, $x_4 = 21$, $x_5 = 99644$, and maximum $P = 3{,}545{,}348$

EXERCISES

5.1 Maximize $P = 2x_1 + 31x_2$ subject to $0 \le x_1 \le 999{,}999$, $0 \le x_2 \le 999{,}999$, $x_1 + x_2 \le 1{,}500{,}000$, and $x_1 + 6x_2 \le 3{,}000{,}000$.

5.2 Maximize $P = 6x_1 + 10x_2 + 9x_3^2$ subject to $0 \le x_1 \le 999{,}999$, $0 \le x_2 \le 999{,}999$, $0 \le x_3 \le 999{,}999$, $.85x_1 + 2.63x_2 + 18x_3 \le 5{,}000{,}000$, and $x_1 + x_3 \le 800{,}000$.

5.3 Minimize $C = .58x_1 + 5.21x_2 + 6.253x_3 - 2.1x_4$ subject to $0 \le x_1 \le 999{,}999$, $0 \le x_2 \le 999{,}999$, $0 \le x_3 \le 999{,}999$, $0 \le x_4 \le 999{,}999$, $x_1 + x_2 + x_3 \le 700{,}000$, $x_3 + x_4 \le 200{,}000$, and $x_1 + x_2 + x_3 x_4 \le 3{,}000{,}000$.

5.4 A farmer can earn a profit of $200 per acre on onions, $100 per acre on carrots, and $125 on radishes. Because of a fertilizer shortage he can only obtain 3000 lbs. of Fertilizer A and 2000 lbs. of Fertilizer B. Onions require 50 lbs. of each fertilizer per acre, radishes require 25 lbs. of each fertilizer per acre, and carrots require 30 lbs. of Fertilizer A and 10 lbs. of Fertilizer B per acre. The farmer has a 100-acre farm. Maximize his profit. (Hint: Maximize $P = 200x + 125y + 100z$ subject to $x \geq 0$, $y \geq 0$, $z \geq 0$, $x + y + z \leq 100$, $50x + 25y + 30z \leq 3000$, and $50x + 25y + 10z \leq 2000$.)

5.5 The following chart shows the profit and catalyst requirements per unit for each of three different grades of steel beams:

	Profit per unit ($)	Catalyst per beam in units
High-grade beams	100	10
Medium-grade beams	80	5
Low-grade beams	55	4

The plant capacity is 1000 beams per day total in any combination. 6600 units of catalyst a day are available during the current shortage. The firm can always sell all beams of any grade that are produced.

Maximize the profit during the catalyst shortage. (Hint: Maximize $P = 100x + 80y + 55z$ subject to $x \geq 0$, $y \geq 0$, $z \geq 0$, $x + y + z \leq 1000$, and $10x + 5y + 4z \leq 6600$.)

5.6 The following chart shows the profit and natural gas requirements per unit for each of six different types of plastic fittings:

Fitting	Profit per fitting ($)	Units of natural gas per fitting
1	5.00	20
2	4.20	16
3	3.65	10
4	2.00	5
5	1.90	2
6	1.60	2

The plant capacity is 10,000 fittings per week in any combination. There are 80,000 units of natural gas per week available due to a temporary shortage.

Maximize the profit per week from the fittings. (Hint: Mazimize $P = 5.00x_1 + 4.20x_2 + 3.65x_3 + 2.00x_4 + 1.90x_5 + 160x_6$ subject to $x_i \geq 0$, $i = 1,6$, $20x_1 + 16x_2 + 10x_3 + 5x_4 + 2x_5 + 2x_6 \leq 80,000$, and $x_1 + x_2 + x_3 + x_4 + x_5 + x_6 \leq 10,000$.)

5.7 Research and Development is starting up ten new production processes. The table below shows the profit per unit per week and the number of engineers required per week per unit from each process:

Process	Profit per unit per week ($)	Engineers per unit per week
1	1000	10
2	600	5
3	200	3
4	100	2
5	750	6
6	350	4
7	200	2
8	150	1
9	600	5
10	210	2

No more than a total of 50 units can be produced per week. Each process must generate at least two units a week. There are 200 engineers available.

Maximize the profit. (Hint: Maximize $P = 1000x_1 + 600x_2 + 200x_3 + 100x_4 + 750x_5 + 350x_6 + 200x_7 + 150x_8 + 600x_9 + 210x_{10}$ subject to $x_i \geq 2$ for all i, $x_1 + x_2 + x_3 + x_4 + x_5 + x_6 + x_7 + x_8 + x_9 + x_{10} \leq 50$, and $10x_1 + 5x_2 + 3x_3 + 2x_4 + 6x_5 + 4x_6 + 2x_7 + x_8 + 5x_9 + 2x_{10} \leq 200$.)

5.8 Maximize $P = 20x + 15y$ subject to $x \geq 0, y \geq 0, x + y \leq 168, 10x + 5y \leq 1000$, and $5x + 10y \leq 1000$.

CHAPTER 6

Integer Programming Problems with Many Variables

The graphs which begin this chapter present the sampling distributions of the feasible solutions of three more integer programming problems. Notice that their tails are reasonably thick. Also, remember that as access to computers increases (through having one's own minicomputer or a good on-line system) and as they increase in speed, the random sample approach will be able to produce a value that will be extremely close to the very end (true optimum) of the distribution.

Additional Monte Carlo integer programming examples follow the graphs.

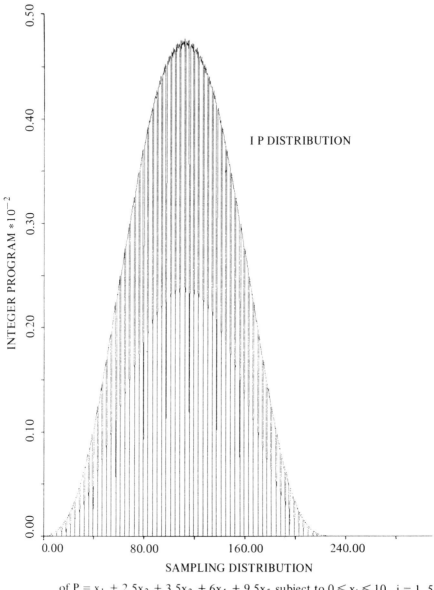

Figure 6.1

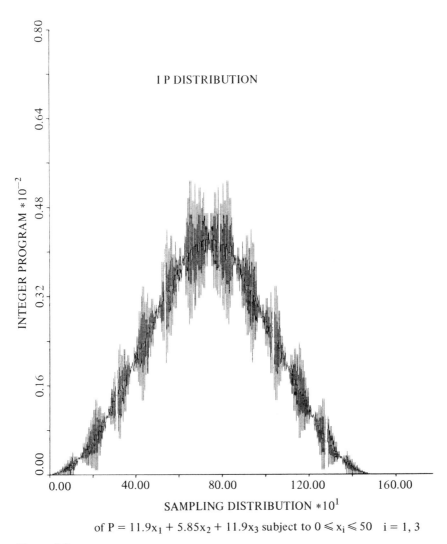

Figure 6.2

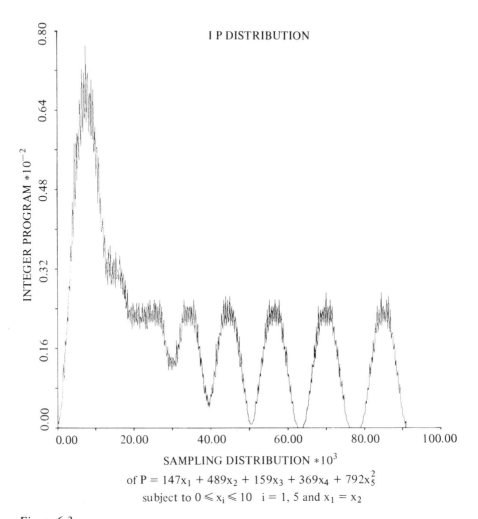

Figure 6.3

EXAMPLE 6.1

The SXR Forestry Company manufactures 40 products (plywood, different cuts of lumber, pressed board, paneling, paper products, etc.) from logging and manufacturing processes. The products (products 1 through 40) contribute a daily per unit profit in cents, respectively, as follows: 215, 116, 670, 924, 510, 600, 424, 942, 43, 369, 408, 52, 319, 214, 851, 394, 88, 124, 17, 779, 278, 258, 271, 281, 326, 819, 485, 454, 297, 53, 136, 796, 114, 43, 80, 268, 179, 78, 105, and 281. The table below shows how much time (in 1/2-minute units) is required in each of the three departments to make one unit each of the forty products:

Time required (1/2-minutes)

Product	Department 1	Department 2	Department 3
1	8	5	3
2	11	3	4
3	6	2	6
4	1	7	2
5	7	7	2
6	9	3	3
7	10	6	7
8	3	2	10
9	11	15	3
10	11	8	7
11	2	16	2
12	1	1	16
13	16	2	3
14	18	2	3
15	2	7	9
16	1	7	8
17	1	2	9
18	2	2	7
19	3	4	6
20	4	3	16
21	7	2	12
22	6	13	1
23	2	8	3
24	2	2	14
25	1	3	7
26	2	4	13
27	1	3	6
28	8	2	16
29	10	1	3
30	2	10	2
31	1	6	1
32	9	3	2

33	1	4	8
34	9	1	3
35	2	8	2
36	4	6	7
37	10	3	1
38	8	4	2
39	6	6	6
40	1	2	5

Each department has no more than 25,000 man or machine 1/2-minutes available per day. Also, between 0 and 99 of each item must be produced. Find the number of each product that should be made to maximize the profit. The relevant information is summarized below:

$$P = 215x_1 + 116x_2 + 670x_3 + 924x_4 + 510x_5 + 600x_6 + 424x_7 + 942x_8$$
$$+ 43x_9 + 369x_{10} + 408x_{11} + 52x_{12} + 319x_{13} + 214x_{14} + 851x_{15} + 394x_{16} +$$
$$88x_{17} + 124x_{18} + 17x_{19} + 779x_{20} + 278x_{21} + 258x_{22} + 271x_{23} + 281x_{24} +$$
$$326x_{25} + 819x_{26} + 485x_{27} + 454x_{28} + 297x_{29} + 53x_{30} + 136x_{31} + 796x_{32} +$$
$$114x_{33} + 43x_{34} + 80x_{35} + 268x_{36} + 179x_{37} + 78x_{38} + 105x_{39} + 281x_{40}$$

subject to $0 \le x_i \le 99$ for $i = 1,40$ and

$$8x_1 + 11x_2 + 6x_3 + x_4 + 7x_5 + 9x_6 + 10x_7 + 3x_8 + 11x_9 + 11x_{10} + 2x_{11} +$$
$$x_{12} + 16x_{13} + 18x_{14} + 2x_{15} + x_{16} + x_{17} + 2x_{18} + 3x_{19} + 4x_{20} + 7x_{21} + 6x_{22} +$$
$$2x_{23} + 2x_{24} + x_{25} + 2x_{26} + x_{27} + 8x_{28} + 10x_{29} + 2x_{30} + x_{31} + 9x_{32} + x_{33} +$$
$$9x_{34} + 2x_{35} + 4x_{36} + 10x_{37} + 8x_{38} + 6x_{39} + x_{40} \le 25{,}000,$$

$$5x_1 + 3x_2 + 2x_3 + 7x_4 + 7x_5 + 3x_6 + 6x_7 + 2x_8 + 15x_9 + 8x_{10} + 16x_{11} +$$
$$x_{12} + 2x_{13} + 2x_{14} + 7x_{15} + 7x_{16} + 2x_{17} + 2x_{18} + 4x_{19} + 3x_{20} + 2x_{21} +$$
$$13x_{22} + 8x_{23} + 2x_{24} + 3x_{25} + 4x_{26} + 3x_{27} + 2x_{28} + x_{29} + 10x_{30} + 6x_{31} +$$
$$3x_{32} + 4x_{33} + x_{34} + 8x_{35} + 6x_{36} + 3x_{37} + 4x_{38} + 6x_{39} + 2x_{40} \le 25{,}000$$

and

$$3x_1 + 4x_2 + 6x_3 + 2x_4 + 2x_5 + 3x_6 + 7x_7 + 10x_8 + 3x_9 + 7x_{10} + 2x_{11} +$$
$$16x_{12} + 3x_{13} + 3x_{14} + 9x_{15} + 8x_{16} + 9x_{17} + 7x_{18} + 6x_{19} + 16x_{20} + 12x_{21}$$
$$+ x_{22} + 3x_{23} + 14x_{24} + 7x_{25} + 13x_{26} + 6x_{27} + 16x_{28} + 3x_{29} + 2x_{30} + x_{31}$$
$$+ 2x_{32} + 8x_{33} + 3x_{34} + 2x_{35} + 7x_{36} + x_{37} + 2x_{38} + 6x_{39} + 5x_{40} \le 25{,}000$$

Also, due to the structure and composition of the trees being logged, at least a certain number of units of each product must be produced each day. These constraints are summarized below and should be added to the maximization problem:

$$x_i \geq 10 \qquad i = 1,20$$
$$x_i \geq 20 \qquad i = 21,40$$

Now, again we have far too many possible points to check for the true maximum profit value so we will do a Monte Carlo technique on a random sample of 2000 points and take the point from these that produces the maximum P.

Due to the large number of variables, we will use subscripted variables wherever possible. However, if the profit function and/or constraints had to be written out individually term by term, the technique would still work. It would just take more time to write the maximizing program. The program is the same in structure as previous ones.

```
      DIMENSION IX(40),Y(40)
      INTEGER X(40)
      PMAX=-1.0 E67
      CALL RSTART(2727277,3737375)
      DO 1 I=1,2000
      DO 20 J=1,20
  400 CONTINUE
      Y(J)=UNI(0)
      X(J)=Y(J)*100.
      IF(X(J).LE.9) GO TO 400
   20 CONTINUE
      DO 21 J=21,40
  401 CONTINUE
      Y(J)=UNI(0)
      X(J)=Y(J)*100.
      IF(X(J).LE.19) GO TO 401
   21 CONTINUE
      IF(8*X(1)+11*X(2)+6*X(3)+X(4)+7*X(5)+9*X(6)+10*X(7)+3*X(8)
     A+11*X(9)+11*X(10)+2*X(11)+X(12)+16*X(13)+18*X(14)+2*X(15)+X(16)
     A+X(17)+2*X(18)+3*X(19)+4*X(20)+7*X(21)+6*X(22)+2*X(23)+2*X(24)
     A+X(25)+2*X(26)+X(27)+8*X(28)+10*X(29)+2*X(30)+X(31)+9*X(32)
     A+X(33)+9*X(34)+2*X(35)+4*X(36)+10*X(37)+8*X(38)+6*X(39)
     A+X(40).GT.25000) GO TO 1
      IF(5*X(1)+3*X(2)+2*X(3)+7*X(4)+7*X(5)+3*X(6)+6*X(7)+2*X(8)
     A+15*X(9)+8*X(10)+16*X(11)+X(12)+2*X(13)+2*X(14)+7*X(15)+7*X(16)
     A+2*X(17)+2*X(18)+4*X(19)+3*X(20)+2*X(21)+13*X(22)+8*X(23)+2*X(24)
     A+3*X(25)+4*X(26)+3*X(27)+2*X(28)+X(29)+10*X(30)+6*X(31)+3*X(32)
     A+4*X(33)+X(34)+8*X(35)+6*X(36)+3*X(37)+4*X(38)+6*X(39)+
     A2*X(40).GT.25000) GO TO 1
      IF(3*X(1)+4*X(2)+6*X(3)+2*X(4)+2*X(5)+3*X(6)+7*X(7)+10*X(8)
     A+3*X(9)+7*X(10)+2*X(11)+16*X(12)+3*X(13)+3*X(14)+9*X(15)+8*X(16)
     A+9*X(17)+7*X(18)+6*X(20)+12*X(21)+X(22)+3*X(23)+14*X(24)+6*X(19)
     A+7*X(25)+13*X(26)+6*X(27)+16*X(28)+3*X(29)+2*X(30)+X(31)+2*X(32)
     A+8*X(33)+3*X(34)+2*X(35)+7*X(36)+X(37)+2*X(38)+6*X(39)+10*X(20)+
     A5*X(40).GT.25000) GO TO 1
      P=215*X(1)+116*X(2)+670*X(3)+924*X(4)+510*X(5)
     A+600*X(6)+424*X(7)+942*X(8)+43*X(9)+369*X(10)
     A+408*X(11)+52*X(12)+319*X(13)+214*X(14)+851*X(15)
```

```
A+394*X(16)+88*X(17)+124*X(18)+17*X(19)+779*X(20)
A+278*X(21)+258*X(22)+271*X(23)+281*X(24)+326*X(25)
A+819*X(26)+485*X(27)+454*X(28)+297*X(29)+53*X(30)
A+136*X(31)+796*X(32)+114*X(33)+43*X(34)+80*X(35)
A+268*X(36)+179*X(37)+78*X(38)+105*X(39)+281*X(40)
      IF(P.GT.PMAX) GO TO 2
      GO TO 1
2     CONTINUE
      DO 6 N=1,40
6     IX(N)=X(N)
      PMAX=P
1     CONTINUE
      WRITE(6,3)IX(1),IX(2),IX(3),IX(4),IX(5),IX(6),IX(7),IX(8),
     AIX(9),IX(10),IX(11),IX(12),IX(13),IX(14),IX(15),IX(16),
     AIX(17),IX(18),IX(19),IX(20),IX(21),IX(22),IX(23),IX(24),
     AIX(25),IX(26),IX(27),IX(28),IX(29),IX(30),IX(31),IX(32),
     AIX(33),IX(34),IX(35),IX(36),IX(37),IX(38),IX(39),IX(40)
3     FORMAT('0',40I10)
      WRITE(6,4)PMAX
4     FORMAT('0',E16.7)
      STOP
      END


              THE PRINTOUT IS

     48   73   16   86   49   99   94   79
     98   86   94   33   95   80   53   86
     87   50   39   78   47   72   97   98
     73   86   99   81   77   95   28   95
     58   23   55   70   35   82   32   94

          0.1030361E 07
```

The solution is:

$x_1 = 48$, $x_2 = 73$, $x_3 = 16$, $x_4 = 86$, $x_5 = 49$, $x_6 = 99$, $x_7 = 94$, $x_8 = 79$,

$x_9 = 98$, $x_{10} = 86$, $x_{11} = 94$, $x_{12} = 33$, $x_{13} = 95$, $x_{14} = 80$, $x_{15} = 53$,

$x_{16} = 86$, $x_{17} = 87$, $x_{18} = 50$, $x_{19} = 39$, $x_{20} = 78$, $x_{21} = 47$, $x_{22} = 72$,

$x_{23} = 97$, $x_{24} = 98$, $x_{25} = 73$, $x_{26} = 86$, $x_{27} = 99$, $x_{28} = 81$, $x_{29} = 77$,

$x_{30} = 95$, $x_{31} = 28$, $x_{32} = 95$, $x_{33} = 58$, $x_{34} = 23$, $x_{35} = 55$, $x_{36} = 70$,

$x_{37} = 35$, $x_{38} = 82$, $x_{39} = 32$, $x_{40} = 94$, and maximum $P = 1,030,361$

Therefore, the SXR Forestry Company should produce

Product	Units	Product	Units	Product	Units	Product	Units
1	48	11	94	21	47	31	28
2	73	12	33	22	72	32	95
3	16	13	95	23	97	33	58
4	86	14	80	24	98	34	23
5	49	15	53	25	73	35	55
6	99	16	86	26	86	36	70
7	94	17	87	27	99	37	35
8	79	18	50	28	81	38	82
9	98	19	39	29	77	39	32
10	86	20	78	30	95	40	94

to yield a profit of \$10,303.61 per day.

EXAMPLE 6.2
Maximize

$P = 50x_1 + 150x_2 + 100x_3 + 92x_4 + 55x_5 + 12x_6 + 11x_7 + 10x_8 + 8x_9 + 3x_{10} + 114x_{11} + 90x_{12} + 87x_{13} + 91x_{14} + 58x_{15} + 16x_{16} + 19x_{17} + 22x_{18} + 21x_{19} + 32x_{20} + 53x_{21} + 56x_{22} + 118x_{23} + 192x_{24} + 52x_{25} + 204x_{26} + 250x_{27} + 295x_{28} + 82x_{29} + 30x_{30} + 29x_{31}^2 - 2x_{32}^2 + 9x_{33}^2 + 94x_{34} + 15x_{35}^3 + 17x_{36}^2 - 15x_{37} - 2x_{38} + x_{39}^2 + 3x_{40}^4 + 52x_{41} + 57x_{42}^2 - x_{43}^2 + 12x_{44} + 21x_{45} + 6x_{46} + 7x_{47} - x_{48} + x_{49} + x_{50} + 119x_{51} + 82x_{52} + 75x_{53} + 18x_{54} + 16x_{55} + 12x_{56} + 6x_{57} + 7x_{58} + 3x_{59} + 6x_{60} + 12x_{61} + 13x_{62} + 18x_{63} + 7x_{64} + 3x_{65} + 19x_{66} + 22x_{67} + 3x_{68} + 12x_{69} + 9x_{70} + 18x_{71} + 19x_{72} + 12x_{73} + 8x_{74} + 5x_{75} + 2x_{76} + 16x_{77} + 17x_{78} + 11x_{79} + 12x_{80} + 9x_{81} + 12x_{82} + 11x_{83} + 14x_{84} + 16x_{85} + 3x_{86} + 9x_{87} + 10x_{88} + 3x_{89} + x_{90} + 12x_{91} + 3x_{92} + 12x_{93} - 2x_{94}^2 - x_{95} + 6x_{96} + 7x_{97} + 4x_{98} + x_{99} + 2x_{100}$

subject to $x_i \geq 0$ $i = 1,100$ $x_i \leq 99$ $i = 1,100,$

$\sum_{i=1}^{100} x_i \leq 7500$, and $\sum_{i=1}^{50} 10x_i + \sum_{i=51}^{100} x_i \leq 42000$

We will try the Monte Carlo approach on 10,000 sample points.

```
DIMENSION IX(100),Y(100)
INTEGER X(100)
PMAX=-1.0 E51
```

```
      CALL RSTART(7373737,5555555)
      DO 1 I=1,10000
      DO 10 J=1,100
      Y(J)=UNI(0)
10    X(J)=Y(J)*100.
      SOT=0.0
      DO 55 KA=1,100
55    SOT=SOT+X(KA)
      IF(SOT.GT.7500) GO TO 1
      SOC=0.0
      DO 58 II=1,50
58    SOC=SOC+X(II)
      TSOC=10*SOC
      SOA=0.0
      DO 59 III=51,100
59    SOA=SOA+X(III)
      TOTAL=TSOC+SOA
      IF(TOTAL.GT.42000) GO TO 1
      P=50*X(1)+150*X(2)+100*X(3)+92*X(4)+55*X(5)+12*X(6)+11*X(7)+
     A10*X(8)+8*X(9)+3*X(10)+114*X(11)+90*X(12)+87*X(13)+91*X(14)+
     A58*X(15)+16*X(16)+19*X(17)+22*X(18)+21*X(19)+32*X(20)+
     A53*X(21)+56*X(22)+118*X(23)+192*X(24)+52*X(25)+204*X(26)+
     A250*X(27)+295*X(28)+82*X(29)+30*X(30)+29*X(31)**2
     A-2*X(32)**2+9*X(33)**2+94*X(34)+15*X(35)**3+17*X(36)**2
     A-15*X(37)-2*X(38)+X(39)**2+3*X(40)**4
     A+52*X(41)+57*X(42)**2-X(43)**2+12*X(44)+21*X(45)
     A+6*X(46)+7*X(47)-X(48)+X(49)+X(50)+119*X(51)
     A+82*X(52)+75*X(53)+18*X(54)+16*X(55)+12*X(56)+6*X(57)
     A+7*X(58)+3*X(59)+6*X(60)+12*X(61)+13*X(62)+18*X(63)
     A+7*X(64)+3*X(65)+19*X(66)+22*X(67)+3*X(68)+12*X(69)
     A+9*X(70)+18*X(71)+19*X(72)+12*X(73)+8*X(74)+5*X(75)+
     A2*X(76)+16*X(77)+17*X(78)+11*X(79)+12*X(80)+
     A9*X(81)+12*X(82)+11*X(83)+14*X(84)+16*X(85)+3*X(86)+
     A9*X(87)+10*X(88)+3*X(89)+X(90)+12*X(91)
     A+3*X(92)+12*X(93)-2*X(94)**2-X(95)+6*X(96)
     A+7*X(97)+4*X(98)+X(99)+2*X(100)
      IF(P.GT.PMAX) GO TO 2
      GO TO 1
2     CONTINUE
      DO 6 L=1,100
6     IX(L)=X(L)
      PMAX=P
1     CONTINUE
      WRITE(6,3)IX
3     FORMAT('0',10I10/('0',10I10))
      WRITE(6,4)PMAX
4     FORMAT('0',I10)
      STOP
      END
```

THE PRINTOUT IS

```
51 10 90 85 35 36 75 98 99 30
56 23 10 56 98 94 63  8 27 92
10 66 69 10 39 38 49  8 95 96
86 14  1 55 98 64  8  1 18 99
84 78  4 19 85 33 59 95 57 48
37 95 62 82 62 62 87 38 95 14
91 21 72 85 68 69 30 30 85 93
73 19 26 62 94 59 53 11  0  1
 2 26 43 50 42 93 27 71 61 93
44 94 15 92  8 18 42 27 66 49
```

1209143390

Note lines 10 through 17 ($soc = 0.0$, etc.) check to see if

$$\sum_{i=1}^{50} 10x_i + \sum_{i=51}^{100} x_i \le 42000$$

where Σ stands for summing all the terms governed by the subscripts. The solution is:

$x_1 = 51, x_2 = 10, x_3 = 90, x_4 = 85, x_5 = 35, x_6 = 36, x_7 = 75, x_8 = 98,$

$x_9 = 99, x_{10} = 30, x_{11} = 56, x_{12} = 23, x_{13} = 10, x_{14} = 56, x_{15} = 98, x_{16} = 94,$

$x_{17} = 63, x_{18} = 8, x_{19} = 27, x_{20} = 92, x_{21} = 10, x_{22} = 66, x_{23} = 69, x_{24} = 10,$

$x_{25} = 39, x_{26} = 38, x_{27} = 49, x_{28} = 8, x_{29} = 95, x_{30} = 96, x_{31} = 86,$

$x_{32} = 14, x_{33} = 1, x_{34} = 55, x_{35} = 98, x_{36} = 64, x_{37} = 8, x_{38} = 1, x_{39} = 18,$

$x_{40} = 99, x_{41} = 84, x_{42} = 78, x_{43} = 4, x_{44} = 19, x_{45} = 85, x_{46} = 33, x_{47} = 59,$

$x_{48} = 95, x_{49} = 57, x_{50} = 48, x_{51} = 37, x_{52} = 95, x_{53} = 62, x_{54} = 82,$

$x_{55} = 62, x_{56} = 62, x_{57} = 87, x_{58} = 38, x_{59} = 95, x_{60} = 14, x_{61} = 91, x_{62} = 21,$

$x_{63} = 72, x_{64} = 85, x_{65} = 68, x_{66} = 69, x_{67} = 30, x_{68} = 30, x_{69} = 85,$

$x_{70} = 93, x_{71} = 73, x_{72} = 19, x_{73} = 26, x_{74} = 62, x_{75} = 94, x_{76} = 59, x_{77} = 53,$

$x_{78} = 11, x_{79} = 0, x_{80} = 1, x_{81} = 2, x_{82} = 26, x_{83} = 43, x_{84} = 50, x_{85} = 42,$

$x_{86} = 93, x_{87} = 27, x_{88} = 71, x_{89} = 61, x_{90} = 93, x_{91} = 44, x_{92} = 94,$

$x_{93} = 15, x_{94} = 92, x_{95} = 8, x_{96} = 18, x_{97} = 42, x_{98} = 27, x_{99} = 66,$

$x_{100} = 49$, and maximum $P = \$12,091,433.90$.

IMPROVING THE EFFICIENCY OF PROGRAMS

1. Consider the problem to maximize $P = 7x^2 - xy + 3y^2 + xy^2$ subject to $x \ge 0,$

$y \geq 0$, and $x + y \leq 5000$. The constraints show that $0 \leq x \leq 5000$ and $0 \leq y \leq 5000$. Therefore, there are $5001 \times 5001 = 25,010,001$ combinations to try.

However, we could exploit the fact that as x ranges from 0 to 5000, y must range from 0 to $5000 - x$. The program would look like this:

```
       INTEGER X,Y,P,BIG
       BIG=-999999
       DO 1 I=1,5001
       X=I-1
       K=5000-X
       DO 1 J=1,K
       Y=J-1
       P=7*X**2-X*Y+3*Y**2+X*Y**2
       IF(P.GT.BIG) GO TO 2
       GO TO 1
2      IX=X
       IY=Y
       BIG=P
1      CONTINUE
       WRITE(6,3)IX,IY,BIG
3      FORMAT('0',3I10)
       STOP
       END
```

If this approach is tried on a Monte Carlo simulation, then multiply the second random number by $5000 - x + 1$ which will guarantee that $x + y \leq 5000$ (still referring to the previous inequality).

If the constraint was $x + y + z + w \leq 5000$, then multiply the first random number by 5001. Multiply the second random number by $5001 - x$. Multiply the third random number by $5001 - x - y$. Multiply the fourth random number by $5001 - x - y - z$. This could introduce a slight bias in the random process, however it shouldn't cause much problem in practice, and there are other "bias free" approaches to the random process.

One bias free approach is to read in four random numbers between 0 and 5000 (referring to $x + y + z + w \leq 5000$) and add them up. If the sum is less than or equal to 5000, use them. If the sum is greater than 5000, divide 5000 into the sum and divide each random number by that quotient. This will "shrink" the random numbers small enough so that $x + y + z + w \leq 5000$.

There are other approaches for more sophisticated problems. The question is, Is it worth the extra programming trouble? I think the answer is sometimes yes.

2. Assume that a function of three variables is constrained by $1 \leq x \leq 1000$, $1 \leq y \leq 1000$, and $1 \leq z \leq 1000$. Therefore, there are $1000 \times 1000 \times 1000 = 1,000,000,000$ possible answers. If this is too many to check on your computer system, consider letting x, y, and z increase by increments of ten instead of one.

Therefore, x could take the values 10, 20, 30, 40, ... , 1000. Y and z could do the same. This way there would only be $100 \times 100 \times 100 = 1{,}000{,}000$ possibilities to check.

This would probably work well in business where there is frequently 10% to 20% estimation error in the model to begin with.

3. Consider the problem maximize $P = 20x_1 + 15x_2 + 19x_3 + 27x_4 + 34x_5 + 42x_6 + 58x_7 + 21x_8 + 90x_9 + 66x_{10} + 15x_{11} + 75x_{12} + 14x_{13} + 88x_{14} + 62x_{15} + 60x_{16} + 58x_{17} + 54x_{18} + 90x_{19} + 29x_{20}$ subject to $x_i \geq 0$ for all i and

$$4x_1 + 5x_2 + 2x_3 + 2x_4 + x_5 + 5x_6 + 6x_7 + 5x_8 + 4x_9 + 3x_{10} + 5x_{11} + 6x_{12} + 2x_{13} + 8x_{14} + 6x_{15} + 5x_{16} + x_{17} + x_{18} + 5x_{19} + 5x_{20} \leq 3800,$$

$$x_1 + x_2 + 8x_3 + 6x_4 + 4x_5 + 2x_6 + 3x_7 + 2x_8 + 4x_9 + 6x_{10} + x_{11} + 2x_{12} + x_{13} + 2x_{14} + 6x_{15} + x_{16} + 3x_{17} + 4x_{18} + 2x_{19} + 5x_{20} \leq 3800,$$

$$3x_1 + 2x_2 + x_3 + 2x_4 + x_5 + x_6 + 3x_7 + x_8 + x_9 + 2x_{10} + 2x_{11} + 2x_{12} + 5x_{13} + x_{14} + x_{15} + x_{16} + 6x_{17} + x_{18} + 5x_{19} + 2x_{20} \leq 3800, \text{ and}$$

$$2x_1 + 2x_2 + 2x_3 + 3x_4 + 2x_5 + 2x_6 + x_7 + 4x_8 + x_9 + x_{10} + 3x_{11} + 2x_{12} + 7x_{13} + 6x_{14} + 2x_{15} + x_{16} + 7x_{17} + 5x_{18} + 3x_{19} + 4x_{20} \leq 3800$$

This is a straight linear programming problem and, of course, could be solved by the simplex method if a simplex package program were obtainable. Also, we could produce a simulated optimum which would be fairly close to the true optimum.

However, let's use our simulation technique along with a little linear programming theory to produce the optimum without resorting to a simplex package program.

First we write a program that reads in twenty random numbers (each time through the loop) and "shrinks" them back inside the constraints as discussed previously. There are no biases this way.

After a few runs of the simulation, the printouts begin to identify certain key variables that tend to have large values, while the others tend to be around zero (relatively speaking).

Now, it is a well-known fact of linear programming theory that in a maximize problem, if all the inequalities are of the less-than type, then the number of nonzero variables in the optimum solution can't exceed the number of inequalities. So in this case, there are no more than four nonzero variables. Let's use this fact.

Six promising (never near zero) variables from the twenty-variable simulation runs were noticed. Therefore, the program was modified so that only six variables were nonzero in the simulation. Then several more runs were made. The printouts are given below:

.000	.000	.000	.000	2.079
.000	.000	.000	460.552	5.451
.000	.000	.000	.000	.000
.000	232.524	134.300	314.508	.000
90924.313				

.000	.000	.000	.000	36.611
.000	.000	.000	482.270	6.769
.000	.000	.000	.000	.000
.000	287.899	58.351	293.384	.000
91349.313				
.000	.000	.000	.000	5.823
.000	.000	.000	468.716	21.681
.000	.000	.000	.000	.000
.000	252.530	104.870	297.347	.000
90884.250				
.000	.000	.000	.000	14.452
.000	.000	.000	557.580	25.045
.000	.000	.000	.000	.000
.000	292.447	1.967	237.136	.000
90736.813				

From the printouts, it looks like x_9, x_{17}, x_{18}, and x_{19} are the nonzero variables. This reduces the model to maximize $P = 90x_9 + 58x_{17} + 54x_{18} + 90x_{19}$ subject to $x_i \geq 0$ and $4x_9 + x_{17} + x_{18} + 5x_{19} \leq 3800$, $4x_9 + 3x_{17} + 4x_{18} + 2x_{19} \leq 3800$, $x_9 + 6x_{17} + x_{18} + 5x_{19} \leq 3800$, and $x_9 + 7x_{17} + 5x_{18} + 3x_{19} \leq 3800$. This is easily solvable through another simulation.

After a few runs, an answer of $x_9 = 564.473$, $x_{17} = 336.546$, $x_{18} = 14.149$, and $x_{19} = 237.936$ produced a P value of 92,500.563.

EXERCISES

6.1   Maximize $P = 6x_1 + 12x_2 + 47x_3 + 58x_4 + 21x_5 + 22x_6 + 4x_7 + 3x_8 + 9x_9 + 22x_{10}$ subject to $0 \leq x_i \leq 99999$, $i = 1,10$, $x_1 + x_5 + x_9 + x_{10} \leq 250,000$, $x_1 + x_2 + x_3 + x_4 + x_5 + x_6 + x_7 + x_8 + x_9 + x_{10} \leq 700,000$, and $x_8 + x_9 + x_{10} \leq 200,000$.

6.2   Maximize $P = 8x_1 + 10x_2 + 18x_3 + 9x_4 + 16x_5 + 12x_6 + 8x_7 + 21x_8 + 22x_9 + 42x_{10} + 28x_{11} + 21x_{12} + 2x_{13} + x_{14}$ subject to

$$0 \leq x_i \leq 99999$$

$$i = 1,14, \quad \sum_{i=1}^{14} x_i \leq 1,000,000,$$

$$\sum_{i=1}^{14} (20 - i)\, x_i \leq 20,000,000$$

6.3   Maximize $C = 10x_1 + 9x_2 + 7x_3 + 6x_4 + x_5 + x_6 + x_7 + 12x_8 + 22x_9 + 2x_{10}$ subject to $0 \leq x_i \leq 99999$, $x_1 + x_2 + x_9 + x_{10} \leq 16,250$, $x_3 + 5x_4 + 7x_5 + x_6 + 9x_7 + x_8 \leq 22,000$, and $x_1 + x_2 + x_3 + x_4 + x_5 + 2x_6 + 19x_7 + 8x_8 + x_9 + x_{10} \leq 1,000,000$.

6.4   Maximize $P = 21x_1 + 19x_2 + 25x_3 + x_4 + 6x_5 + 7x_6 + 9x_7 + 18x_8 + 18x_9 +$

$9x_{10} + x_{11} + 31x_{12} + 17x_{13} + 3x_{14} + 9x_{15} + 10x_{16} + 11x_{17} + 19x_{18} + 19x_{19} + 19x_{20}$
subject to $x_i \geq 0$, $i = 1,20$, and $x_i \leq 9999$, $i = 1,20$,

$$\sum_{i=1}^{20} x_i \leq 100,000$$

$$\sum_{i=1}^{20} 20x_i \leq 1,000,000$$

$$\sum_{i=1}^{20} (21 - i)x_i \leq 1,000,000$$

6.5 We seek to minimize $P = x_1^6 + x_2^5 + x_3 - x_4^4 - x_5^3 - x_6^3 + x_1x_2x_6 - x_3x_4x_5 + 18x_1 - 21x_2 - 23x_3 + 22x_4 + 22x_5 + x_6$ subject to $x_i \geq 0, i = 1,6, x_i \leq 9999, i = 1, 6, x_1 + x_2 + x_3 + x_4 + x_5 + x_6 \leq 30,000, 22x_1 + 5x_2 + 6x_3 + x_4 + x_5 + x_6 \leq 104,000, x_1 + 2x_2 + 3x_3 + x_4 + x_5 + 9x_6 \leq 1920$, and $x_1 + x_2 \leq 41$.

6.6 Maximize $P = 3x_1^2 + 7x_2^2 - 6x_1 - 18x_2 - x_1x_2$ subject to $x_1 \geq 0$, $x_2 \geq 0$, $x_1 \leq 9999$, $x_2 \leq 9999$, $x_1 + x_2 \leq 15,000$, $4x_1 + 4x_2 \leq 500$, $3x_1 + x_2 \leq 20,000$, $x_1 + 12x_2 \leq 600$, $x_1 + 3x_2 \leq 20,000$, and $x_1^2 + 2x_2^2 \leq 80,000,000$.

6.7 Maximize $P = 7x_1 + 9x_2 + 31x_3 + 2x_4$ subject to $x_1 \geq 0$, $x_2 \geq 0$, $x_3 \geq 0$, $x_4 \geq 0$, $x_1 \leq 99$, $x_2 \leq 999$, $x_3 \leq 9999$, $x_4 \leq 99999$, $10x_1 + 1000x_2 + x_3 + x_4 \leq 700,000$, $50x_1 + 500x_2 \leq x_3 + x_4$, and $x_1 + x_2 + x_3 + x_4 \leq 1,000$.

6.8 Minimize $P = 7x_1 + 9x_2 + 31x_3 + 2x_4$ subject to $x_1 \geq 0, x_2 \geq 0, x_3 \geq 0, x_4 \geq 0$, $x_1 \leq 99$, $x_2 \leq 999$, $x_3 \leq 9999$, $x_4 \leq 99999$, $10x_1 + 1000x_2 + x_3 + x_4 \leq 700,000$, $50x_1 + 500x_2 \leq x_3 + x_4$, and $x_1 + x_2 + x_3 + x_4 \leq 1000$.

6.9 The A Company wants to make and market ten products (Product 1, Product 2, ... , Product 10). The first eight products have downward sloping demand curves and the last two have upward sloping demand curves. We wish to find how many of each product should be made in order to maximize profit. We have the following information available.

Product 1 has a price-quantity curve described as $y = -.5x_1 + 40$ and costs \$1 to make. Therefore, the profit equation for Product 1 is:

$$P_1 = x_1y - x_1$$
$$P_1 = x_1(-.5x_1 + 40) - x_1$$
$$P_1 = -.5x_1^2 + 40x_1 - x_1$$
$$P_1 = -.5x_1^2 + 39x_1 \text{ for } 0 \leq x_1 \leq 78$$

Product 2 has a price-quantity curve described as $y = -.5x_2 + 60$ and costs \$1 to make, also. Therefore, the profit equation for Product 2 is:

$$P_2 = x_2y - x_2$$
$$P_2 = x_2(-.5x_2 + 60) - x_2$$

$P_2 = -.5x_2^2 + 60x_2 - x_2$

$P_2 = -.5x_2^2 + 59x_2$ for $0 \le x_2 \le 118$

Product 3 has a price-quantity curve described as $y = -.3x_3 + 50$ and costs $.50 to make. Therefore, the profit equation for Product 3 is:

$P_3 = x_3 y - .5x_3$

$P_3 = x_3(-.3x_3 + 50) - .5x_3$

$P_3 = -.3x_3^2 + 50x_3 - .50x_3$

$P_3 = -.3x_3^2 + 49.5x_3$ for $0 \le x_3 \le 165$

Product 4 has a price-quantity curve described as $y = -.2x_4 + 100$ and costs $1 to make. Therefore, the profit equation for Product 4 is:

$P_4 = x_4 y - x_4$

$P_4 = x_4(-.2x_4 + 100) - x_4$

$P_4 = -.2x_4^2 + 100x_4 - x_4$

$P_4 = -.2x_4^2 + 99x_4$ for $0 \le x_4 \le 495$

Product 5 has a price-quantity curve described as $y = -.2x_5 + 70$ and costs $.90 to make. Therefore, the profit equation for Product 5 is:

$P_5 = x_5 y - x_5$

$P_5 = x_5(-.2x_5 + 70) - .90x_5$

$P_5 = -.2x_5^2 + 70x_5 - .90x_5$

$P_5 = -.2x_5^2 + 69.1x_5$ for $0 \le x_5 \le 346$

Product 6 has a price-quantity curve described as $y = -.25x_6 + 58$ and costs $1.25 to make. Therefore, the profit equation for Product 6 is:

$P_6 = x_6 y - 1.25x_6$

$P_6 = x_6(-.25x_6 + 58) - 1.25x_6$

$P_6 = -.25x_6^2 + 58x_6 - 1.25x_6$

$P_6 = -.25x_6^2 + 56.75x_6$ for $0 \le x_6 \le 227$

Product 7 has a price-quantity curve described as $y = -.60x_7 + 54$ and costs $1.50 to make. Therefore, the profit equation for Product 7 is:

$P_7 = x_7 y - 1.50x_7$

$P_7 = x_7(-.60x_7 + 54) - 1.50x_7$

$P_7 = -.60x_7^2 + 54x_7 - 1.50x_7$

$P_7 = -.60x_7^2 + 52.5x_7$ for $0 \le x_7 \le 88$

Product 8 has a price-quantity curve described as $y = -.5x_8 + 300$ and costs $2.00 to make. Therefore, the profit equation for Product 8 is:

$$P_8 = x_8 y - 2x_8$$
$$P_8 = x_8(-.5x_8 + 300) - 2x_8$$
$$P_8 = -.5x_8^2 + 300x_8 - 2x_8$$
$$P_8 = -.5x_8^2 + 298x_8 \text{ for } 0 \le x_8 \le 596$$

Product 9 has a price-quantity curve described as $y = .2x_9 + 20$ and costs $.50 to make. Therefore, the profit equation for Product 9 is:

$$P_9 = x_9 y - .5x_9$$
$$P_9 = x_9(.2x_9 + 20) - .5x_9$$
$$P_9 = .2x_9^2 + 20x_9 - .5x_9$$
$$P_9 = .2x_9^2 + 19.5x_9 \text{ for } 0 \le x_9$$

Product 10 has a price-quantity curve described as $y = .4x_{10} + 12$ and costs $.40 to make. Therefore, the profit equation for Product 10 is:

$$P_{10} = x_{10} y - .4x_{10}$$
$$P_{10} = x_{10}(.4x_{10} + 12) - .4x_{10}$$
$$P_{10} = .4x_{10}^2 + 12x_{10} - .4x_{10}$$
$$P_{10} = .4x_{10}^2 + 11.6x_{10} \text{ for } 0 \le x_{10}$$

Consequently, the profit equation for the ten products is:

$$P = P_1 + P_2 + P_3 + P_4 + P_5 + P_6 + P_7 + P_8 + P_9 + P_{10}$$

$P = -.5x_1^2 + 39x_1 - .5x_2^2 + 59x_2 - .3x_3^2 + 49.5x_3 - .2x_4^2 + 99x_4 - .2x_5^2 + 69.1x_5 - .25x_6^2 + 56.75x_6 - .60x_7^2 + 52.5x_7 - .5x_8^2 + 298x_8 + .2x_9^2 + 19.5x_9 + .4x_{10}^2 + 11.6x_{10}$. We seek to maximize the function P subject to

$$0 \le x_1 \le 78$$
$$0 \le x_2 \le 118$$
$$0 \le x_3 \le 165$$
$$0 \le x_4 \le 495$$
$$0 \le x_5 \le 346$$
$$0 \le x_6 \le 227$$
$$0 \le x_7 \le 88$$
$$0 \le x_8 \le 596$$
$$0 \le x_9$$
$$0 \le x_{10}$$

$$x_1 + x_2 + x_3 + x_4 + x_5 + x_6 + x_7 + x_8 + x_9 + x_{10} \le 3000$$

$$2x_1 + x_2 + 6x_3 + 3x_4 + 2x_5 + x_6 + x_7 + 2x_8 + 10x_9 + 10x_{10} \le 6000$$

$$x_1 + x_2 + 3x_3 + 3x_4 + 4x_5 + 4x_6 + x_7 + x_8 + 2x_9 + 3x_{10} \leq 4500$$

where these are the man-minutes available and how long each item must spend in each of the three departments that make the ten products.

Write a program to maximize the above system.

6.10 The R Company produces ten products (Product 1, Product 2, ... , Product 10) at a profit of $20, $30, $35, $50, $62, $66, $70, $81, $90, and $100, respectively. The table below shows how much time is required in each of the four departments to make one unit each of the ten products:

Time required (hours)

Product	Department 1	Department 2	Department 3	Department 4
1	1	6	1	5
2	4	1	4	5
3	3	2	3	2
4	2	7	2	1
5	5	3	1	2
6	1	3	4	1
7	2	2	2	3
8	5	1	2	3
9	1	6	1	1
10	1	1	2	5

Each department has no more than 2700 man-hours available per day.

Find the number of units of products 1 through 10 that should be produced to maximize the profit. The relevant information can be summarized as follows: Maximize $P = 20x_1 + 30x_2 + 35x_3 + 50x_4 + 62x_5 + 66x_6 + 70x_7 + 81x_8 + 90x_9 + 100x_{10}$ subject to $x_i \geq 0$, $i = 1,10$,

$$x_1 + 4x_2 + 3x_3 + 2x_4 + 5x_5 + x_6 + 2x_7 + 5x_8 + x_9 + x_{10} \leq 2700$$

$$6x_1 + x_2 + 2x_3 + 7x_4 + 3x_5 + 3x_6 + 2x_7 + x_8 + 6x_9 + x_{10} \leq 2700$$

$$x_1 + 4x_2 + 3x_3 + 2x_4 + x_5 + 4x_6 + 2x_7 + 2x_8 + x_9 + 2x_{10} \leq 2700$$

$$5x_1 + 5x_2 + 2x_3 + x_4 + 2x_5 + x_6 + 3x_7 + 3x_8 + x_9 + 5x_{10} \leq 2700$$

Write a program to maximize the above system.

CHAPTER 7

A Two-Thousand
Variable
Integer
Programming
Problem

Once again, this chapter opens with three integer programming problem distributions. Note that the thickness of their tails and overall shape reassure us that the Monte Carlo integer programming technique produces a nearly optimum answer.

After the graphs, a 2000-variable integer programming problem and its Monte Carlo solution are presented.

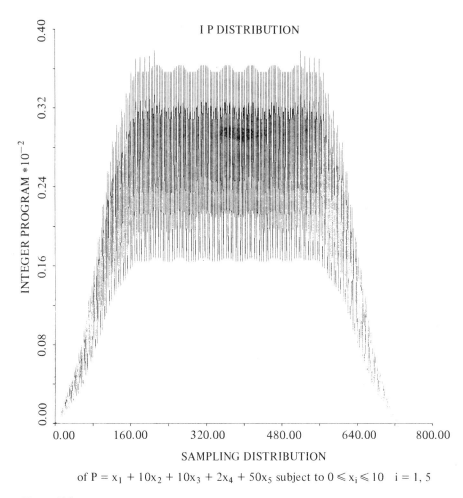

I P DISTRIBUTION

of $P = x_1 + 10x_2 + 10x_3 + 2x_4 + 50x_5$ subject to $0 \leqslant x_i \leqslant 10$ $i = 1, 5$

Figure 7.1

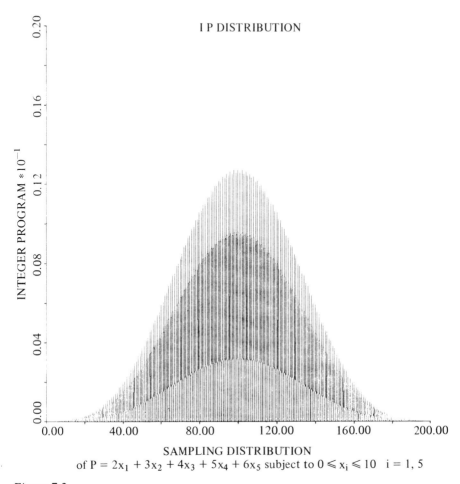

Figure 7.2

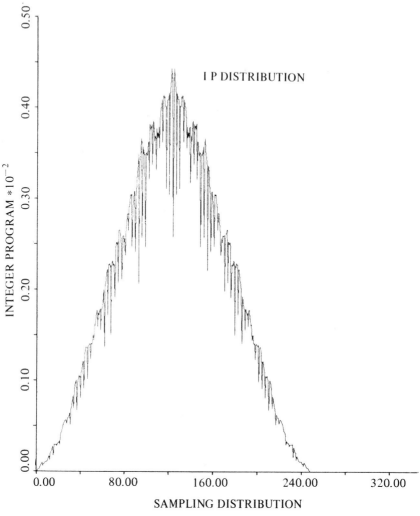

Figure 7.3

of $P = 10x_1 + .5x_2 + 3.8x_3 + .5x_4 + 10x_5$ subject to $0 \leqslant x_i \leqslant 10$ $i = 1, 5$

EXAMPLE

The Z Company manufactures 2000 products (products 1 through 2000) at a profit of $P = |i - 1000| + (-1)^i \times (.0001) + 200$ cents per month where i is the product number and $|\ |$ means absolute value or the whole number amount without the sign. The Z Company must make at least 1000 units of products 1001 through 2000. The total production must not exceed 8,000,000 units and no more than 9,999 units of any product can be produced.

Find the number of each product that should be made to maximize the profit. The relevant information can be summarized as follows:

$$\text{Maximize } P = \sum_{i=1}^{2000}(|i - 1000| + (-1)^i \times (.0001) + 200)x_i$$

where x_i is the number of product i manufactured by the Z Company subject to $0 \le x_i \le 9{,}999$ units for each product and $x_i \ge 1000$ units for $i = 1001 \ldots 2000$

$$\sum_{i=1}^{2000} x_i \le 18{,}000{,}000 \text{ units}$$

Now, quite obviously, we have far too many possible points to check for the true maximum profit value so we will do a Monte Carlo technique on a random sample of 5000 points and take the point from these that gives the maximum P.

Due to the large number of variables, we will use subscripted variables wherever possible. However, if the profit function and/or constraints had to be written out individually term by term, the technique would still work. It would just take more time to write the maximizing program. Note that the profit equation units are cents. The program follows:

```
      DIMENSION IX(2000)
      INTEGER X(2000)
      PMAX=-1.0 E67
      CALL RSTART(28282621,5556579)
      DO 1 I=1,5000
 8    CONTINUE
      DO 20 J=1,1000
      Y=UNI(0)
      X(J)=Y*10000.
 20   CONTINUE
      DO 21 K=1001,2000
 90   CONTINUE
      Y=UNI(0)
      X(K)=Y*10000.
      IF(X(K).LT.1000) GO TO 90
 21   CONTINUE
      SUM=0.0
      DO 22 L=1,2000
 22   SUM=SUM*X(L)
      IF(SUM.GT.18000000) GO TO 8
```

```
      P=0.0
      DO 23 M=1,2000
23    P=P+(ABS(M-1000.)+(-1)**M*(.01)**2+200.)*X(M)
      IF(P.GT.PMAX) GO TO 2
      GO TO 1
2     CONTINUE
      DO 6 N=1,2000
6     IX(N)=X(N)
      PMAX=P
1     CONTINUE
      WRITE(6,3)IX
3     FORMAT('0',10I10/('0',10I10))
      WRITE(6,4)PMAX
4     FORMAT('0',E16.7)
      STOP
      END
```

THE PRINTOUT IS

8575	3245	2296	4567	6737
9319	5278	7794	9266	5447
9283	6670	6474	8814	4612
8347	8569	6296	647	7217
7480	9927	2239	4088	4378
9472	7432	9341	9155	859
2759	8823	8105	9220	2368
1229	6059	5294	7225	5708
9219	3937	649	8466	4948
3492	6420	7092	4767	4770
5718	1377	6797	8386	9140
9363	3913	9210	45	7374
3840	6673	5475	2790	7466
9684	908	8295	1595	4907
5089	6369	2411	7147	1180
2753	5896	595	504	7664
1443	9682	5103	3476	4930

THE PRINTOUT IS (Continued)

8292	5380	7653	7494	6087
9072	9652	6259	688	7795
570	3267	4471	7419	4272
8860	4711	8526	8751	5768
5851	3189	6476	150	2614
4334	2474	5835	2741	3927
8894	8020	8071	6242	4808
2670	2748	2454	9992	7867
7271	2815	1451	3371	7166
2651	1414	4624	5010	8445
5579	7463	4569	241	327
9789	5789	6631	7685	6429
9405	8568	6763	3461	9902
8258	427	8240	5590	9380
5965	1370	4535	4881	8470
6889	5102	8608	5729	6903
9855	7005	3327	6920	1572
7150	8750	8143	109	7366
3209	2961	8884	6653	9962
9896	9712	9213	7861	4252
4760	288	8886	721	4346
9589	8414	4182	9363	8540
6971	4965	7050	7613	2221
4813	8883	9981	9938	9793
9316	7758	2707	6417	4136
7058	5123	7215	7180	8138

THE PRINTOUT IS (Continued)

4209	2006	4155	6870	3826
1126	2320	3784	1820	6861
4783	6950	8647	9328	8147
4927	6235	3065	2273	6048
5834	568	898	280	3593
9035	1871	9911	2628	6564
5732	5319	320	4050	1420
2063	9602	9041	7822	5562
2975	7788	9947	9590	8012
1760	8449	4856	3093	4851
1262	3916	2132	7548	6098
8651	7027	4299	2547	6589
6605	333	2547	2287	794
4183	7952	59	8783	2170
3967	4270	9917	1074	7188
3462	6072	5277	7009	4559
4271	4594	9124	3399	8275
9064	9904	7843	7923	6947
374	9717	4937	2165	8552
1825	3981	7454	8898	6295
7687	9468	7619	501	4432
2081	2591	6817	7584	4148
6629	2442	4992	7967	2878
5561	7457	4696	1057	4076
4942	2965	3310	3175	9255
6954	8425	7968	1980	162

THE PRINTOUT IS (Continued)

3154	7462	6383	1141	9395
6103	2058	7419	5988	9158
1053	3889	3862	8165	4231
1896	3298	2717	6621	5273
2047	4821	496	9589	3065
2088	4939	841	594	5998
640	9856	3367	1498	8689
8643	3660	4171	2082	4950
965	1237	8734	1270	9011
2636	4713	4554	4903	8432
6460	2877	9115	8798	748
5305	5097	2833	1119	1219
7237	2449	9563	5333	5933
7595	2172	4680	8529	9050
7540	3786	4855	5055	6634
4306	6129	8012	2913	5364
5966	7519	1418	836	2251
5978	5610	9851	8616	3037
678	6731	4280	5103	2096
6644	998	6190	8152	3207
5866	6337	5220	4287	8742
3865	4509	2267	3018	7703
9055	5000	8508	6044	9688
3731	5195	7583	8743	4211
6580	1578	245	7269	1403
2995	5340	5087	2460	8973

THE PRINTOUT IS (Continued)

1698	9428	1289	2876	5659
8066	7460	2168	5864	5669
1231	6366	7113	5387	8301
1320	3213	7393	5436	6081
7560	623	5699	8582	202
3976	2032	6406	144	3211
7964	8884	1626	9799	4160
6765	3144	7983	9594	5717
7956	6279	6071	9909	4813
9698	4866	1913	7687	8900
4217	5196	3223	2573	6430
5426	4680	9245	3346	6871
1109	4814	8907	112	506
2026	7597	7347	5713	8149
7476	1513	1790	7117	6590
5491	3629	2356	1474	7637
2553	6584	6526	9896	644
4797	2985	4737	1559	6717
6272	7172	6582	4946	436
8097	4656	5062	8463	5220
5152	3927	7192	7809	2121
2448	5592	1519	8785	9036
5147	9556	1004	24	1103
6403	8485	3281	3320	392
2470	1287	5488	1342	8665
9906	1447	9528	4145	9113

THE PRINTOUT IS (Continued)

7375	2229	6998	1927	8575
4106	7457	7791	9629	7653
9257	6662	6657	9984	9984
50	440	2187	9158	5262
9146	7519	2794	9095	9421
4666	3207	7241	4586	2345
2790	5635	8697	1469	539
11	5209	1156	53	9913
9003	4800	7768	3407	525
2486	187	8743	777	5970
8826	9226	5922	2493	1662
7536	250	3676	9806	5752
6251	5736	8160	7331	545
7287	8812	7289	4428	961
5914	6832	7768	5119	794
8695	5023	1877	6055	9433
2103	7721	7400	4910	2855
2942	1955	5250	3902	6155
1814	5486	6587	142	1574
8158	4784	5277	8603	4124
7316	6773	4796	7816	3727
2017	8559	3201	2171	4221
5781	6699	8158	8662	8543
3299	2906	7743	304	2132
54	1137	6330	7743	9490
7253	8099	3321	7029	2286

THE PRINTOUT IS (Continued)

450	2127	8707	3095	206
3381	8431	153	5037	8847
7742	6832	1310	6371	6434
1263	9666	6630	2783	7023
7089	9323	2136	8904	4202
5072	2609	6	6555	9274
6646	6409	8641	4159	7185
5677	9399	5296	7184	5435
7954	8807	1257	8275	8335
5531	8171	9245	1933	8390
2946	2159	6441	9216	7323
991	31	1270	7338	2592
9509	3722	6749	6993	1211
4331	5084	1523	3381	6578
9038	5021	8783	7506	5987
8364	6298	2507	8357	7579
254	3315	7602	5777	6242
5454	6545	179	2167	1388
8825	451	3280	5621	4204
4632	9949	8005	8488	8883
6908	1495	6796	7320	2750
618	8955	8165	8394	6880
5735	2484	3292	7391	4712
1756	8122	2930	4479	503
2709	1724	5965	271	7937
5176	9627	1172	391	1791

THE PRINTOUT IS (Continued)

7231	7261	8486	5564	7012
1990	8829	5066	930	9990
1565	9480	2793	1434	3460
7854	5984	5220	7462	7785
9551	7245	7506	9827	1406
9993	7296	3842	7382	9710
1824	3552	4897	7407	370
5553	9987	9938	9745	9023
6436	7405	6506	2388	5773
3146	6918	3191	6878	2549
3392	7412	3942	6939	6158
4495	1544	8805	8928	4323
5584	4590	7286	2399	8820
1324	8567	9480	9774	3324
1971	1914	3743	5224	7659
8932	4664	7594	3580	3137
6601	1368	8794	455	3577
7368	2016	5778	6526	7147
4150	576	6099	1410	3563
8693	84	2264	2832	6612
4177	5554	5734	4413	4872
9512	3217	3694	3207	5996
7108	8681	8114	554	299
6805	8135	7565	2178	4974
247	6709	8031	7804	4542
7013	1194	4045	3522	4729

THE PRINTOUT IS (Continued)

6672	7466	4747	1289	5007
8444	5597	7583	5125	2503
8892	4913	2057	8125	8287
7605	1043	7814	7493	4633
9389	2464	9496	4464	1316
7720	4471	7341	3810	6788
6435	7515	7180	5437	8001
9075	2439	2959	5799	8157
6752	7093	1787	6889	5248
9480	9647	2563	8552	8245
2499	2260	6424	8205	1411
4619	5011	8491	5847	8662
9352	8150	4733	5044	7664
4511	1833	5891	1754	7502
9227	7838	3987	3376	4372
5848	5735	1781	9064	8356
8560	6147	9843	3736	3823
9314	1478	5041	6944	6290
5242	4844	1886	7712	9300
6388	4626	9951	7321	4364
2486	2264	1210	6882	9111
1710	4691	2759	4330	1151
7933	7235	2012	6956	3624
9139	2210	1011	6175	7947
2107	1116	7735	6364	8564
4106	7560	8401	2364	8579

THE PRINTOUT IS (Continued)

3940	1909	5986	8735	8539
2613	8827	9443	7208	8265
4713	3893	5029	4992	4687
3191	6962	3050	5642	6402
7634	8188	8811	9104	5328
2199	2965	8000	1308	5848
3312	7239	3619	6564	6814
1800	9477	8645	5962	7962
4115	3031	1146	9595	7250
7146	7627	1444	7126	2561
1230	4335	4936	9150	9534
4854	3314	6195	7343	8306
3742	7701	2521	5815	2204
5459	4812	9735	5101	2993
2046	5339	3617	3654	9368
3315	5580	3639	1612	6917
6996	9718	5341	4585	9437
5356	7203	5010	5231	6287
7280	7884	1781	9729	2342
6494	7879	8828	2057	2889
8819	6907	2072	2922	5179
4773	2023	9179	6864	8573
9657	7810	9765	8299	1902
6723	3217	8797	3821	3754
8135	5018	6894	6200	5156
5129	4370	1026	5615	4455

THE PRINTOUT IS (Continued)

6200	7097	6782	6821	9883
7908	8498	9815	2404	6091
4908	4627	3583	9858	6897
2657	3871	9311	1024	2338
4815	7839	3702	1658	6627
4833	9356	2638	1622	5985
1314	4013	2257	7416	4186
8368	2532	9878	6479	9970
1503	9287	2192	9563	7651
9833	2358	2858	5919	9793
5482	4753	9177	2287	1123
6154	6814	5494	1638	7532
1774	2854	1162	1282	7228
1831	5929	9092	1192	5319
1183	9225	4701	5178	8752
5912	6701	6992	1641	6918
6735	8144	8247	6182	2871
1587	3679	7788	3611	1575
6948	7511	2532	7590	2751
8196	4415	2728	6626	5208
1611	2786	2215	8220	9380
2301	9379	5566	8981	3794
1931	7435	7231	6467	3724
4137	1305	1849	5694	7525
3904	5693	9019	2875	6080
8910	8002	7825	4927	9135

THE PRINTOUT IS (Continued)

9121	9835	6922	3012	5771
7514	3147	1251	9185	3847
7844	3362	9574	7188	6959
7058	9722	4806	1330	4729
6400	5841	7438	2062	5426
3996	5142	4884	3029	4213
8016	8886	1770	7918	1728
9109	9100	2614	3780	9157
3088	3869	9456	6770	7808
5922	5252	8216	2024	8202
2152	3944	4300	3097	5877
7389	1437	2117	9770	9560
9429	8326	5175	6112	5579
2582	5281	8449	3163	2936
9152	8486	8544	4886	2419
1450	3862	5975	4751	4728
5606	1085	6052	6545	4802
9908	6227	8188	3086	4824
1166	3578	3618	2972	5269
4866	1776	6855	5147	9183
8774	9992	5997	7092	8576
7623	8556	2722	9329	1470
4855	5901	1712	7160	7546
7092	5042	6422	3151	1107
8282	9731	3845	5489	8328
8450	5590	7484	4593	9857

THE PRINTOUT IS (Continued)

7342	5332	5918	7514	1822
3300	3399	3578	5205	9021
7283	2506	9483	4340	5112
4406	2884	3496	5021	8661
6773	2687	5168	6822	4416
5095	9084	7095	1020	8802
3627	2541	2606	2762	3120
3857	5064	5670	8439	9605
1677	3619	6619	7139	3259
5302	2484	7179	9696	1715
3024	2701	8990	9632	6875
4561	5494	1911	2017	4906
1280	3524	9615	5975	9316
2117	8858	4091	4820	2102
9227	6444	5615	5691	3612
7143	1039	1948	2333	6460
7765	8449	8786	5470	3747
3248	5759	5320	2641	5067
6627	4160	5317	4457	8884
3193	9198	6447	5896	7347
1020	9992	4705	1283	5348
5089	5700	8399	9090	8946
1865	7279	7571	9915	1345
8835	5921	7367	9163	6771
8156	7989	4530	5278	7881
9201	4277	2851	8609	5990

THE PRINTOUT IS (Continued)

8458	6835	4880	7767	2680
6175	2925	1974	5521	5356
2446	6472	6812	2623	4429
2962	7907	3553	4236	3435
2481	3974	1509	3285	6128
7205	8071	3582	8850	5527
5390	2590	7028	8860	9903
9680	8948	6568	8872	4119
4869	2139	9009	4800	7717
3098	9137	6937	9385	3880
8813	7952	8392	8788	7192
4062	9638	1271	3818	5026
5787	9489	4849	3690	8494
7750	3009	2767	9517	2194
7512	5324	4330	8063	9411
3897	8678	6992	3848	6334
6547	2275	4726	7873	4704
7364	1853	4836	2336	1919
7100	5325	8046	9699	5021
2832	1807	5347	5818	6781
8324	8917	8584	1247	8707
1142	8487	7491	9130	7359
1985	5672	6167	5957	7784
4608	7592	4078	6141	5590
2248	3175	8820	4341	6659
5384	4329	7518	6144	9201

THE PRINTOUT IS (Continued)

9907	6630	4012	8545	5155
4026	7759	2071	9564	8743
6380	9589	4360	5168	1769
4098	8663	5094	2597	9730
5006	2468	9751	6295	3407
1359	5119	8481	4814	2548
1963	8841	5379	2706	7822
2576	5056	7153	7407	3734
1805	7218	7062	7411	8732
4246	6888	3111	6673	2038
2173	4693	8601	9376	8829
8594	2097	5235	2534	8092
5744	1631	8085	3833	6858
9114	2958	5723	7710	4749
9108	1902	9434	9488	2020
6727	2176	2514	5496	2651
2722	2475	9804	5700	5964
4480	3204	8903	4581	7359
2921	1292	1460	7129	9639
3668	5253	8505	3753	5964
2011	8382	2197	7738	6653
1765	8117	2815	3832	7656
1449	9788	5684	6010	4904
5334	7864	9176	4281	3099
2467	4266	3389	1941	1144
9392	6058	1819	6389	1959

THE PRINTOUT IS (Continued)

4252	7881	9013	3147	7763
8253	9644	3591	4743	6141
4153	9651	6303	3062	1647
2320	9095	3689	8478	8347
3775	7525	1173	9318	5346
8210	1145	2978	7562	8563
3324	2868	7294	7951	2059
6194	4710	7563	2992	9879
2342	5143	9779	2383	6286
6268	1029	9761	9304	7973
4100	2836	5170	9971	3296
2964	2858	7064	8202	5637
9999	9256	5546	9968	9892
9633	8772	5929	6626	6395
8729	4818	8729	9233	6836
7911	5941	4449	3218	9270
6654	6493	9073	6000	4341
2041	3172	5440	6650	5793
6286	5581	6908	1217	5133

.7734272E 10

Therefore, the solution is:

$x_1 = 8575$, $x_2 = 3245$, $x_3 = 2296$, $x_4 = 4567, \ldots, x_{10} = 5447, \ldots,$
$x_{200} = 2221$, $x_{201} = 4813$, $x_{202} = 8883$, $x_{203} = 9981, \ldots, x_{400} = 748,$
$x_{401} = 5305, \ldots, x_{2000} = 5133$, and maximum $P = 7734272000$ per month

Therefore, the company should produce 8575 units of Product 1, 3245 units of Product 2, 2296 units of Product 3, 4567 units of Product 4, ... , 5447 units of Product 10, ... , 2221 units of Product 200, 4813 units of Product 201, 8883 units of

Product 202, 9981 units of Product 203, ... , 748 units of Product 400, 5305 units of Product 401, ... , and 5133 units of Product 2000 each month to realize a monthly profit of $77,342,720.00

This program looks at a random sample of 5000 combinations of production for the 2000 products. Therefore, the probability of at least one of the 5000 P values being in the upper .001 region of the distribution of all feasible solutions is one minus the probability that none of the 5000 combinations lands in the upper .001 region. Therefore, P (at least one P value in upper .001 region) = $1 - .999^{5000}$ = .99328. Therefore, the odds are better than 100 to 1 that the maximum P value ($77,342,720) is in the upper .001 region and hence is near the true optimum.*

Just recently the author has been introduced to interactive computing with on-line computer terminals. With that type of system (or one's own minicomputer), it is recommended that a larger problem, like the above (or any problem in Part Two), be run dozens of times. On the interactive terminals, this can be done by just pushing a few buttons each time once the initial run is made. This would produce dozens of independent solutions. The programmer could then take the best of these. This would give the programmer a feeling of security in regard to the optimum obtained, and justifiably so.

Also, this approach will begin to reinforce and reveal directly to the user the truly amazing fact (which justifies the Monte Carlo integer programming approach) that there are thousands of nearly optimum good solutions and not just one perfect one with all the rest being no good.

COMMENTS ON THE PROGRAM

Again, the same structure as in previous problems is used to write this program. But, because we have so many variables and as a review, let's go over this program line by line.

Lines 1 and 2 declare two sets of 2000-integer variables (integer variables only use whole numbers, no decimals), $IX(1)$, $IX(2)$, ... , $IX(2000)$ and $X(1)$, $X(2)$, ... , $X(2000)$ for use in the program. The x array is used in the search and computation part of the program. The IX array is used in the storage area to eventually store and print the optimum solution.

Line 3 declares PMAX (the variable that stores the optimum P value) to be a very small number so that the first real P value will be greater than this PMAX value. This way the search for the optimum gets started in the right direction. Line 4 calls the subprogram which generates our random number sequence. Lines 5 through 20 read in the various solution possibilities and check them to see if they satisfy the constraints. Specifically, line 5 says that 5000 different combinations of the 2000 product amounts will be checked for the optimum combination. Lines 7 through 10

---

*The program has looked at 50,000 additional samples and found the optimum to still be 77,342,720.00. Therefore, the probability that this answer is in the upper .0001 region of the distribution of the answers is $1 - .9999^{55,000}$ = .9959143.

set the first 1000 variables equal to various random whole numbers between 0 and 9,999 as prescribed in the problem. Line 8 reads in a seven-digit random number between 0 and .9999999. In line 9, Y*10000. shifts the decimal over four places. Setting Y*10000. equal to X(J) truncates the remaining decimals giving X(J) a random whole number between 0 and 9999.

Lines 11 through 16 make random whole number assignments between 1000 and 9999 to variables 1001 through 2000 (as prescribed in the problem) in the same fashion as lines 7 through 10 did for the first 1000 variables. The only difference is that line 15 checks to see if each random variable value is 1000 or more, as required in the problem. If it isn't, GO TO 90 orders it to read another random number (and to keep reading them in) until a satisfactory one is found.

Lines 17, 18, and 19 add up the variable values and check to see if their total is less than or equal to 18,000,000:

$$\sum_{i=1}^{2000} x \leq 18,000,000$$

If the total is not less than 18,000,000, GO TO 8 (in line 20) orders the computer to go back and read in a new group of 2000 values for the variables. This way 5000 combinations which meet the constraints are checked.

Lines 21 through 23 calculate P, and line 24 checks the current P value to see if it is larger than the current stored optimum value of PMAX. If the current P value is greater than PMAX, then GO TO 2 is followed and lines 27 through 29 store the new current optimum solution in the 2001 variables provided there.

If P is not greater than PMAX, then line 25 (GO TO 1) sends the computer to the end of the loop (1 CONTINUE) and then back up to line 5 to repeat the process 4,999 more times. Lines 31 and 32 output the optimum combination of product values (in order across the rows, $[x_1, x_2, \ldots, x_{2000}]$).

Lines 33 and 34 print the optimum P value which results from this optimum product mix.

EXERCISES

7.1 Maximize $P = x_1 + 9x_2 + 21.7x_3 + 16.2x_4 + 7x_5 + x_6$ subject to $0 \leq x_1 \leq 158$, $0 \leq x_2 \leq 800$, $0 \leq x_3 \leq 6450$, $0 \leq x_4 \leq 9000$, $0 \leq x_5 \leq 600$, $0 \leq x_6 \leq 700$, $100x_1 + 50x_2 + 5x_3 + 4x_4 + 10x_5 + 12x_6 \leq 60,000$, and $x_1 + x_2 + x_3 + x_4 + x_5 + x_6 \leq 1000$.

7.2 Maximize

$$P = \sum_{i=1}^{20} (28 - i) x_i$$

subject to, $0 \leq x_i \leq 800$, $i = 1,10$, $0 \leq x_i \leq 5000$, $i = 11,18$, $0 \leq x_{19} \leq 120$, $0 \leq x_{20} \leq 650$, and

$$\sum_{i=1}^{20} (20 - i)x_i \leq 300,000$$

7.3 Minimize $C = 10x_1 + 8x_2 + x_3 + 9x_4 + 10x_5$ subject to $0 \leq x_1 \leq 400$, $0 \leq x_2 \leq 4000$, $0 \leq x_3 \leq 952$, $0 \leq x_4 \leq 150$, $0 \leq x_5 \leq 3000$, $x_1 + x_2 + x_3 + x_4 + x_5 \geq 1000$, $x_2 + x_5 \leq 6000$, and $x_1 + x_3 + x_4 \leq 1000$.

7.4 Write down any integer program problem you can think of. The more complicated and theoretically unsolvable the problem is the better for this example. Use the Monte Carlo approach to take a random sample of about one million possible solutions and find the optimum solution of this sample.

Then look at the graphs of the sampling distributions of feasible solutions of the integer programming problems in the text. This will help to convince you that we can get an essentially optimum solution every time.

CHAPTER 8

The Unlimited Future of Monte Carlo Integer Programming

As in previous chapters, this one also opens with three distributions of the feasible solutions of selected integer programming problems. If readers wish additional justification, there are several dozen more distributions in Appendix A. As mentioned before, Appendix B explains the technique used to generate these distributions (and any other small sample statistical distributions, for that matter) in case readers would like to experiment on their own.

This chapter introduces some ideas for making computer programs more efficient on large integer programming problems. It presents a few transportation problems (linear and nonlinear). It also offers a general discussion of what the author feels is the widespread, simple, and virtually unlimited usefulness of the techniques presented in this text. The point is made that if one can write the optimization problem down, it can be optimized using the techniques in this text and a modern-day and/or future-day computer.

These discussions and examples follow the graphs.

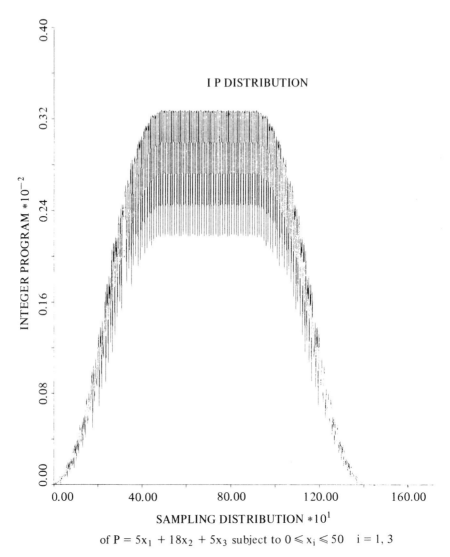

Figure 8.1

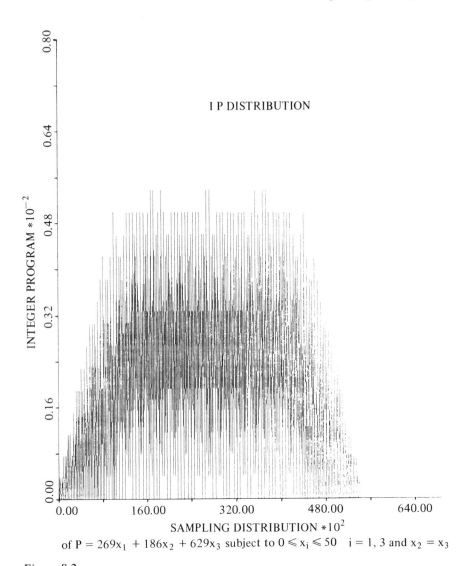

Figure 8.2

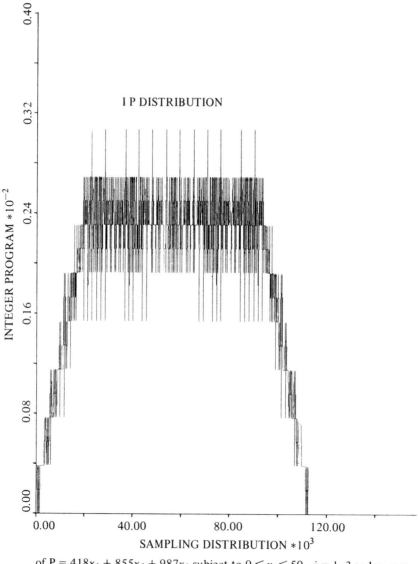

of P = 418x$_1$ + 855x$_2$ + 987x$_3$ subject to 0 ≤ x$_i$ ≤ 50   i = 1, 3 and x$_2$ = x$_3$

Figure 8.3

Transportation Problems

Classic transportation problems are just special cases of regular integer and linear programming problems. However, due to their special nature, they should be treated with care.

EXAMPLE 8.1

Company T has three warehouses stocking Product XA and three customers (A, B, and C) who need supplies of Product XA. A needs 41 units per week of Product XA; B needs 52 units per week of XA; and C needs 47 units per week of XA. This totals to 140 units of XA demanded per week. On a weekly basis, Warehouse 1 has 30 units of XA to deliver, Warehouse 2 has 70 units, and Warehouse 3 has 40 units. This totals to 140 units of XA available per week. The cost of delivering one unit from each warehouse i to each customer j is given in the following table:

	Delivery cost ($)		
To customer	Warehouse 1	Warehouse 2	Warehouse 3
A	1.10	1.18	1.35
B	1.58	1.03	1.16
C	.92	.88	1.30

How should the 140 units per week be delivered in order to minimize the cost of delivery?

The problem can be summarized as follows: Minimize $C = 110A1 + 158B1 + 92C1 + 118A2 + 103B2 + 88C2 + 135A3 + 116B3 + 130C3$ subject to $A1 \geq 0$, $B1 \geq 0$, $C1 \geq 0$, $A2 \geq 0$, $B2 \geq 0$, $C2 \geq 0$, $A3 \geq 0$, $B3 \geq 0$, $C3 \geq 0$, and

$$A1 + B1 + C1 = 30 \quad W1 \qquad A1 + A2 + A3 = 41$$
$$A2 + B2 + C2 = 70 \quad W2 \qquad B1 + B2 + B3 = 52$$
$$A3 + B3 + C3 = 40 \quad W3 \qquad C1 + C2 + C3 = 47$$

There are so many possibilities to check that we will use the Monte Carlo approach on a sample of 1,000,000 points and take the minimum from these.

```
      DIMENSION Y(6)
      INTEGER A1,B1,C1,A2,B2,C2,A3,B3,C3,CMIN
      CMIN=9999999
      CALL RSTART(2626261,5858589)
      DO 1 I=1,100000
101   CONTINUE
      Y(1)=UNI(0)
      A1=Y(1)*100.
      IF(A1.EQ.0.OR.A1.GT.42) GO TO 101
      A1=A1-1
102   Y(2)=UNI(0)
      A2=Y(2)*100.
```

```
      IF(A2.EQ.0.OR.A2.GT.42.OR.A1+A2.GT.42) GO TO 102
      A2=A2-1
      A3=41-A1-A2
201   CONTINUE
      Y(3)=UNI(0)
      B1=Y(3)*100.
      IF(B1.EQ.0.OR.B1.GT.53) GO TO 201
      B1=B1-1
202   CONTINUE
      Y(4)=UNI(0)
      B2=Y(4)*100.
      IF(B2.EQ.0.OR.B2.GT.53.OR.B1+B2.GT.53) GO TO 202
      B2=B2-1
      B3=52-B1-B2
301   CONTINUE
      Y(5)=UNI(0)
      C1=Y(5)*100.
      IF(C1.EQ.0.OR.C1.GT.48) GO TO 301
      C1=C1-1
302   CONTINUE
      Y(6)=UNI(0)
      C2=Y(6)*100.
      IF(C2.EQ.0.OR.C2.GT.48.OR.C1+C2.GT.48) GO TO 302
      C2=C2-1
      C3=47-C1-C2
      IF(A1+B1+C1.NE.30) GO TO 1
      IF(A2+B2+C2.NE.70) GO TO 1
      IF(A3+B3+C3.NE.40) GO TO 1
      C=110*A1+158*B1+92*C1+118*A2+103*B2+88*C2
     X+135*A3+116*B3+130*C3
      IF(C.LT.CMIN) GO TO 2
      GO TO 1
  2   IA1=A1
      IB1=B1
      IC1=C1
      IA2=A2
      IB2=B2
      IC2=C2
      IA3=A3
      IB3=B3
      IC3=C3
      CMIN=C
  1   CONTINUE
      WRITE(6,3)IA1,IB1,IC1,IA2,IB2,IC2,IA3,IB3,IC3,CMIN
  3   FORMAT('0',10I10)
      STOP
      END
```

THE PRINTOUT IS

25   0   5   14   19   37   2   33   5   14823

The best solution is:

A1 = 25	B1 = 0	C1 = 5
A2 = 14	B2 = 19	C2 = 37
A3 = 2	B3 = 33	C3 = 5

minimum C = 14823

Therefore, each week the company should ship

A1 = 25 units from Warehouse 1 to Customer A
A2 = 14 units from Warehouse 2 to Customer A
A3 = 2 units from Warehouse 3 to Customer A
B1 = 0 units from Warehouse 1 to Customer B
B2 = 19 units from Warehouse 2 to Customer B
B3 = 33 units from Warehouse 3 to Customer B
C1 = 5 units from Warehouse 1 to Customer C
C2 = 37 units from Warehouse 2 to Customer C
C3 = 5 units from Warehouse 3 to Customer C
to realize a minimum cost of $148.23 per week

Rather than spending time trying to explain this program (the reader can study it as an exercise), we will point out that there is a more general and efficient way to approach transportation problems. It will be presented while solving the remaining transportation examples in this chapter.

Let's do the above example over again using a more sophisticated approach. First, we make the following variable changes for convenience's sake:

A1 becomes x_1, B1 becomes x_2, C1 becomes x_3,

A2 becomes x_4, B2 becomes x_5, C2 becomes x_6,

A3 becomes x_7, B3 becomes x_8, C3 becomes x_9

The problem can now be written as: Minimize C = $110x_1$ + $158x_2$ + $92x_3$ + $118x_4$ + $103x_5$ + $88x_6$ + $135x_7$ + $116x_8$ + $130x_9$ subject to $x_i \geq 0$, i = 1,9, and $x_1 + x_2 + x_3$ = 30, $x_4 + x_5 + x_6$ = 70, $x_7 + x_8 + x_9$ = 40, $x_1 + x_4 + x_7$ = 41, $x_2 + x_5 + x_8$ = 52, and $x_3 + x_6 + x_9$ = 47.

What we propose to do is solve the system of six equations with nine unknowns for the general solution (all solutions). We will then random sample thousands or millions of feasible solutions from the general solution and take the combination of the nine variables that minimize C. We must remember that we only accept solutions that have nonnegative values for all of the variables. Only nonnegative values make sense in most practical transportation problems. Notice that this approach will work just as well with nonlinear objective functions as with linear ones. This makes possible the solution of nonlinear transportation problems from an easy approach. Writing out the equations we get:

$$x_1 + x_2 + x_3 + 0x_4 + 0x_5 + 0x_6 + 0x_7 + 0x_8 + 0x_9 = 30$$
$$0x_1 + 0x_2 + 0x_3 + x_4 + x_5 + x_6 + 0x_7 + 0x_8 + 0x_9 = 70$$
$$0x_1 + 0x_2 + 0x_3 + 0x_4 + 0x_5 + 0x_6 + x_7 + x_8 + x_9 = 40$$
$$x_1 + 0x_2 + 0x_3 + x_4 + 0x_5 + 0x_6 + x_7 + 0x_8 + 0x_9 = 41$$
$$0x_1 + x_2 + 0x_3 + 0x_4 + x_5 + 0x_6 + 0x_7 + x_8 + 0x_9 = 52$$
$$0x_1 + 0x_2 + x_3 + 0x_4 + 0x_5 + x_6 + 0x_7 + 0x_8 + x_9 = 47$$

This system can be solved by hand calculation or a computer subroutine. The solution is not difficult, but we will just give the result here so as not to divert from our main task.* However, review of a few pages of linear algebra or a package computer program is all that is needed to obtain the solution. Our general solution (all solutions) is:

x_5 arbitrary   (anything)

x_6 arbitrary   (anything)

x_8 arbitrary   (anything)

x_9 arbitrary   (anything)

$$x_1 = x_5 + x_6 + x_8 + x_9 - 69$$
$$x_2 = -x_5 - x_8 + 52$$
$$x_3 = -x_6 - x_9 + 47$$
$$x_4 = -x_5 - x_6 + 70$$
$$x_7 = -x_8 - x_9 + 40$$

Keeping in mind that all of the x's must be nonnegative, we select x_5, x_6, x_8, and x_9 to be greater than or equal to zero. Also, $x_8 + x_9$ must be less than or equal to 40 (from $x_7 + x_8 + x_9 = 40$) and $x_5 + x_6$ must be less than or equal to 70 (from $x_4 + x_5 + x_6 = 70$). The program reflecting these facts is below:

```
INTEGER X(9),CMIN,OKN,IX(9)
OKN=0
CMIN=9999999
CALL RSTART(1616161,1515151)
DO 1 I=1,100000
Y=UNI(0)
X(8)=Y*41
Z=UNI(0)
X(9)=Z*(40-X(8)+1)
Y1=UNI(0)
X(5)=Y1*71
Y2=UNI(0)
X(6)=Y2*(71-X(5))
```

*See Appendix C for a review of solving systems of equations.

```
      X(1)=X(5)+X(6)+X(8)+X(9)
      X(2)=-(X(5)+X(8))
      X(3)=-X(6)-X(9)
      X(4)=-X(5)-X(6)
      X(7)=-X(8)-X(9)
      X(1)=X(1)-69
      X(2)=X(2)+52
      X(3)=X(3)+47
      X(4)=X(4)+70
      X(5)=X(5)+0
      X(6)=X(6)+0
      X(7)=X(7)+40
      X(8)=X(8)+0
      X(9)=X(9)+0
      DO 188 KAA=1,9
      IF(X(KAA).LT.0) GO TO 1
188   CONTINUE
      OKN=OKN+1
      C=110*X(1)+158*X(2)+92*X(3)+118*X(4)+103*X(5)+
     A88*X(6)+135*X(7)+116*X(8)+130*X(9)
      IF(C.LT.CMIN) GO TO 2
      GO TO 1
  2   CONTINUE
      DO 800 KA=1,9
800   IX(KA)=X(KA)
      CMIN=C
  1   CONTINUE
      WRITE(6,3)IX(1),IX(2),IX(3),IX(4),IX(5),IX(6),IX(7),IX(8),IX(9)
  3   FORMAT('0',9I10)
      WRITE(6,4)CMIN
  4   FORMAT('0',I10)
      WRITE(6,5)OKN
  5   FORMAT('0',I10)
      STOP
      END
```

THE PRINTOUT IS

29   0   1   12   12   46   0   40   0   14622

13548

The solution is:

$x_1 = 29$, $x_2 = 0$, $x_3 = 1$, $x_4 = 12$, $x_5 = 12$, $x_6 = 46$, $x_7 = 0$, $x_8 = 40$, $x_9 = 0$, and minimum C equals 14622

Therefore, each week the company should ship:

$x_1 = 29$ units from Warehouse 1 to Customer A

$x_4 = 12$ units from Warehouse 2 to Customer A

$x_7 =$ 0 units from Warehouse 3 to Customer A
$x_2 =$ 0 units from Warehouse 1 to Customer B
$x_5 =$ 12 units from Warehouse 2 to Customer B
$x_8 =$ 40 units from Warehouse 3 to Customer B
$x_3 =$ 1 unit from Warehouse 1 to Customer C
$x_6 =$ 46 units from Warehouse 2 to Customer C
$x_9 =$ 0 units from Warehouse 3 to Customer C
to realize a minimum cost of \$146.22 per week

Line 1 of the program declares the appropriate variables as in previous Monte Carlo integer programming problems. X(9) declares the 9 x variables. IX(9) declares the 9 storage variables (to store the current minimum). CMIN is the variable that stores the current minimum and OKN keeps count of the number of nonnegative feasible solutions. Line 2 initializes OKN to zero. Line 3 initializes CMIN to be a very large number so that the initial comparison with the initial C value will have C being the smaller of the two values and hence cause the first solution to be stored. Line 4 calls the random number subprogram. Line 5 starts the loop and tells the computer to go from line 5 to line 39 100,000 times. Line 6 assigns a seven-digit random number between 0 and .9999999 to Y. In line 7, X(8) = Y*41 changes that number to a number between 0 and 40 inclusive. (The rule is always multiply by one more than your upper bound for the variable.) Line 8 reads in another random number and line 9 assures that X(9) will be between 0 and 40-X(8) as required. Similar results follow for X(5) and X(6) in lines 10 through 13, reflecting the constraint $x_4 + x_5 + x_6 = 70$.

Lines 14 through 27 produce values for the other variables (lines 23, 24, 26, and 27 aren't really necessary, but were put in to organize the solution). Lines 28 through 30 check to make sure that all values x_1 through x_9 are nonnegative. If there is one or more negative variable then the program follows GO TO 1 in line 29 and skips that solution. If the values are all nonnegative, then line 31 adds 1 to the counter variable OKN. Line 32 evaluates the function for the first solution and line 33 checks to see if it is the smallest so far. If it is (it will be the first time), then the computer follows GO TO 2 and goes to the storage area and stores the optimum solution so far in IX(1), IX(2), IX(3), ... , IX(9), CMIN in lines 37 and 38. With line 39 the computer goes back to line 5 and repeats the process 99,999 more times. After running through the loop 100,000 times, it writes the solution with lines 40 through 43. It also writes the number of the 100,000 solutions that were free of any negative values, in this case 13,548. So the probability of the solution being in the upper .001 region of the distribution of nonnegative feasible solutions is $1 - .999^{13547}$ equals $1 - .0000012978 = .9999987022$, a virtual certainty.

Just to be sure that we aren't biasing our result by reading in too many large values for x_8 and x_5, we adjust their bounds from 40 and 70 to 30 and 60 and run the program again. Then, we lower these bounds to 20 and 50 and run the program again. As can be seen, in this case better answers were not produced.

```
      INTEGER X(9),IX(9),CMIN,OKN
      OKN=0
      CMIN=9999999
      CALL RSTART(12222221,1456789)
      DO 1 I=1,100000
      Y=UNI(0)
      X(8)=Y*31
      Z=UNI(0)
      X(9)=Z*(30-X(8)+1)
      Y1=UNI(0)
      X(5)=Y1*61
      Y2=UNI(0)
      X(6)=Y2*(61-X(5))
      X(1)=X(5)+X(6)+X(8)+X(9)
      X(2)=-(X(5)+X(8))
      X(3)=-X(6)-X(9)
      X(4)=-X(5)-X(6)
      X(7)=-X(8)-X(9)
      X(1)=X(1)-69
      X(2)=X(2)+52
      X(3)=X(3)+47
      X(4)=X(4)+70
      X(5)=X(5)+0
      X(6)=X(6)+0
      X(7)=X(7)+40
      X(8)=X(8)+0
      X(9)=X(9)+0
      DO 188 KAA=1,9
      IF(X(KAA).LT.0) GO TO 1
188   CONTINUE
      OKN=OKN+1
      C=110*X(1)+158*X(2)+92*X(3)+118*X(4)+103*X(5)
     A+88*X(6)+135*X(7)+116*X(8)+130*X(9)
      IF(C.LT.CMIN) GO TO 2
      GO TO 1
2     CONTINUE
      DO 800 KA=1,9
800   IX(KA)=X(KA)
      CMIN=C
1     CONTINUE
      WRITE(6,3)IX(1),IX(2),IX(3),IX(4),IX(5),IX(6),IX(7),IX(8),IX(9)
3     FORMAT('0',9I10)
      WRITE(6,4)CMIN
4     FORMAT('0',I10)
      WRITE(6,5)OKN
5     FORMAT('0',I10)
      STOP
      END
```

```
              THE PRINTOUT IS
   21   0   9   10   22   38   10   30   0   14758
                    15837
```

```
      INTEGER X(9),IX(9),CMIN,OKN
      OKN=0
      CMIN=9999999
      CALL RSTART(3434343,5656565)
      DO 1 I=1,100000
      Y=UNI(0)
      X(8)=Y*21
      Z=UNI(0)
      X(9)=Z*(20-X(8)+1)
      Y1=UNI(0)
      X(5)=Y1*51
      Y2=UNI(0)
      X(6)=Y2*(51-X(5))
      X(1)=X(5)+X(6)+X(8)+X(9)
      X(2)=-(X(5)+X(8))
      X(3)=-X(6)-X(9)
      X(4)=-X(5)-X(6)
      X(7)=-X(8)-X(9)
      X(1)=X(1)-69
      X(2)=X(2)+52
      X(3)=X(3)+47
      X(4)=X(4)+70
      X(5)=X(5)+0
      X(6)=X(6)+0
      X(7)=X(7)+40
      X(8)=X(8)+0
      X(9)=X(9)+0
      DO 188 KAA=1,9
      IF(X(KAA).LT.0) GO TO 1
188   CONTINUE
      OKN=OKN+1
      C=110*X(1)+158*X(2)+92*X(3)+118*X(4)+103*X(5)+
     A88*X(6)+135*X(7)+116*X(8)+130*X(9)
      IF(C.LT.CMIN) GO TO 2
      GO TO 1
  2   CONTINUE
      DO 800 KA=1,9
800   IX(KA)=X(KA)
      CMIN=C
  1   CONTINUE
      WRITE(6,3)IX(1),IX(2),IX(3),IX(4),IX(5),IX(6),IX(7),IX(8),IX(9)
  3   FORMAT('0',9I10)
      WRITE(6,4)CMIN
  4   FORMAT('0',I10)
      WRITE(6,5)OKN
  5   FORMAT('0',I10)
      STOP
      END
```

                        THE PRINTOUT IS
      1   0   29   20   32   18   20   20   0   15038
                              1295

If we wanted to look for a better answer still, we could go back to the 40 and 70 bounds (the best answer-producing bounds) and run the program five or ten more times which would probably produce the true optimum or point out where it is if we don't already have it.

In the current theory and practice of transportation problems, it is required that the objective function (the one to be maximized or minimized) be linear (no squared terms, powers, or special functions—just multiples of variables added together). This can lead to a very impractical model, since many transportation costs are nonlinear (the unit costs increase or decrease as the quantity transported changes).*

However, our technique works just as easily on nonlinear transportation problems. So let's do the previous example again, only this time x_9 is raised to the 1.5 power and the additional conditions of $x_8 + x_9 = 30$ and $x_5 + x_6 = 60$ hold. The problem is to minimize $C = 110x_1 + 158x_2 + 92x_3 + 118x_4 + 103x_5 + 88x_6 + 135x_7 + 116x_8 + 130x_9^{1.5}$ subject to $x_i \geq 0$, $i = 1,9$, $x_1 + x_2 + x_3 = 30$, $x_4 + x_5 + x_6 = 70$, $x_7 + x_8 + x_9 = 40$, $x_1 + x_4 + x_7 = 41$, $x_2 + x_5 + x_8 = 52$, $x_3 + x_6 + x_9 = 47$, $x_5 + x_6 = 60$, and $x_8 + x_9 = 30$. Everything is as before except for X(9)**1.5 at the end of the objective function, and $x_5 + x_6 = 60$ and $x_8 + x_9 = 30$ are taken care of when the random numbers are read in for x_5, x_6, x_8, and x_9. The program follows:

```
INTEGER X(9),IX(9),CMIN,OKN
OKN=0
CMIN=9999999
CALL RSTART(8989899,3535353)
DO 1 I=1,100000C
Y=UNI(0)
X(8)=Y*31
Z=UNI(0)
X(9)=Z*(30-X(8)+1)
Y1=UNI(0)
X(5)=Y1*61
Y2=UNI(0)
X(6)=Y2*(61-X(5))
X(1)=X(5)+X(6)+X(8)+X(9)
X(2)=-(X(5)+X(8))
X(3)=-X(6)-X(9)
X(4)=-X(5)-X(6)
X(7)=-X(8)-X(9)
X(1)=X(1)-69
X(2)=X(2)+52
X(3)=X(3)+47
X(4)=X(4)+70
X(5)=X(5)+0
X(6)=X(6)+0
X(7)=X(7)+40
```

*Also fixed charges, start-up costs, supply and demand considerations, and price discounts for buying in quantity can make the objective function nonlinear, to mention only a few cases.

```
       X(8)=X(8)+0
       X(9)=X(9)+0
       DO 188 KAA=1,9
       IF(X(KAA).LT.0) GO TO 1
188    CONTINUE
       OKN=OKN+1
       C=110*X(1)+158*X(2)+92*X(3)+118*X(4)+103*X(5)+
       A88*X(6)+135*X(7)+116*X(8)+130*X(9)**1.5
       IF(C.LT.CMIN) GO TO 2
       GO TO 1
  2    CONTINUE
       DO 800 KA=1,9
800    IX(KA)=X(KA)
       CMIN=C
  1    CONTINUE
       WRITE(6,3)IX(1),IX(2),IX(3),IX(4),IX(5),IX(6),IX(7),IX(8),IX(9)
  3    FORMAT('0',9I10)
       WRITE(6,4)CMIN
  4    FORMAT('0',I10)
       WRITE(6,5)OKN
  5    FORMAT('0',I10)
       STOP
       END
```

THE PRINTOUT IS

     21   0   9   10   22   38   10   30   0   14758

                       15837

The solution is:

$x_1 = 21, x_2 = 0, x_3 = 9, x_4 = 10, x_5 = 22, x_6 = 38, x_7 = 10, x_8 = 30, x_9$
$= 0$, and minimum $C = 14758$

Therefore, each week the company should ship:

$x_1 = 21$ units from Warehouse 1 to Customer A
$x_4 = 10$ units from Warehouse 2 to Customer A
$x_7 = 10$ units from Warehouse 3 to Customer A
$x_2 = 0$ units from Warehouse 1 to Customer B
$x_5 = 22$ units from Warehouse 2 to Customer B
$x_8 = 30$ units from Warehouse 3 to Customer B
$x_3 = 9$ units from Warehouse 1 to Customer C
$x_6 = 38$ units from Warehouse 2 to Customer C
$x_9 = 0$ units from Warehouse 3 to Customer C
to realize a minimum cost of $147.58

EXAMPLE 8.2

Company TA has five warehouses stocking Product XB and five customers (A, B, C, D, E) that need supplies of Product XB. A needs 82 units per week of Product XB while B, C, D, and E need 60, 48, 52, and 58 units, respectively, per week. This totals to 300 units of XB demanded per week. Warehouse 1 has 50 units of XB available per week and warehouses 2, 3, 4, and 5 have 55, 60, 65, and 70 units per week available, respectively. This totals to 300 units available per week. The cost of delivering one unit from each warehouse to each customer is given in the following table:

To customer	Ware-house 1	Ware-house 2	Ware-house 3	Ware-house 4	Ware-house 5
			Delivery cost per unit (\$)		
A	1.19	1.92	2.04	1.58	3.18
B	2.21	2.15	1.58	4.03	3.60
C	2.14 units$^{1.5}$	1.66	2.06	1.42	2.09
D	3.10	2.62	1.09	1.71	3.15
E	2.51	2.11	2.01	2.48	3.16 units$^{1.5}$

How should the 300 units per week be delivered in order to minimize the cost of delivery?

The problem can be summarized as follows:

$$\text{Minimize } C = 119A1 + 221B1 + 214C1^{1.5} + 310D1 + 251E1$$
$$+ 192A2 + 215B2 + 166C2 + 262D2 + 211E2$$
$$+ 204A3 + 158B3 + 206C3 + 109D3 + 201E3$$
$$+ 158A4 + 403B4 + 142C4 + 171D4 + 248E4$$
$$+ 318A5 + 360B5 + 209C5 + 315D5 + 316E5^{1.5}$$

subject to all variables greater than or equal to zero and,

$$A1 + B1 + C1 + D1 + E1 = 50$$
$$A2 + B2 + C2 + D2 + E2 = 55$$
$$A3 + B3 + C3 + D3 + E3 = 60$$
$$A4 + B4 + C4 + D4 + E4 = 65$$
$$A5 + B5 + C5 + D5 + E5 = 70$$
$$A1 + A2 + A3 + A4 + A5 = 82$$
$$B1 + B2 + B3 + B4 + B5 = 60$$
$$C1 + C2 + C3 + C4 + C5 = 48$$
$$D1 + D2 + D3 + D4 + D5 = 52$$
$$E1 + E2 + E3 + E4 + E5 = 58$$

We make the following variable changes for convenience's sake in solving the system of equations (10 equations and 25 unknowns) and writing the Monte Carlo program to minimize the transportation cost:

$A1$ becomes x_1, $B1$ becomes x_2, $C1$ becomes x_3, $D1$ becomes x_4,

$E1$ becomes x_5, $A2$ becomes x_6, $B2$ becomes x_7, $C2$ becomes x_8,

$D2$ becomes x_9, $E2$ becomes x_{10}, $A3$ becomes x_{11}, $B3$ becomes x_{12},

$C3$ becomes x_{13}, $D3$ becomes x_{14}, $E3$ becomes x_{15}, $A4$ becomes x_{16},

$B4$ becomes x_{17}, $C4$ becomes x_{18}, $D4$ becomes x_{19}, $E4$ becomes x_{20},

$A5$ becomes x_{21}, $B5$ becomes x_{22}, $C5$ becomes x_{23}, $D5$ becomes x_{24},

and $E5$ becomes x_{25}

Now, the problem can be written as follows:

$$\begin{aligned}
\text{Minimize } C = {}& 119x_1 + 221x_2 + 214x_3^{1.5} + 310x_4 + 251x_5 + 192x_6 + 215x_7 \\
& + 166x_8 + 262x_9 + 211x_{10} + 204x_{11} + 158x_{12} + 206x_{13} \\
& + 109x_{14} + 201x_{15} + 158x_{16} + 403x_{17} + 142x_{18} + 171x_{19} \\
& + 248x_{20} + 318x_{21} + 360x_{22} + 209x_{23} + 315x_{24} + 316x_{25}^{1.5}
\end{aligned}$$

subject to $x_i \geq 0$, $i = 1,25$, and

$$x_1 + x_2 + x_3 + x_4 + x_5 = 50$$
$$x_6 + x_7 + x_8 + x_9 + x_{10} = 55$$
$$x_{11} + x_{12} + x_{13} + x_{14} + x_{15} = 60$$
$$x_{16} + x_{17} + x_{18} + x_{19} + x_{20} = 65$$
$$x_{21} + x_{22} + x_{23} + x_{24} + x_{25} = 70$$
$$x_1 + x_6 + x_{11} + x_{16} + x_{21} = 82$$
$$x_2 + x_7 + x_{12} + x_{17} + x_{22} = 60$$
$$x_3 + x_8 + x_{13} + x_{18} + x_{23} = 48$$
$$x_4 + x_9 + x_{14} + x_{19} + x_{24} = 52$$
$$x_5 + x_{10} + x_{15} + x_{20} + x_{25} = 58$$

We will solve the system of 10 equations and 25 unknowns and then random sample from the feasible solutions that satisfy the system of equations (and all x's are nonnegative). We will take the combination that minimizes C. Notice again that the nonlinear objective function presents no problem.

The solution of the system of equations can be solved by hand calculation or a computer subroutine. The author did this system and the other systems of equations in this chapter by hand with pencil and paper. It was not difficult, but the subroutine approach is recommended for larger systems of equations. Our general solution (all solutions) is:

x_7 arbitrary   (anything)

x_8 arbitrary   (anything)

x_9 arbitrary   (anything)

x_{10} arbitrary   (anything)

x_{12} arbitrary   (anything)

x_{13} arbitrary   (anything)

x_{14} arbitrary   (anything)

x_{15} arbitrary   (anything)

x_{17} arbitrary   (anything)

x_{18} arbitrary   (anything)

x_{19} arbitrary   (anything)

x_{20} arbitrary   (anything)

x_{22} arbitrary   (anything)

x_{23} arbitrary   (anything)

x_{24} arbitrary   (anything)

x_{25} arbitrary   (anything)

$$x_1 = x_7 + x_8 + x_9 + x_{10} + x_{12} + x_{13} + x_{14} + x_{15} + x_{17}$$
$$+ x_{18} + x_{19} + x_{20} + x_{22} + x_{23} + x_{24} + x_{25} - 168$$

$$x_2 = -x_7 - x_{12} - x_{17} - x_{22} + 60$$

$$x_3 = -x_8 - x_{13} - x_{18} - x_{23} + 48$$

$$x_4 = -x_9 - x_{14} - x_{19} - x_{24} + 52$$

$$x_5 = -x_{10} - x_{15} - x_{20} - x_{25} + 58$$

$$x_6 = -x_7 - x_8 - x_9 - x_{10} + 55$$

$$x_{11} = -x_{12} - x_{13} - x_{14} - x_{15} + 60$$

$$x_{16} = -x_{17} - x_{18} - x_{19} - x_{20} + 65$$

$$x_{21} = -x_{22} - x_{23} - x_{24} - x_{25} + 70$$

Keeping in mind that all of the x's must be nonnegative, we select x_7, x_8, x_9, x_{10}, x_{12}, x_{13}, x_{14}, x_{15}, x_{17}, x_{18}, x_{19}, x_{20}, x_{22}, x_{23}, x_{24}, and x_{25} to be greater than or equal to zero.

Also, $x_7 + x_8 + x_9 + x_{10}$ must be less than or equal to 55 (from $x_6 + x_7 + x_8 + x_9 + x_{10} = 55$). This is reflected in lines 6 through 13 in the program given below. Also, $x_{12} + x_{13} + x_{14} + x_{15}$ must be less than or equal to 60 (from $x_{11} + x_{12} + x_{13} + x_{14} + $

$x_{15} = 60$), as shown in lines 14 through 21. $X_{17} + x_{18} + x_{19} + x_{20}$ must be less than or equal to 65 (from $x_{16} + x_{17} + x_{18} + x_{19} + x_{20} = 65$), displayed in lines 22 through 29 in the program. $X_{22} + x_{23} + x_{24} + x_{25}$ must be less than or equal to 70 (from $x_{21} + x_{22} + x_{23} + x_{24} + x_{25} = 70$), reflected in lines 30 through 36 in the program.

The program is identical in structure to the programs used to solve the 3×3 transportation problems earlier in this chapter.

```
INTEGER X(25),IX(25),CMIN,OKN
OKN=0
CMIN=9999999
CALL RSTART(1818181,1919191)
DO 1 I=1,100000
R1=UNI(0)
X(7)=R1*56
R2=UNI(0)
X(8)=R2*(56-X(7))
R3=UNI(0)
X(9)=R3*(56-X(7)-X(8))
R4=UNI(0)
X(10)=R4*(56-X(7)-X(8)-X(9))
S1=UNI(0)
X(12)=S1*61
S2=UNI(0)
X(13)=S2*(61-X(12))
S3=UNI(0)
X(14)=S3*(61-X(12)-X(13))
S4=UNI(0)
X(15)=S4*(61-X(12)-X(13)-X(14))
T1=UNI(0)
X(17)=T1*66
T2=UNI(0)
X(18)=T2*(66-X(17))
T3=UNI(0)
X(19)=T3*(66-X(17)-X(18))
T4=UNI(0)
X(20)=T4*(66-X(17)-X(18))
U1=UNI(0)
X(22)=U1*71
U2=UNI(0)
X(23)=U2*(71-X(22))
U3=UNI(0)
X(24)=U3*(71-X(22)-X(23))
U4=UNI(0)
X(25)=U4*(71-X(22)-X(23)-X(24))
X(1)=X(7)+X(8)+X(9)+X(10)+X(12)+X(13)+X(14)+X(15)+
AX(17)+X(18)+X(19)+X(20)+X(22)+X(23)+X(24)+X(25)
X(2)=-(X(7)+X(12)+X(17)+X(22))
X(3)=-(X(8)+X(13)+X(18)+X(23))
X(4)=-(X(9)+X(14)+X(19)+X(24))
X(5)=-(X(10)+X(15)+X(20)+X(25))
X(6)=-(X(7)+X(8)+X(9)+X(10))
```

```
      X(11)=-(X(12)+X(13)+X(14)+X(15))
      X(16)=-(X(17)+X(18)+X(19)+X(20))
      X(21)=-(X(22)+X(23)+X(24)+X(25))
      X(1)=X(1)-168
      X(2)=X(2)+60
      X(3)=X(3)+48
      X(4)=X(4)+52
      X(5)=X(5)+58
      X(6)=X(6)+55
      X(11)=X(11)+60
      X(16)=X(16)+65
      X(21)=X(21)+70
      DO 18 K=1,25
      IF(X(K).LT.0) GO TO 1
18    CONTINUE
      OKN=OKN+1
      C=119*X(1)+221*X(2)+214*X(3)**1.5+310*X(4)+251*X(5)
      A+192*X(6)+215*X(7)+166*X(8)+262*X(9)+211*X(10)
      A+204*X(11)+158*X(12)+206*X(13)+109*X(14)+201*X(15)
      A+158*X(16)+403*X(17)+142*X(18)+171*X(19)+248*X(20)
      A+318*X(21)+360*X(22)+209*X(23)+315*X(24)+316*X(25)**1.5
      IF(C.LT.CMIN) GO TO 2
      GO TO 1
2     CONTINUE
      DO 800 KA=1,25
800   IX(KA)=X(KA)
      CMIN=C
1     CONTINUE
      WRITE(6,3)IX(1),IX(2),IX(3),IX(4),IX(5),
      AIX(6),IX(7),IX(8),IX(9),IX(10),
      AIX(11),IX(12),IX(13),IX(14),IX(15),
      AIX(16),IX(17),IX(18),IX(19),IX(20),
      AIX(21),IX(22),IX(23),IX(24),IX(25)
3     FORMAT('0',25I10)
      WRITE(6,4)CMIN
4     FORMAT('0',I10)
      WRITE(6,5)OKN
5     FORMAT('0',I10)
      STOP
      END
```

THE PRINTOUT IS

22	10	5	8	5
11	37	3	3	1
26	2	2	26	4
11	4	2	1	47
12	7	36	14	1

66234

109

The solution is:

$$x_1 = 22, x_2 = 10, x_3 = 5, x_4 = 8, x_5 = 5, x_6 = 11, x_7 = 37, x_8 = 3,$$
$$x_9 = 3, x_{10} = 1, x_{11} = 26, x_{12} = 2, x_{13} = 2, x_{14} = 26, x_{15} = 4,$$
$$x_{16} = 11, x_{17} = 4, x_{18} = 2, x_{19} = 1, x_{20} = 47, x_{21} = 12, x_{22} = 7, x_{23} = 36,$$
$$x_{24} = 14, x_{25} = 1, \text{ and minimum } C = 66234$$

Therefore, the company should ship:

x_1 = 22 units from Warehouse 1 to Customer A

x_2 = 10 units from Warehouse 1 to Customer B

x_3 = 5 units from Warehouse 1 to Customer C

x_4 = 8 units from Warehouse 1 to Customer D

x_5 = 5 units from Warehouse 1 to Customer E

x_6 = 11 units from Warehouse 2 to Customer A

x_7 = 37 units from Warehouse 2 to Customer B

x_8 = 3 units from Warehouse 2 to Customer C

x_9 = 3 units from Warehouse 2 to Customer D

x_{10} = 1 unit from Warehouse 2 to Customer E

x_{11} = 26 units from Warehouse 3 to Customer A

x_{12} = 2 units from Warehouse 3 to Customer B

x_{13} = 2 units from Warehouse 3 to Customer C

x_{14} = 26 units from Warehouse 3 to Customer D

x_{15} = 4 units from Warehouse 3 to Customer E

x_{16} = 11 units from Warehouse 4 to Customer A

x_{17} = 4 units from Warehouse 4 to Customer B

x_{18} = 2 units from Warehouse 4 to Customer C

x_{19} = 1 unit from Warehouse 4 to Customer D

x_{20} = 47 units from Warehouse 4 to Customer E

x_{21} = 12 units from Warehouse 5 to Customer A

x_{22} = 7 units from Warehouse 5 to Customer B

x_{23} = 36 units from Warehouse 5 to Customer C

x_{24} = 14 units from Warehouse 5 to Customer D

x_{25} = 1 unit from Warehouse 5 to Customer E

Just to be sure that we aren't biasing our result by reading in too many large values for x_7, x_{12}, x_{17} and, x_{22}, we lower their bounds some in the next program. The program is identical to the preceding one except for this change. Actually, in a more thorough investigation the variables should be switched around and values read in at all levels.

```
INTEGER X(25),IX(25),CMIN,OKN
OKN=0
CMIN=9999999
CALL RSTART(1818171,5352523)
DO 1 I=1,100000
R1=UNI(0)
X(7)=R1*41
R2=UNI(0)
X(8)=R2*(41-X(7))
R3=UNI(0)
X(9)=R3*(41-X(7)-X(8))
R4=UNI(0)
X(10)=R4*(41-X(7)-X(8)-X(9))
S1=UNI(0)
X(12)=S1*46
S2=UNI(0)
X(13)=S2*(46-X(12))
S3=UNI(0)
X(14)=S3*(46-X(12)-X(13))
S4=UNI(0)
X(15)=S4*(46-X(12)-X(13)-X(14))
T1=UNI(0)
X(17)=T1*46
T2=UNI(0)
X(18)=T2*(46-X(17))
T3=UNI(0)
X(19)=T3*(46-X(17)-X(18))
T4=UNI(0)
X(20)=T4*(46-X(17)-X(18))
U1=UNI(0)
X(22)=U1*51
U2=UNI(0)
X(23)=U2*(51-X(22))
U3=UNI(0)
X(24)=U3*(51-X(22)-X(23))
U4=UNI(0)
X(25)=U4*(51-X(22)-X(23)-X(24))
X(1)=X(7)+X(8)+X(9)+X(10)+X(12)+X(13)+X(14)+X(15)+
AX(17)+X(18)+X(19)+X(20)+X(22)+X(23)+X(24)+X(25)
X(2)=-(X(7)+X(12)+X(17)+X(22))
X(3)=-(X(8)+X(13)+X(18)+X(23))
X(4)=-(X(9)+X(14)+X(19)+X(24))
X(5)=-(X(10)+X(15)+X(20)+X(25))
X(6)=-(X(7)+X(8)+X(9)+X(10))
X(11)=-(X(12)+X(13)+X(14)+X(15))
X(16)=-(X(17)+X(18)+X(19)+X(20))
X(21)=-(X(22)+X(23)+X(24)+X(25))
```

```
      X(1)=X(1)-168
      X(2)=X(2)+60
      X(3)=X(3)+48
      X(4)=X(4)+52
      X(5)=X(5)+58
      X(6)=X(6)+55
      X(11)=X(11)+60
      X(16)=X(16)+65
      X(21)=X(21)+70
      DO 18 K=1,25
      IF(X(K).LT.0) GO TO 1
 18   CONTINUE
      OKN=OKN+1
      C=119*X(1)+221*X(2)+214*X(3)**1.5+310*X(4)+251*X(5)
     A+192*X(6)+215*X(7)+166*X(8)+262*X(9)+211*X(10)
     A+204*X(11)+158*X(12)+206*X(13)+109*X(14)+201*X(15)
     A+158*X(16)+403*X(17)+142*X(18)+171*X(19)+248*X(20)
     A+318*X(21)+360*X(22)+209*X(23)+315*X(24)+316*X(25)**1.5
      IF(C.LT.CMIN) GO TO 2
      GO TO 1
  2   CONTINUE
      DO 800 KA=1,25
800   IX(KA)=X(KA)
      CMIN=C
  1   CONTINUE
      WRITE(6,3)IX(1),IX(2),IX(3),IX(4),IX(5),
     AIX(6),IX(7),IX(8),IX(9),IX(10),
     AIX(11),IX(12),IX(13),IX(14),IX(15),
     AIX(16),IX(17),IX(18),IX(19),IX(20),
     AIX(21),IX(22),IX(23),IX(24),IX(25)
  3   FORMAT('0',25I10)
      WRITE(6,4)CMIN
  4   FORMAT('0',I10)
      WRITE(6,5)OKN
  5   FORMAT('0',I10)
      STOP
      END
```

THE PRINTOUT IS

1	19	0	11	19
16	25	4	0	10
19	9	5	23	4
23	0	18	1	23
23	7	21	17	2

65893

427

The solution is:

$x_1 = 1, x_2 = 19, x_3 = 0, x_4 = 11, x_5 = 19, x_6 = 16, x_7 = 25, x_8 = 4,$
$x_9 = 0, x_{10} = 10, x_{11} = 19, x_{12} = 9, x_{13} = 5, x_{14} = 23, x_{15} = 4,$
$x_{16} = 23, x_{17} = 0, x_{18} = 18, x_{19} = 1, x_{20} = 23, x_{21} = 23, x_{22} = 7, x_{23} = 21,$
$x_{24} = 17, x_{25} = 2,$ and minimum $C = 65893$

This solution is based on more samples, 427, and it has a lower minimum 65,893 than the previous program. Therefore, we will focus our search in this area of the solution. We set up 16 nested DO loops to search nearly all of the combinations around $x_7, x_8, x_9, x_{10}, x_{12}, x_{13}, x_{14}, x_{15}, x_{17}, x_{18}, x_{19}, x_{20}, x_{22}, x_{23}, x_{24},$ and x_{25} for a better optimum.

This program ends up looking at an additional 1,679,471 all nonnegative solutions and selecting

$x_1 = 18, x_2 = 13, x_3 = 0, x_4 = 3, x_5 = 16, x_6 = 11, x_7 = 27, x_8 = 4,$
$x_9 = 2, x_{10} = 11, x_{11} = 14, x_{12} = 11, x_{13} = 5, x_{14} = 25, x_{15} = 5, x_{16} = 20,$
$x_{17} = 0, x_{18} = 18, x_{19} = 3, x_{20} = 24, x_{21} = 19, x_{22} = 9, x_{23} = 21, x_{24} = 19,$
and $x_{25} = 2$

producing a minimum of 63471.

```
INTEGER X(25),IX(25),CMIN,OKN
OKN=0
CMIN=9999999
DO 1 I=25,27
X(7)=I
DO 1 J=3,4
X(8)=J
DO 1 L=1,3
X(9)=L-1
DO 1 M=10,11
X(10)=M
DO 1 MA=9,11
X(12)=MA
DO 1 II=4,5
X(13)=II
DO 1 JJ=23,25
X(14)=JJ
DO 1 LL=4,5
X(15)=LL
DO 1 MM=1,3
X(17)=MM-1
DO 1 NN=17,18
X(18)=NN
DO 1 III=1,3
X(19)=III
DO 1 JJJ=23,24
```

```
      X(20)=JJJ
      DO 1 LLL=7,9
      X(22)=LLL
      DO 1 MMM=20,21
      X(23)=MMM
      DO 1 NNN=17,19
      X(24)=NNN
      DO 1 IA=2,3
      X(25)=IA
      X(1)=X(7)+X(8)+X(9)+X(10)+X(12)+X(13)+X(14)+X(15)+
     AX(17)+X(18)+X(19)+X(20)+X(22)+X(23)+X(24)+X(25)
      X(2)=-(X(7)+X(12)+X(17)+X(22))
      X(3)=-(X(8)+X(13)+X(18)+X(23))
      X(4)=-(X(9)+X(14)+X(19)+X(24))
      X(5)=-(X(10)+X(15)+X(20)+X(25))
      X(6)=-(X(7)+X(8)+X(9)+X(10))
      X(11)=-(X(12)+X(13)+X(14)+X(15))
      X(16)=-(X(17)+X(18)+X(19)+X(20))
      X(21)=-(X(22)+X(23)+X(24)+X(25))
      X(1)=X(1)-168
      X(2)=X(2)+60
      X(3)=X(3)+48
      X(4)=X(4)+52
      X(5)=X(5)+58
      X(6)=X(6)+55
      X(11)=X(11)+60
      X(16)=X(16)+65
      X(21)=X(21)+70
      DO 18 K=1,25
      IF(X(K).LT.0) GO TO 1
   18 CONTINUE
      OKN=OKN+1
      C=119*X(1)+221*X(2)+214*X(3)**1.5+310*X(4)+251*X(5)
     A+192*X(6)+215*X(7)+166*X(8)+262*X(9)+211*X(10)
     A+204*X(11)+158*X(12)+206*X(13)+109*X(14)+201*X(15)
     A+158*X(16)+403*X(17)+142*X(18)+171*X(19)+248*X(20)
     A+318*X(21)+360*X(22)+209*X(23)+315*X(24)+316*X(25)**1.5
      IF(C.LT.CMIN) GO TO 2
      GO TO 1
    2 CONTINUE
      DO 800 KA=1,25
  800 IX(KA)=X(KA)
      CMIN=C
    1 CONTINUE
      WRITE(6,3)IX(1),IX(2),IX(3),IX(4),IX(5),
     AIX(6),IX(7),IX(8),IX(9),IX(10),
     AIX(11),IX(12),IX(13),IX(14),IX(15),
     AIX(16),IX(17),IX(18),IX(19),IX(20),
     AIX(21),IX(22),IX(23),IX(24),IX(25)
    3 FORMAT('0',25I10)
      WRITE(6,4)CMIN
    4 FORMAT('0',I10)
```

```
     WRITE(6,5)OKN
5    FORMAT('0',I10)
     STOP
     END


          THE PRINTOUT IS

18      13      0      3      16
11      27      4      2      11
14      11      5     25       5
20       0     18      3      24
19       9     21     19       2

          63471

          1679471
```

Therefore, the company should ship:

x_1 = 18 units from Warehouse 1 to Customer A

x_2 = 13 units from Warehouse 1 to Customer B

x_3 =   0 units from Warehouse 1 to Customer C

x_4 =   3 units from Warehouse 1 to Customer D

x_5 = 16 units from Warehouse 1 to Customer E

x_6 = 11 units from Warehouse 2 to Customer A

x_7 = 27 units from Warehouse 2 to Customer B

x_8 =   4 units from Warehouse 2 to Customer C

x_9 =   2 units from Warehouse 2 to Customer D

x_{10} = 11 units from Warehouse 2 to Customer E

x_{11} = 14 units from Warehouse 3 to Customer A

x_{12} = 11 units from Warehouse 3 to Customer B

x_{13} =   5 units from Warehouse 3 to Customer C

x_{14} = 25 units from Warehouse 3 to Customer D

x_{15} =   5 units from Warehouse 3 to Customer E

x_{16} = 20 units from Warehouse 4 to Customer A

x_{17} =   0 units from Warehouse 4 to Customer B

x_{18} = 18 units from Warehouse 4 to Customer C

x_{19} =   3 units from Warehouse 4 to Customer D

x_{20} = 24 units from Warehouse 4 to Customer E

x_{21} = 19 units from Warehouse 5 to Customer A

x_{22} = 9 units from Warehouse 5 to Customer B

x_{23} = 21 units from Warehouse 5 to Customer C

x_{24} = 19 units from Warehouse 5 to Customer D

x_{25} = 2 units from Warehouse 5 to Customer E

Oil Refinery Problem Solved as a Transportation Problem*

EXAMPLE 8.3

An oil refinery can obtain five grades of crude oil. It uses the crudes to make three products. The following table shows what percentage of a unit of each crude becomes Product 1, Product 2, and Product 3. For example, 1 unit of crude oil 1 yields .3 units of Product 1, .35 units of Product 2, and .30 units of Product 3. The refinery is required to produce 400 units of Product 1, 450 units of Product 2, and 550 units of Product 3.

Product	Percentage yield of the five crudes					Units required
	1	2	3	4	5	
1	.30	.25	.30	.25	.35	400
2	.35	.30	.25	.25	.25	450
3	.30	.40	.40	.40	.30	550

In addition, there are limited supplies. We can obtain at most 600 units of Crude 1, 1500 units of Crude 2, 600 units of Crude 3, 200 units of Crude 4, and 400 units of Crude 5.

Also, the limited supply and demand factors cause the prices for the crudes to be nonlinear (vary with the amount purchased). If x_i is the number of units purchased of crude i, the cost equation is given as

$$C = \$4.02x_1^{1.06} + \$5.18x_2^{1.09} + \$4.58x_3^{1.11} + \$3.82x_4^{1.15} + \$4.48x_5^{.94}$$

The problem is to select the right amounts of the various crudes to satisfy the yield requirements of 400, 450, and 550 units and at the same time minimize C.

Therefore, the problem can be stated as: Minimize $C = 4.02x_1^{1.06} + 5.18x_2^{1.09} + 4.58x_3^{1.11} + 3.82x_4^{1.15} + 4.48x_5^{.94}$ subject to $.30x_1 + .25x_2 + .30x_3 + .25x_4 + .35x_5 = 400$, $.35x_1 + .30x_2 + .25x_3 + .25x_4 + .25x_5 = 450$, $.30x_1 + .40x_2 + .40x_3 + .40x_4 + .30x_5 = 550$, $0 \le x_1 \le 600$, $0 \le x_2 \le 1500$, $0 \le x_3 \le 600$, $0 \le x_4 \le 200$, and $0 \le x_5 \le 400$.

*This problem was first published in COMPSTAT 1978, pp. 377–379 © Physica-Verlag, Vienna (Austria).

Using the general transportation problem approach, we solve the system of three equations and five unknowns. Then, we random sample from these solutions, looking at one million solutions subject to the inequality constraints placed on the x_i's, and take the solution that produces the minimum C value. The general solution (all solutions) for the 3×5 system is:

x_4 arbitrary   (anything)

x_5 arbitrary   (anything)

$x_1 = 394.7368 + .210526x_4 - .789474x_5$

$x_2 = 842.1053 - .684211x_4 + 1.923077x_5$

$x_3 = 236.8421 - .47368x_4 - 1.47368x_5$

We incorporate this solution into the program given below:

```
INTEGER X(5),OKN
REAL RX(5),IX(5)
OKN=0
CMIN=9999999
CALLRSTART(1234567,8912345)
DO 1 I=1,1000000
R1=UNI(0)
X(4)=R1*201
R2=UNI(0)
X(5)=R2*401
RX(1)=394.7368+.210526*X(4)-.789474*X(5)
RX(2)=842.1053-.684211*X(4)+1.923077*X(5)
RX(3)=236.8421-.47368*X(4)-1.47368*X(5)
IF(RX(1).LT.0.OR.RX(1).GT.600) GO TO 1
IF(RX(2).LT.0.OR.RX(2).GT.1500) GO TO 1
IF(RX(3).LT.0.OR.RX(3).GT.600) GO TO 1
OKN=OKN+1
C=4.02*RX(1)**1.06+5.18*RX(2)**1.09+4.58*RX(3)**1.11
A+3.82*X(4)**1.15+4.48*X(5)**.94
IF(C.LT.CMIN) GO TO 2
GO TO 1
2 CONTINUE
IX(1)=RX(1)
IX(2)=RX(2)
IX(3)=RX(3)
IX(4)=RX(4)
IX(5)=RX(5)
CMIN=C
1 CONTINUE
WRITE(6,3)IX(1),IX(2),IX(3),IX(4),IX(5)
3 FORMAT('0',5F14.5)
WRITE(6,4)CMIN
4 FORMAT('0',F14.5)
WRITE(6,5)OKN
5 FORMAT('0',I10)
```

```
STOP
END
```

```
            THE PRINTOUT IS

436.84155   705.26294   142.10611   200.00000   0.0

            11935.40234

            322034
```

The solution is:

$x_1 = 436.84$, $x_2 = 705.26$, $x_3 = 142.11$, $x_4 = 200$, $x_5 = 0$, and minimum $C = 1193540$

322,034 solutions were looked at (some were repeated) to provide this optimum. (Actually, there were only 201 $\times$ 401 $=$ 80,601 unique solutions.) So, we could have just put this in two nested loops and looked at them all. However, the Monte Carlo approach is more general and works better on very large problems, as stated before.

In this case, the true minimum cost is produced by using 436.84 units of Crude 1, 705.26 units of Crude 2, 142.11 units of Crude 3, 200 units of Crude 4, and no units of Crude 5. This gives a minimum cost of $11,935.40.

Suppose that the next week the oil company discovers that an oil embargo, a North Sea oil find, and the Alaskan Pipeline have combined to change the cost equation to

$$C = 3.58x_1^{.88} + 5.92x_2^{1.04} + 2.95x_3^{.98} + 4.01x_4^{1.02} + 5.02x_5^{1.08}$$

We decide to run the program again with the new cost equation. The run is shown below:

```
C     SECOND OIL PROBLEM
      INTEGER X(5),OKN
      REAL RX(5),IX(5)
      OKN=0
      CMIN=9999999
      CALL RSTART(7654323,7876543)
      DO 1 I=1,1000000
      R1=UNI(0)
      X(4)=R1*201
      R2=UNI(0)
      X(5)=R2*401
      RX(1)=394.7368+.210526*X(4)-.789474*X(5)
      RX(2)=842.1053-.684211*X(4)+1.923077*X(5)
      RX(3)=236.8421-.47368*X(4)-1.47368*X(5)
      IF(RX(1).LT.0.OR.RX(1).GT.600) GO TO 1
```

```
    IF(RX(2).LT.0.OR.RX(2).GT.1500) GO TO 1
    IF(RX(3).LT.0.OR.RX(3).GT.600) GO TO 1
    OKN=OKN+1
    C=3.58*RX(1)**.88+5.92*RX(2)**1.04+2.95*RX(3)**.98+
    A4.01*X(4)**1.02+5.02*X(5)**1.08
    IF(C.LT.CMIN) GO TO 2
    GO TO 1
  2 CONTINUE
    IX(1)=RX(1)
    IX(2)=RX(2)
    IX(3)=RX(3)
    IX(4)=RX(4)
    IX(5)=RX(5)
    CMIN=C
  1 CONTINUE
    WRITE(6,3)IX(1),IX(2),IX(3),IX(4),IX(5)
  3 FORMAT('0',5F14.5)
    WRITE(6,4)CMIN
  4 FORMAT('0',F14.5)
    WRITE(6,5)OKN
  5 FORMAT('0',I10)
    STOP
    END
```

THE PRINTOUT IS

436.84155   705.26294   142.10611   200.00000   0.0

7452.86719

322034

The solution is to use exactly the same amounts of each crude as before. The net result with the new cost structure is to reduce costs to $7,452.87. Therefore, the problem is insensitive to cost changes at this level. The program can be modified, monitored, maintained, and rerun as new changes in constraints or costs arise.

Hints to Improve Performance of the Optimization Process

FOCUS SEARCH

Any optimization problem can be run on-line (at a terminal) where results come back to the programmer in seconds or minutes. Therefore, run a Monte Carlo integer program ten or twenty times and notice in what region of the feasible solution space the answers are landing. They will almost certainly always land in the same area (or, at most, a couple of areas). Then, the programmer can set up loops to focus the search for the optimum in this area. The loops will examine all (or almost all) of the feasible solutions in this area and generally produce an improved optimum and usually the true optimum.

As computer speeds and on-line computers and minicomputers become commonplace, this will almost surely guarantee discovery of the true optimum in a matter of a few minutes.

INCREASING THE EFFICIENCY OF LARGE PROGRAMS

An optimization problem with many variables (say, 50 or so) may present a problem which can be overcome easily. With many variables and many constraints, most groups of random numbers read in as possible solutions will fail to meet the constraints. It could conceivably happen that of 1,000,000 such groups read in, only a few dozen or a few hundred would meet the constraints. This is inefficient. Therefore, one can structure the program so that all random number groups are transformed, if necessary, to meet the constraints. This way, if the computer reads in 1,000,000 such groups, it will get one million feasible solutions (ones that meet the constraints).

To accomplish this (only recommended for problems with many variables), have the computer read in a random number group (proposed solution). If it meets the constraints, proceed as usual. However, if it fails to meet the constraints, have the program jump to an area where it takes the constraints' inequality totals and divides by the constraints' upper bounds. Then, search all these quotients for the largest value, add .01 to this for safety, and divide all the random number values by this result. This will produce transformed random numbers that meet the constraints. This only really works on the less than or equal constraints. However, they are usually the only ones that present any difficulty as far as efficiency is concerned.

Statistical Distributions of the Possible Solutions

It might be interesting to consider again the distributions of the possible solutions as an aid to determining how good an answer we can get using Monte Carlo techniques and how likely we are to get it.

Assume that we have any probability distribution, for example, the one in Figure 8.4. Now, if this is the probability distribution of the possible solutions of an integer programming maximization problem, then, we are interested in getting one of the large values in the distribution for the "best" solution to our Monte Carlo integer programming problem. The question might naturally arise if we take a random sample of one million possible solutions (like we do in a Monte Carlo approach), what is the probability of getting an answer that is in the upper .001 percent area and hence a pretty good solution?

We have two events: success (S) if we get a profit value large enough to be in the upper .001 percent area, and no success (N) if we get a profit value in the lower

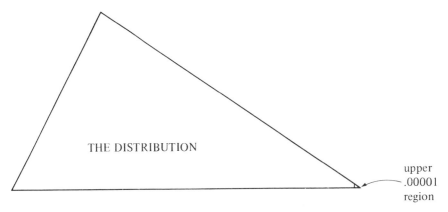

Figure 8.4

99.999 percent of the distribution. Therefore, $P(S) = .00001$ and $P(N) = .99999$. The question is, what is the probability of getting at least one S (we only need one) in one million independent trials? We seek

$$P(1) + P(2) + P(3) + P(4) + \ldots + P(1000000)$$

But, this is just $1 - P(0)$ where $P(0)$ is the probability of no successes.

Therefore, $1 - P(0) = 1 - .99999^{1000000} = .9999546024$ is the probability of getting a good answer, where a good answer is defined as one that is in the upper .001 percent area of the possible solutions probability distribution. Similar results would follow for different levels of confidence and different numbers of points looked at.

Let's note that technically having a solution in the upper .001 percent or .01 percent area of the solution values distribution doesn't necessarily guarantee that the solution is within .001 percent or .01 percent of the true optimum value. It is possible that the solution distribution could look like Figure 8.5. Then, we could get a solution in the upper .001 percent area but the true optimum might be much larger.

However, this is almost impossible in any true "real world" application. The constraints and function to be optimized would have to be very unusual, to say the least, to produce this kind of discontinuity. This just isn't worth worrying about. Also, if there were a remote extreme solution point like this, it would be sensitive to any slight change and hence maybe impractical anyway.

Much has been written about finding the exact corner points in a convex polygon because according to the theory of linear programming the optimum solution must occur at one of these extreme points. However, the theory of linear programming assumes linearity of the objective function and all constraints to realize its results. Frequently, in applications these conditions are not met or if they are met when the problem is formulated they may change over time. Therefore, quite a case could be made for choosing a "good" solution near the temporary or contrived optimum. Our

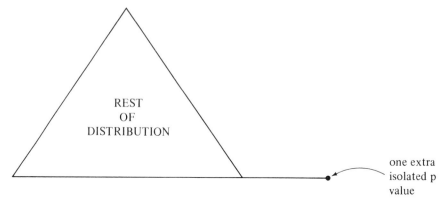

REST
OF
DISTRIBUTION

one extra
isolated p
value

Figure 8.5

work does this very simply, easily, and at very little cost. It can be universally applied to any optimization problem under any constraints. Also, the solution should hold up well under changes in constraints or changes in the optimization function.

Appendix A presents more graphs of the distribution function of the possible solutions of various integer programming problems. They are all nicely behaved and would not cause the extreme value problem mentioned above. Readers are encouraged to generate some solution distributions for other integer programming problems to help convince themselves that there is not much to worry about on this account.

One technique used to solve an integer programming problem is to solve the corresponding linear programming problem and then to take an integer solution near the optimum. The author has no quarrel with this approach.* It is clever and useful. One reason for it being that the linear programming problem is solvable and the integer programming problem is not.

Therefore, it seems that we should be allowed to turn this around (now that we can solve integer programming problems) and solve a linear programming problem by solving the corresponding integer programming problem with Monte Carlo techniques and then using this answer (or a fractional one near it) as the linear programming solution. Remember also that our objective function and our constraints don't have to meet any conditions for solution. We just look at a few million possibilities regardless of the problem and take the optimum value.

The preceding discussion, of course, holds for objective functions to be minimized. Analogous arguments for the lower .001 percent area of the distribution could be made. Everything else is the same except that you are looking for the smallest function value instead of the largest.

---

*Our approach is better for 0–1 programming problems, though.

Conclusion

This work was done in FORTRAN IV because it is the most widely used language and it is ideal for any quantitative problem area that one is studying. However, these programs could be changed easily into other languages such as BASIC, APL or PL-1 to name just a few. The approach would remain the same. Also, if random number generation is not available on one's computer system, it would be possible to arrange the DO-loops to just look at several thousand values (when in fact there were trillions of points to check). The loops could be systematically arranged to, say, do every 10th point in the loop. With this approach if there were, say, ten variables, then only $.1^{10}$ of the points would be examined. This approach is so systematic that it might be more likely to miss the optimum point by quite a bit. This decision can be left up to the user.

However, the author believes that the Monte Carlo approach is far superior because it is not systematic and also because it can be used to check a million random points and then a million more as many times as the user wishes, depending on how much accuracy is required. For that matter, if a manager or researcher wanted to run a minicomputer all night to check billions of points, this could easily be done yielding an even better answer based on more points. It seems that most minicomputers are turned off for the majority of the 168 hours in each week. If this is the case, they could be working on the Monte Carlo integer programming problems for part of that time.

Appendices

APPENDIX A

Sampling Distributions of Feasible Solutions of Selected Integer Programming Problems

Presented in this appendix are the sampling distributions of feasible solutions of numerous integer programming problems. Again, these distributions and all other ones that the author generated have thick tails (no isolated extreme points). This tends to reassure us that we are getting very nearly optimum answers with the Monte Carlo approach. Appendix B follows with an explanation of the process used to generate these distributions.

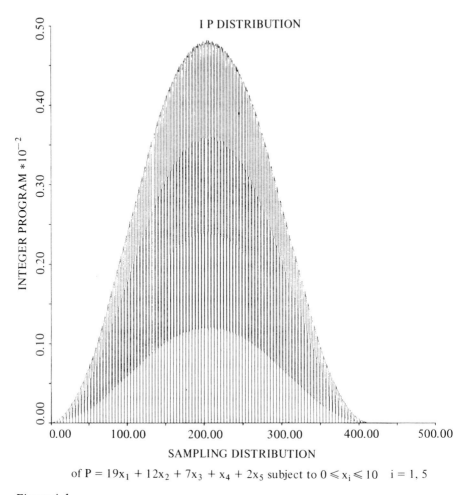

Figure A.1

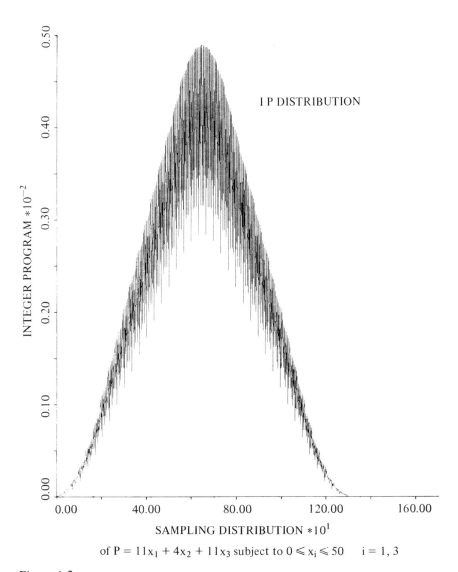

I P DISTRIBUTION

of $P = 11x_1 + 4x_2 + 11x_3$ subject to $0 \leqslant x_i \leqslant 50$ $i = 1, 3$

Figure A.2

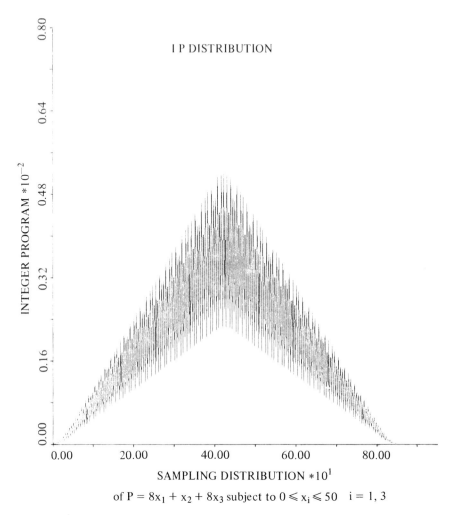

Figure A.3

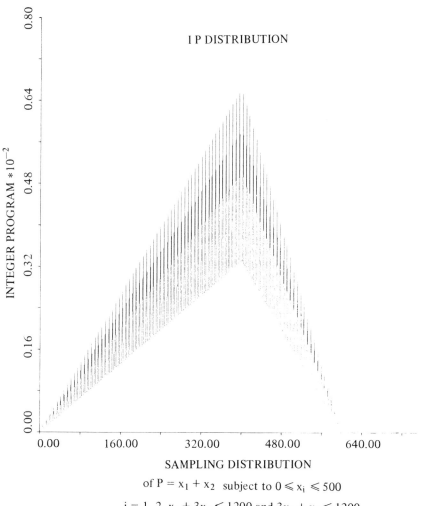

Figure A.4

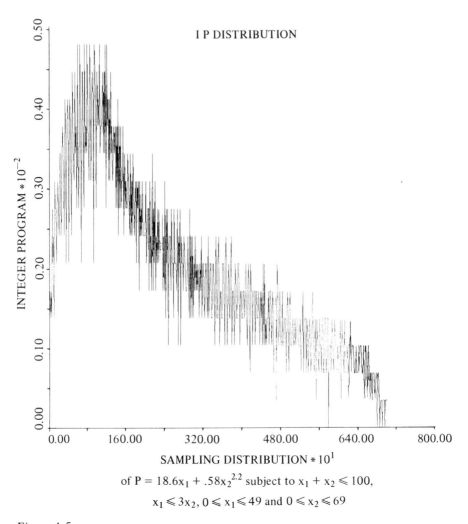

Figure A.5

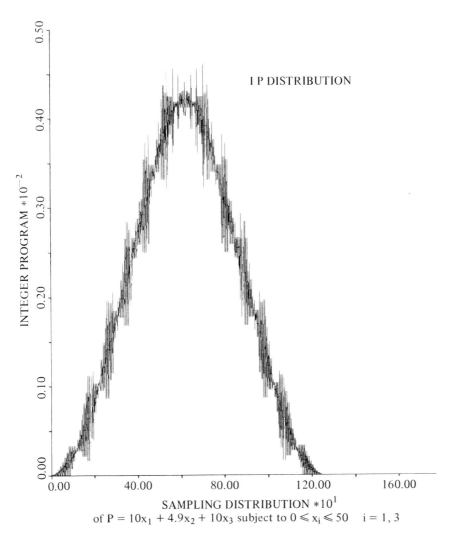

Figure A.6

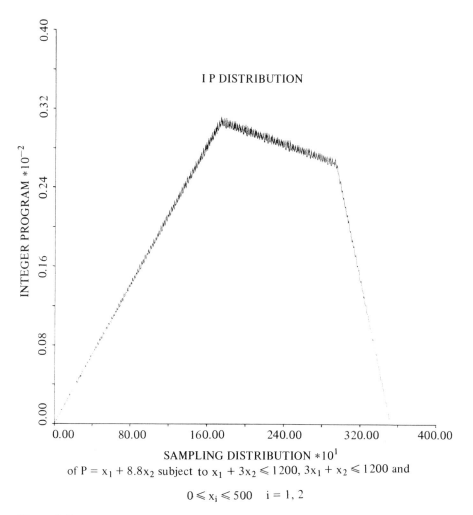

Figure A.7

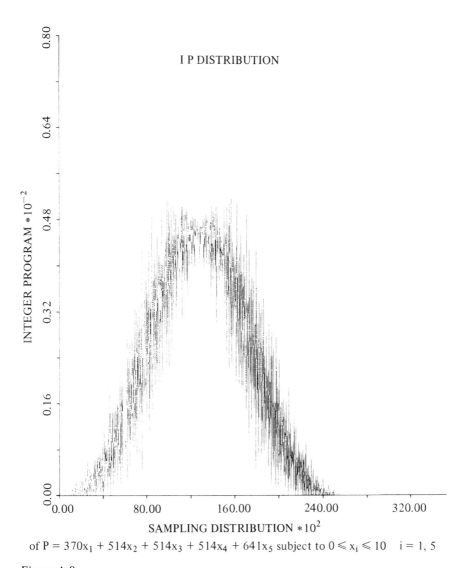

SAMPLING DISTRIBUTION $*10^2$

of $P = 370x_1 + 514x_2 + 514x_3 + 514x_4 + 641x_5$ subject to $0 \leqslant x_i \leqslant 10$ $i = 1, 5$

Figure A.8

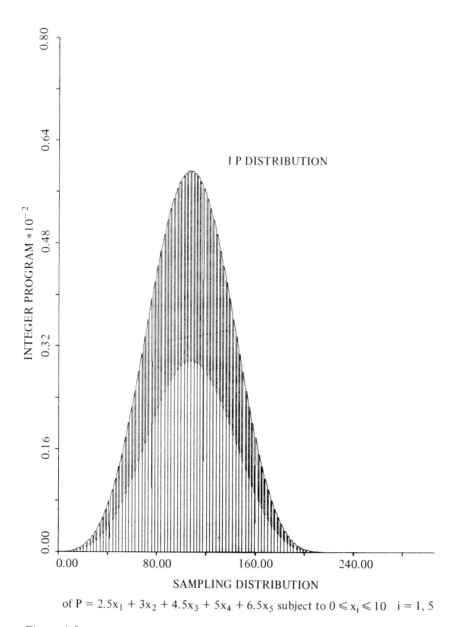

of P = $2.5x_1 + 3x_2 + 4.5x_3 + 5x_4 + 6.5x_5$ subject to $0 \leqslant x_i \leqslant 10$ i = 1, 5

Figure A.9

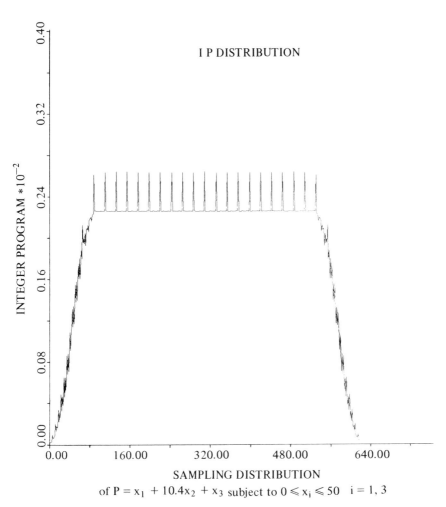

Figure A.10

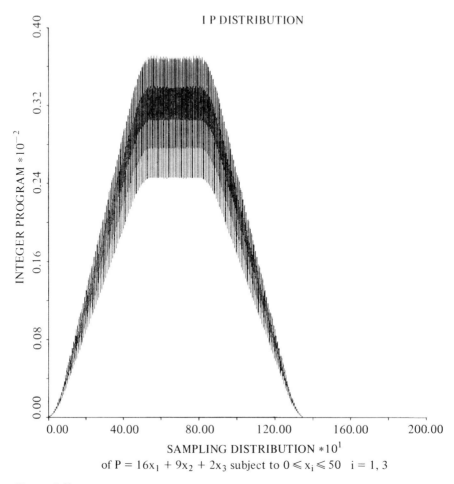

Figure A.11

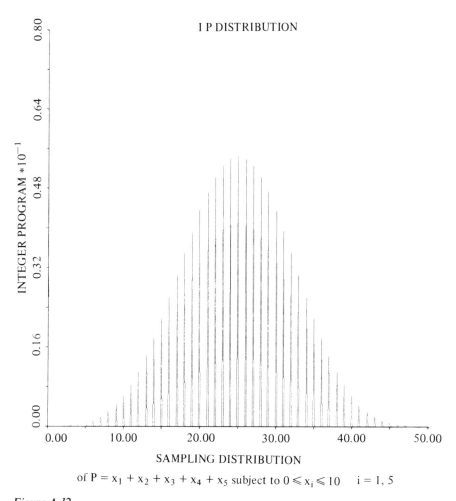

I P DISTRIBUTION

SAMPLING DISTRIBUTION

of $P = x_1 + x_2 + x_3 + x_4 + x_5$ subject to $0 \leqslant x_i \leqslant 10$ $i = 1, 5$

Figure A.12

How to Obtain Sampling Distributions of Feasible Solutions of Integer Programming Problems

The sampling distribution of a statistic is a formula or graph which describes or shows exactly where and with what probability the statistic value occurs. Distributions are defined so that their probabilities add up to one (or the area under the curve is one if the distribution is continuous).

We are very interested in the true sampling distributions of the objective function in an integer programming problem (subject to the constraints). We are interested in these distributions for general knowledge and to show that there are no isolated extreme points. We want to demonstrate that the tails of these distributions are thick enough to justify a Monte Carlo search for an optimum, even with the largest of integer programming problems.

To do this, we generated the sampling distributions of the feasible solutions of integer programming problems. Many of them appear in this text. All of them had thick tails, tending to reassure us of the appropriateness of the random sample Monte Carlo technique.

This appendix contains FORTRAN IV programs that produced four integer programming distributions. The approach is the same in all cases. First, we must have an integer programming problem with a finite number of possibilities. Then, within the limits of your computer (probably 1,000,000 to 1,000,000,000 possible solutions) one can find any sampling distribution.

Have one nested DO-loop for each variable. Set up the loops to look at all possible feasible solutions and find the maximum and minimum. Take their difference and divide it by 512 (or whatever number of histogram intervals you wish). Usually using 2^k (k, a whole number) intervals makes the histogram part of the program easier to write.

Next, set up the 513 histogram interval boundaries and the 512 histogram interval midpoints. Then, set up a new section with one nested DO-loop for each variable as before. Only this time through the loops, put each feasible solution in the interval to which it belongs. This is done by adding one to the correct interval counter variable each time a value lands in that interval. At the end of the loops, divide the interval counter totals by the total number of feasible solutions and graph the resulting distribution.

The first two programs presented did not search for the maximum and minimum in the beginning, because it was obvious from the problem what they were. However, the last two programs did search for the maximum and the minimum before producing the histograms. This is because the constraints made it difficult to predict the maximum or minimum.

The distributions produced from these programs were graphed on a Calcomp plotter. Each plot has 512 peaks. The total of the peak heights is one by definition. The three CALL statements at the end of each program accessed the Calcomp plotter on our computer system. These commands may differ in your computer, but the FORTRAN IV programs should transfer easily.

The DO 10 loop in the programs finds the correct histogram interval for each feasible solution, ignoring all the rest. It only generates the one interval it needs each time. Histogram programs can be written that have each pigeonhole interval physically present in the program. However, they tend to be very large inflexible programs.

Note the very few changes that are required in going from one program to the next. For instance, we never have to alter the histogram loop (as long as we are content with 512 intervals). This is good because that loop is a bit complicated. We only have to change the number of nested loops and the function and constraints depending on the problem. The programs follow.

SAMPLING DISTRIBUTION OF $P = x_1 + x_2 + x_3 + x_4 + x_5$
subject to $0 \le x_i \le 10$, $i = 1,5$

```
DIMENSION S(512), BOUND(513), CENT(514), P(514)
BIG=50
SS=0
```

```
        D=50/512.
        DO 50 K=1,512
 50     S(K)=0.
        DO 4 I=1,11
        X1=I-1
        DO 4 J=1,11
        X2=J-1
        DO 4 K=1,11
        X3=K-1
        DO 4 L=1,11
        X4=L-1
        DO 4 M=1,11
        X5=M-1
        PF=X1+X2+X3+X4+X5
        RLKI=SS
        RUKI=BIG
        RMKI=(RUKI-RLKI)/2.+RLKI
        DO 10 JJJ=1,9
        IF(PF-RMKI)8,8,9
 8      RLKI=RLKI
        RMMKI=RMKI
        RMKI=RLKI+(RMKI-RLKI)/2.
        RUKI=RMMKI
        GO TO 10
 9      RLKI=RMKI
        RMKI=RMKI+(RUKI-RMKI)/2.
        RUKI=RUKI
 10     CONTINUE
        NNNN=(RUKI-SS+D/2.)/D
        S(NNNN)=S(NNNN)+1.
 4      CONTINUE
        DO 5000 I=1,512
 5000   P(I)=S(I)/161051.
        WRITE(6,3030)P
 3030   FORMAT('0',10F11.8/('0',10F11.8))
        SUMOFP=0.
        DO 328 II=1,512
 328    SUMOFP=SUMOFP+P(II)
        WRITE(6,3015)SUMOFP
 3015   FORMAT('0',F15.7)
        DO 12 III=1,513
        XXX=III-1
 12     BOUND(III)=SS+XXX*D
        WRITE(6,3025)BOUND
 3025   FORMAT('0',8F14.3/('0',8F14.3))
        DO 990 I=1,512
        J=I+1
 990    CENT(I)=(BOUND(I)+BOUND(J))/2.
        CALL PLOTID('DTIS    ','NUMBER')
        CALL CALCO1(CENT,P,514,-1,-1,1)
        CALL PLTEND(15.0)
        STOP
        END
```

SAMPLING DISTRIBUTION OF $P = .5x_1 + x_2 + 1.5x_3 + x_4 + x_5$ subject to $0 \le x_i \le 10, \quad i = 1,5$

```
      DIMENSION S(512), BOUND(513), CENT(514), P(514)
      BIG=50
      SS=0
      D=50/512.
      DO 50 K=1,512
  50  S(K)=0.
      DO 4 I=1,11
      X1=I-1
      DO 4 J=1,11
      X2=J-1
      DO 4 K=1,11
      X3=K-1
      DO 4 L=1,11
      X4=L-1
      DO 4 M=1,11
      X5=M-1
      PF=.5*X1+X2+1.5*X3+X4+X5
      RLKI=SS
      RUKI=BIG
      RMKI=(RUKI-RLKI)/2.+RLKI
      DO 10 JJJ=1,9
      IF(PF-RMKI)8,8,9
   8  RLKI=RLKI
      RMMKI=RMKI
      RMKI=RLKI+(RMKI-RLKI)/2.
      RUKI=RMMKI
      GO TO 10
   9  RLKI=RMKI
      RMKI=RMKI+(RUKI-RMKI)/2.
      RUKI=RUKI
  10  CONTINUE
      NNNN=(RUKI-SS+D/2.)/D
      S(NNNN)=S(NNNN)+1.
   4  CONTINUE
      DO 5000 I=1,512
5000  P(I)=S(I)/161051.
      WRITE(6,3030)P
3030  FORMAT('0',10F11.8/('0',10F11.8))
      SUMOFP=0.
      DO 328 II=1,512
 328  SUMOFP=SUMOFP+P(II)
      WRITE(6,3015)SUMOFP
3015  FORMAT('0',F15.7)
      DO 12 III=1,513
      XXX=III-1
  12  BOUND(III)=SS+XXX*D
      WRITE(6,3025)BOUND
3025  FORMAT('0',8F14.3/('0',8F14.3))
      DO 990 I=1,512
```

```
       J=I+1
990    CENT(I)=(BOUND(I)+BOUND(J))/2.
       CALL PLOTID('DTIS     ','NUMBER')
       CALL CALCO1(CENT,P,514,-1,-1,1)
       CALL PLTEND(15.0)
       STOP
       END
```

SAMPLING DISTRIBUTION OF $P = .01x_1^2 + 2x_2$
subject to $0 \le x_i \le 500$, $i = 1,2$, $x_1 + x_2 \le 500$, and $3x_1 + x_2 \le 1200$

```
       DIMENSION S(512), BOUND(513), CENT(514), P(514)
       N=0
       BIG=-1.E71
       SS=1.E70
       DO 50 K=1,512
50     S(K)=0.
       DO 1 I=1,501
       X1=I-1
       DO 1 J=1,501
       X2=J-1
       IF(X1+X2.GT.500) GO TO 1
       IF(3*X1+X2.GT.1200) GO TO 1
       PF=.01*X1**2+2*X2
       IF(PF.GT.BIG)BIG=PF
       IF(PF.LT.SS)SS=PF
1      CONTINUE
       WRITE(6,3010)SS,BIG
3010   FORMAT('0',2F15.7)
       D=(BIG-SS)/512.
       DO 4 I=1,501
       X1=I-1
       DO 4 J=1,501
       X2=J-1
       IF(X1+X2.GT.500) GO TO 4
       IF(3*X1+X2.GT.1200) GO TO 4
       PF=.01*X1**2+2*X2
       N=N+1
       RLKI=SS
       RUKI=BIG
       RMKI=(RUKI-RLKI)/2.+RLKI
       DO 10 JJJ=1,9
       IF(PF-RMKI)8,8,9
8      RLKI=RLKI
       RMMKI=RMKI
       RMKI=RLKI+(RMKI-RLKI)/2.
       RUKI=RMMKI
       GO TO 10
9      RLKI=RMKI
       RMKI=RMKI+(RUKI-RMKI)/2.
       RUKI=RUKI
```

```
  10  CONTINUE
      NNNN=(RUKI-SS+D/2.)/D
      S(NNNN)=S(NNNN)+1.
   4  CONTINUE
      DO 5000 I=1,512
5000  P(I)=S(I)/N
      WRITE(6,30)N
  30  FORMAT('0',I10)
      WRITE(6,3030)P
3030  FORMAT('0',10F11.8/('0',10F11.8))
      SUMOPF=0.
      DO 328 II=1,512
 328  SUMOPF=SUMOPF+P(II)
      WRITE(6,3015)SUMOPF
3015  FORMAT('0',F15.7)
      DO 12 III=1,513
      XXX=III-1
  12  BOUND(III)=SS+XXX*D
      WRITE(6,3025)BOUND
3025  FORMAT('0',8F14.3/('0',8F14.3))
      DO 990 I=1,512
      J=I+1
 990  CENT(I)=(BOUND(I)+BOUND(J))/2.
      CALL PLOTID('DTIS    ','NUMBER')
      CALL CALCO1(CENT,P,514,-1,-1,1)
      CALL PLTEND(15.0)
      STOP
      END
```

SAMPLING DISTRIBUTION OF $P = 18.2x_1 + 6.1x_2$
subject to $0 \le x_i \le 500$, $i = 1,2$, and $x_1 + 3x_2 \le 1200$

```
      DIMENSION S(512), BOUND(513), CENT(514), P(514)
      N=0
      BIG=-1.E71
      SS=1.E70
      DO 50 K=1,512
  50  S(K)=0.
      DO 1 I=1,501
      X1=I-1
      DO 1 J=1,501
      X2=J-1
      IF(X1+3*X2.GT.1200) GO TO 1
      PF=18.2*X1+6.1*X2
      IF(PF.GT.BIG)BIG=PF
      IF(PF.LT.SS)SS=PF
   1  CONTINUE
      WRITE(6,3010)SS,BIG
3010  FORMAT('0',2F15.7)
      D=(BIG-SS)/512.
      DO 4 I=1,501
```

```
      X1=I-1
      DO 4 J=1,501
      X2=J-1
      IF(X1+3*X2.GT.12000) GO TO 4
      PF=18.2*X1+6.1*X2
      N=N+1
      RLKI=SS
      RUKI=BIG
      RMKI=(RUKI-RLKI)/2.+RLKI
      DO 10 JJJ=1,9
      IF(PF-RMKI)8,8,9
   8  RLKI=RLKI
      RMMKI=RMKI
      RMKI=RLKI+(RMKI-RLKI)/2.
      RUKI=RMMKI
      GO TO 10
   9  RLKI=RMKI
      RMKI=RMKI+(RUKI-RMKI)/2.
      RUKI=RUKI
  10  CONTINUE
      NNNN=(RUKI-SS+D/2.)/D
      S(NNNN)=S(NNNN)+1.
   4  CONTINUE
      DO 5000 I=1,512
5000  P(I)=S(I)/N
      WRITE(6,30)N
  30  FORMAT('0',I10)
      WRITE(6,3030)P
3030  FORMAT('0',10F11.8/('0',10F11.8))
      SUMOFP=0.
      DO 328 II=1,512
 328  SUMOFP=SUMOFP+P(II)
      WRITE(6,3015)SUMOFP
3015  FORMAT('0',F15.7)
      DO 12 III=1,513
      XXX=III-1
  12  BOUND(III)=SS+XXX*D
      WRITE(6,3025)BOUND
3025  FORMAT('0',8F14.3/('0',8F14.3))
      DO 990 I=1,512
      J=I+1
 990  CENT(I)=(BOUND(I)+BOUND(J))/2.
      CALL PLOTID('DTIS    ','NUMBER')
      CALL CALCO1(CENT,P,514,-1,-1,1)
      CALL PLTEND(15.0)
      STOP
      END
```

APPENDIX C

How to Solve a System of Equations

For a thorough treatment of solving systems of equations, the reader should consult one of the many fine books on linear algebra.

However, a brief review of the "diagonal technique" is presented here. There are, of course, other ways to solve systems of equations, but this technique has the additional benefit of being easy to program into a computer.

EXAMPLE 1
Solve the following system of equations:

$$x + 5y = 10$$
$$3x + 12y = 28$$

First we write down the coefficients (with all the x's in one column, the y's in another column, and equal to a constant column) without the variables, plus signs or equals signs. They are understood. This gives us

1	5	10
3	12	28

Our objective is to rearrange and/or change this matrix of numbers into

1	0	a
0	1	b

This will give us the solution $x = a$ and $y = b$ if we use only the three elementary matrix operations which at any stage keep the solution space the same as it was with the beginning system of equations. The rules are

1. At any point, any two rows can be interchanged without changing the solution space.
2. At any point, any row can be multiplied or divided by any number (except zero) without changing the solution space.
3. At any point, any row can have added to it a multiple of another row without changing the solution space.

So the idea is to put a 1 in the upper-left corner of the matrix and then 0's underneath it. Then put the next 1 down the main diagonal and then 0's everywhere else in that column, and so on until you have something like

x	y	z	w	u	
1	0	0	0	0	6
0	1	0	0	0	4
0	0	1	0	0	3
0	0	0	1	0	9
0	0	0	0	1	-2

at which point the solution to this system would be

$$x = 6$$
$$y = 4$$
$$z = 3$$
$$w = 9$$
$$u = -2$$

Now look back to our example of

$$x + 5y = 10$$
$$3x + 12y = 28$$

so

1	5	10
3	12	28

-3 times row 1 added to row 2
(rule 3)

1	5	10
0	−3	−2

row two divided by −3
(rule 2)

1	5	10
0	1	2/3

−5 times row 2 added to row 1
(rule 3)

1	0	20/3
0	1	2/3

Therefore, $x = 20/3$ and $y = 2/3$ is the solution to this system.

EXAMPLE 2
Solve the following system:

$$2x + 14y = 30$$
$$2x + 9y = 60$$

so

2	14	30
2	9	60

row 1 divided by 2
(rule 2)

1	7	15
2	9	60

−2 times row 1 added to row 2
(rule 3)

1	7	15
0	−5	30

row 2 divided by −5
(rule 2)

1	7	15
0	1	−6

−7 times row 2 added to row 1
(rule 3)

1	0	57
0	1	−6

Therefore $x = 57$ and $y = -6$ is the solution to this system.

EXAMPLE 3

Solve the following system:

$$x + 3y + 5z = 100$$
$$2x + 9y + 30z = 50$$

When the number of equations does not equal the number of unknowns, just proceed as before (trying to put 1's down the diagonal and 0's everywhere else) and then interpret the results. Therefore,

1	3	5	100
2	9	30	50

add -2 times row 1 to row 2
(rule 3)

1	3	5	100
0	3	20	-150

divide row 2 by 3
(rule 2)

1	3	5	100
0	1	20/3	-50

add -3 times row 2 to row 1
(rule 3)

1	0	-15	250
0	1	20/3	-50

Therefore

$$x - 15z = 250$$
$$y + (20/3)z = -50$$

so with z arbitrary

$$x = 15z + 250$$
$$y = -(20/3)z - 50$$

In this case we have many solutions. By letting z take different values, the appropriate x and y values are produced from $x = 15z + 250$ and $y = -(20/3)z - 50$.

EXAMPLE 4

If you started with four equations and six unknowns and the final matrix was

x	y	z	w	u	v	
1	0	0	0	6	3	21
0	1	0	0	4	-2	27

0	0	1	0	8	3	− 12
0	0	0	1	5	16	8

then this would represent

$$x + 6u + 3v = 21$$
$$y + 4u - 2v = 27$$
$$z + 8u + 3v = -12$$
$$w + 5u + 16v = 8$$

so the solution would be for arbitrary u and v

$$x = 21 - 6u - 3v$$
$$y = 27 - 4u + 2v$$
$$z = -12 - 8u - 3v$$
$$w = 8 - 5u - 16v$$

For more practice, consult a linear algebra book.

Additional Business Examples

EXAMPLE 1

The advertising department in the K Company is trying to develop the most effective advertising strategy given their budgetary and other constraints. They have five possible ads to choose from. They are:

Ad 1   Sponsoring television show A
       (limit of at most 10 times)
Ad 2   Sponsoring television show B
       (limit of at most 15 times)
Ad 3   Sponsoring radio show C
       (limit of at most 8 times)
Ad 4   A one-page ad in magazine T
       (limit of at most 4 times)
Ad 5   A Sunday newspaper ad of four pages
       (limit of at most twice)

These limits are all in the time period of the next 8 months. The budget for the next 8 months is $1,000,000.

The costs of the ads and their profit ratings relative to each other (a rating of 2 is twice as productive saleswise as a 1, etc.) are given below:

Ad	Cost per unit ($)	Profit rating	Number of units
1	150,000	14	x_1
2	90,000	8	x_2
3	10,000	3	x_3
4	5,000	2.4	x_4
5	15,000	3.9	x_5

Management wants to do at least one Sunday newspaper ad (ad 5) and at least 2 sponsorships of television show B (ad 2). What advertising strategy will maximize the profit rating subject to the constraints?

We seek to maximize $P = 14x_1 + 8x_2 + 3x_3 + 2.4x_4 + 3.9x_5$ subject to $0 \le x_1 \le 10$, $2 \le x_2 \le 15$, $0 \le x_3 \le 8$, $0 \le x_4 \le 4$, $1 \le x_5 \le 2$, and $150,000x_1 + 90,000x_2 + 10,000x_3 + 5,000x_4 + 15,000x_5 \le 1,000,000$. The program follows:

```
C    ADVERTISING    STRATEGY
        INTEGER X1,X2,X3,X4,X5,P,PMAX
        PMAX=-999999
        DO 1 I=1,11
        X1=I-1
        DO 1 J=2,15
        X2=J
        DO 1 K=1,9
        X3=K-1
        DO 1 L=1,5
        X4=L-1
        DO 1 M=1,2
        X5=M
        IF(150000*X1+90000*X2+10000*X3+5000*X4+15000*X5.GT.1000000)
        AGO TO 1
        P=14*X1+8*X2+3*X3+2.4*X4+3.9*X5
        IF(P.GT.PMAX) GO TO 2
        GO TO 1
    2   IX1=X1
        IX2=X2
        IX3=X3
        IX4=X4
        IX5=X5
        PMAX=P
    1   CONTINUE
        WRITE(108,3)IX1,IX2,IX3,IX4,IX5,PMAX
    3   FORMAT('0',5I5,I12)
```

```
STOP
END

        THE PRINTOUT IS

    4   3   8   4   2     121
```

Therefore, the K Company should select x_1 = 4 units of ad 1, x_2 = 3 units of ad 2, x_3 = 8 units of ad 3, x_4 = 4 units of ad 4, and x_5 = 2 units of ad 5 to earn a maximum profit rating of 121.

EXAMPLE 2

The KMA Company has analyzed their holding, ordering, and shortage (or stockout) costs and determined that their cost equation is $C = q^2 - 96q + 2406$, where q is the constant quantity ordered with each placement of an order. If the demand for the product will not exceed 300 during the time period under consideration (so $0 \leq q \leq 300$), what is the order quantity q that will minimize the cost C?

```
C   EOQ  ECONOMIC  ORDER  QUANTITY  PROBLEM
        INTEGER C, Q, CMIN
        CMIN=999999
        DO 1 I=1,301
        Q=I-1
        C=Q**2-96*Q+2406
        IF(C.LT.CMIN) GO TO 2
        GO TO 1
    2   IQ=Q
        CMIN=C
    1   CONTINUE
        WRITE(108,3)IQ,CMIN
    3   FORMAT('0',I12,I12)
        STOP
        END


        THE PRINTOUT IS

        48        102
```

Therefore, ordering a quantity of q = 48 each time will yield a minimum cost of C = 102.

EXAMPLE 3

The International Falls Power Company wants to build a transmission line connecting five different cities. The line does not have to loop back to the city it started from but it must go through each city. The distances between the cities are given below. Write a program to find the minimum distance between the cities and hence minimize the length and therefore the cost of construction in this case.

Distance in miles

City City	1	2	3	4	5
1	0	75	48	92	104
2	75	0	58	106	200
3	48	58	0	75	120
4	92	106	75	0	90
5	104	200	120	90	0

The program follows:

```
C   MINIMIZE TRANSMISSION LINE DISTANCE
        INTEGER D(5,5),DMIN,D
        DMIN=999999
        D(1,2)=75
        D(2,1)=75
        D(1,3)=48
        D(3,1)=48
        D(1,4)=92
        D(4,1)=92
        D(1,5)=104
        D(5,1)=104
        D(2,3)=58
        D(3,2)=58
        D(2,4)=106
        D(4,2)=106
        D(2,5)=200
        D(5,2)=200
        D(3,4)=75
        D(4,3)=75
        D(3,5)=120
        D(5,3)=120
        D(4,5)=90
        D(5,4)=90
        DO 1 I=1,5
        DO 1 J=1,5
        DO 1 K=1,5
        DO 1 L=1,5
        DO 1 M=1,5
        IF(I.EQ.J.OR.I.EQ.K.OR.I.EQ.L.OR.I.EQ.M) GO TO 1
        IF(J.EQ.K.OR.J.EQ.L.OR.J.EQ.M) GO TO 1
        IF(K.EQ.L.OR.K.EQ.M) GO TO 1
        IF(L.EQ.M) GO TO 1
        D=D(I,J)+D(J,K)+D(K,L)+D(L,M)
        IF(D.LT.DMIN) GO TO 2
```

```
      GO TO 1
   2  I1=I
      J1=J
      K1=K
      L1=L
      M1=M
      MD1=D(I,J)
      MD2=D(J,K)
      MD3=D(K,L)
      MD4=D(L,M)
      DMIN=D
   1  CONTINUE
C  WE WILL PRINT SUBSCRIPTS AND VALUES
      WRITE(108,3)I1,J1,K1,L1,M1,MD1,MD2,MD3,MD4,DMIN
   3  FORMAT('0',5I5,4I6,I10)
      STOP
      END
```

THE PRINTOUT IS

2	1	3	4	5	75	48	75	90	288

Therefore, build the line from city 2 to 1 to 3 to 4 to 5 for a minimum distance of 288 miles.

EXAMPLE 4

The T Company makes $5 per unit on Product A and $10 per unit on Product B. However, they both compete for the same labor resources. It takes 6 minutes of time in Department I, 10 minutes in Department II, and 17 minutes in Department III to make one unit of A. It takes 5 minutes in Department I, 12 minutes in Department II, and 20 minutes in Department III to make one unit of B. There are 2000 man-minutes of time available per time period in each department. Also, if any of Product A is produced, there is a fixed start-up cost (product testing and insurance) of $14 per time period. And if any of Product B is produced, there is a fixed start-up cost (product testing and insurance) of $22 per time period. Find the product mix strategy to maximize profit.

Maximize $P = 5x + 10y - 14x_a - 22y_a$ subject to $x \geq 0$, $y \geq 0$, $6x + 5y \leq 2000$, $10x + 12y \leq 2000$, and $17x + 20y \leq 2000$, where $x_a = 0$ if $x = 0$, $x_a = 1$ if $x > 0$, $y_a = 0$ if $y = 0$, and $y_a = 1$ if $y > 0$. The program follows:

```
C  FIXED COST PRODUCT MIX PROBLEM
      INTEGER X,Y,P,PMAX
      PMAX=-999999
      DO 1 I=1,118
      X=I-1
      DO 1 J=1,101
```

```
      Y=J-1
      IF(6*X+5*Y.GT.2000) GO TO 1
      IF(10*X+12*Y.GT.2000) GO TO 1
      IF(17*X+20*Y.GT.2000) GO TO 1
      P=5*X+10*Y-36
      IF(X.EQ.0) P=P+14
      IF(Y.EQ.0) P=P+22
      IF(P.GT.PMAX) GO TO 2
      GO TO 1
2     IX=X
      IY=Y
      PMAX=P
1     CONTINUE
      WRITE(108,3) IX,IY,PMAX
3     FORMAT('0',2I10,I12)
      STOP
      END


      THE PRINTOUT IS

      0    100    978
```

Therefore, the T Company should make $x = 0$ units of Product A and $y = 100$ units of Product B to obtain a maximum profit of \$978 per time period.

EXAMPLE 5

Consider the following job assignment problem. Six jobs must be completed. There are six machines available for the work. Each job can be done on one and only one machine. The cost of doing each job on each individual machine is given in the table below:

	Time required					
Job	Machine 1	Machine 2	Machine 3	Machine 4	Machine 5	Machine 6
1	44	602	678	895	326	959
2	558	353	577	866	305	813
3	24	189	878	683	285	442
4	862	848	569	831	555	470
5	848	689	364	957	267	426
6	954	952	669	174	37	215

Find the assignment of each job to each machine that minimizes the total cost.

```
C   JOB ASSIGNMENT STRATEGY PROBLEM
    INTEGER U(6),V(6),W(6),X(6),Y(6),Z(6),C,CMIN
    PMAX=-999999
    U(1)=44
    U(2)=602
    U(3)=678
    U(4)=895
    U(5)=326
    U(6)=959
    V(1)=558
    V(2)=353
    V(3)=577
    V(4)=866
    V(5)=305
    V(6)=813
    W(1)=24
    W(2)=189
    W(3)=878
    W(4)=683
    W(5)=285
    W(6)=442
    X(1)=862
    X(2)=848
    X(3)=569
    X(4)=831
    X(5)=555
    X(6)=470
    Y(1)=848
    Y(2)=689
    Y(3)=364
    Y(4)=957
    Y(5)=267
    Y(6)=426
    Z(1)=954
    Z(2)=952
    Z(3)=669
    Z(4)=174
    Z(5)=37
    Z(6)=215
    DO 1 I=1,6
    DO 1 J=1,6
    DO 1 K=1,6
    DO 1 L=1,6
    DO 1 M=1,6
    DO 1 N=1,6
    IF(I.EQ.J.OR.I.EQ.K.OR.I.EQ.L.OR.I.EQ.M.OR.I.EQ.N) GO TO 1
    IF(J.EQ.K.OR.J.EQ.L.OR.J.EQ.M.OR.J.EQ.N) GO TO 1
    IF(K.EQ.L.OR.K.EQ.M.OR.K.EQ.N) GO TO 1
    IF(L.EQ.M.OR.L.EQ.N) GO TO 1
    IF(M.EQ.N) GO TO 1
    C=U(I)+V(J)+W(K)+X(L)+Y(M)+Z(N)
    IF(C.LT.CMIN) GO TO 2
    GO TO 1
```

```
2   IX1=U(I)
    IX2=V(J)
    IX3=W(K)
    IX4=X(L)
    IX5=Y(M)
    IX6=Z(N)
    CMIN=C
1   CONTINUE
    WRITE(108,3)IX1,IX2,IX3,IX4,IX5,IX6,CMIN
3   FORMAT('0',6I8,I12)
    STOP
    END
```

THE PRINTOUT IS

44   305   189   470   364   174   1546

Therefore, the solution is $x_1 = 44$, $x_2 = 305$, $x_3 = 189$, $x_4 = 470$, $x_5 = 364$, and $x_6 = 174$. So Job 1 should be done on Machine 1; Job 2 on Machine 5; Job 3 on Machine 2; Job 4 on Machine 6; Job 5 on Machine 3, and Job 6 on Machine 4.

EXAMPLE 6
Deliveries of various products need to be made to firms in Chicago. The products are to be sent by air freight. Due to a scheduling problem, only two planes are immediately available. Their combined capacity is 50,000 lbs. The products, weights, and profit returns are listed below:

Product	Weight (lbs.)	Profit ($)
A	7,000	200
B	14,000	600
C	9,000	310
D	6,000	204
E	17,000	315
F	12,000	209
G	10,000	380
H	22,000	1,000
I	8,000	150
J	4,000	80
K	6,000	72

To maximize the immediate profit (the rest will be shipped later at a slight loss), which products should be shipped? The program follows:

```
C   CARGO LOADING PROBLEM
    INTEGER X1,X2,X3,X4,X5,X6,X7,X8,X9,X10,X11,PMAX,P
    PMAX=-999999
    DO 1 I=1,2
    X1=I-1
    DO 1 J=1,2
    X2=J-1
    DO 1 K=1,2
    X3=K-1
    DO 1 L=1,2
    X4=L-1
    DO 1 M=1,2
    X5=M-1
    DO 1 N=1,2
    X6=N-1
    DO 1 IA=1,2
    X7=IA-1
    DO 1 JA=1,2
    X8=JA-1
    DO 1 KA=1,2
    X9=KA-1
    DO 1 LA=1,2
    X10=LA-1
    DO 1 MA=1,2
    X11=MA-1
    IF(7000*X1+14000*X2+9000*X3+6000*X4+17000*X5+
   A12000*X6+10000*X7+22000*X8+8000*X9+4000*X10+
   A6000*X11.GT.50000) GO TO 1
    P=200*X1+600*X2+310*X3+204*X4+315*X5+209*X6
   A+380*X7+1000*X8+150*X9+80*X10+72*X11
    IF(P.GT.PMAX) GO TO 2
    GO TO 1
  2 IX1=X1
    IX2=X2
    IX3=X3
    IX4=X4
    IX5=X5
    IX6=X6
    IX7=X7
    IX8=X8
    IX9=X9
    IX10=X10
    IX11=X11
    PMAX=P
  1 CONTINUE
    WRITE(108,3)IX1,IX2,IX3,IX4,IX5,IX6
   A,IX7,IX8,IX9,IX10,IX11,PMAX
  3 FORMAT('0',11I4,I12)
    STOP
    END
```

```
                    THE PRINTOUT IS
  0    1    0    0    0    0    1    1    0    1    0       2060
```

Therefore, products B, G, H, and J should be shipped to Chicago to gain a maximum profit of $2060.

EXAMPLE 7

The Pacific Palisades Company has two factories and two warehouses. The supplies and demands of the factories and warehouses, respectively, and the unit shipping costs are shown in the table below:

	Shipping costs		
	To	To	
Factory	Warehouse 1	Warehouse 2	Supply
1	$50	$65	400
2	$70	$40	500
Demand	300	600	

There are the following fixed charges which are incurred only if a nonzero amount is shipped from factory to warehouse:

Factory 1 to Warehouse 1 $ 800

Factory 1 to Warehouse 2 2000

Factory 2 to Warehouse 1 1500

Factory 2 to Warehouse 2   600

We seek the shipment pattern that will minimize the cost. This can be summarized as

Minimize $C = 50x_{11} + 800y_{11} + 65x_{12} + 2000y_{12} + 70x_{21} + 1500y_{21} + 40x_{22} + 600y_{22}$

subject to

$x_{11} \geq 0, x_{12} \geq 0, x_{21} \geq 0, x_{22} \geq 0,$

$x_{11} + x_{12} = 400$

$x_{21} + x_{22} = 500$

$x_{11} + x_{21} = 300$

$x_{12} + x_{22} = 600$

and

$y_{11} = 1$ if $x_{11} > 0$ and $y_{11} = 0$ if $x_{11} = 0$

$y_{12} = 1$ if $x_{12} > 0$ and $y_{12} = 0$ if $x_{12} = 0$

$y_{21} = 1$ if $x_{21} > 0$ and $y_{21} = 0$ if $x_{21} = 0$

$y_{22} = 1$ if $x_{22} > 0$ and $y_{22} = 0$ if $x_{22} = 0$

First we will solve the system of equations:

$$x_{11} + x_{12} \qquad\qquad = 400$$
$$x_{12} + \qquad x_{22} = 600$$
$$x_{21} + x_{22} = 500$$
$$x_{11} + \qquad x_{21} \qquad = 300$$

Using the row diagonalization method discussed in Appendix C, we get:

1	1	0	0	400
0	1	0	1	600
0	0	1	1	500
1	0	1	0	300
1	1	0	0	400
0	1	0	1	600
0	0	1	1	500
0	−1	1	0	−100
1	0	0	−1	−200
0	1	0	1	600
0	0	1	1	500
0	0	1	1	500
1	0	0	−1	−200
0	1	0	1	600
0	0	1	1	500
0	0	0	0	0

Therefore, the solution is:

$$x_{11} - x_{22} = -200$$
$$x_{12} + x_{22} = 600$$
$$x_{21} + x_{22} = 500$$

or for $200 \leq x_{22} \leq 500$, then

$$x_{11} = x_{22} - 200$$
$$x_{12} = 600 - x_{22}$$
$$x_{21} = 500 - x_{22}$$

Keeping in mind the fixed-charge terms, the program follows:

```
C   FIXED  CHARGE  TRANSPORTATION  PROBLEM
        INTEGER X11,X12,X21,X22,C,CMIN
        CMIN=999999
        DO 1 I=200,500
        X22=I
        X11=X22-200
        X12=600-X22
        X21=500-X22
        C=50*X11+65*X12+70*X21+40*X22+800+2000+1500+600
        IF(X11.EQ.0) C=C-800
        IF(X12.EQ.0) C=C-2000
        IF(X21.EQ.0) C=C-1500
        IF(X22.EQ.0) C=C-600
        IF(C.LT.CMIN) GO TO 2
        GO TO 1
   2    IX11=X11
        IX12=X12
        IX21=X21
        IX22=X22
        CMIN=C
   1    CONTINUE
        WRITE(108,3)IX11,IX12,IX21,IX22,CMIN
   3    FORMAT('0',4I8,I12)
        STOP
        END

                THE PRINTOUT IS

        300    100    0    500    44900
```

Therefore, the company should ship 300 units from Factory 1 to Warehouse 1, 100 units from Factory 1 to Warehouse 2, and 500 units from Factory 2 to Warehouse 2 in order to minimize the cost.

EXAMPLE 8

The Algoma Midwest Company is considering funding five projects over part or all of the next three years. The project costs (per year) and their estimated yearly return are given below:

Project	Constant Yearly Cost ($)	Return (%)	
1	800,000	10 times $i^{1.5}$	
2	600,000	12	where i
3	1,100,000	5 times i	is the
4	450,000	3 times i	year number
5	1,900,000	6	(either 1, 2, 3)

No more than 2,000,000 can be invested in any one year. What investment plan will maximize the total dollar return for the three years combined? The program is given below:

```
C   CAPITAL BUDGETING PROBLEM
        INTEGER X11,X21,X31,X41,X51
        INTEGER X12,X22,X32,X42,X52
        INTEGER X13,X23,X33,X43,X53
        PMAX=-999999
        DO 1 I1=1,2
        X11=I1-1
        DO 1 J1=1,2
        X21=J1-1
        DO 1 K1=1,2
        X31=K1-1
        DO 1 L1=1,2
        X41=L1-1
        DO 1 M1=1,2
        X51=M1-1
        DO 1 I2=1,2
        X12=I2-1
        DO 1 J2=1,2
        X22=J2-1
        DO 1 K2=1,2
        X32=K2-1
        DO 1 L2=1,2
        X42=L2-1
        DO 1 M2=1,2
        X52=M2-1
        DO 1 I3=1,2
        X13=I3-1
        DO 1 J3=1,2
        X23=J3-1
        DO 1 K3=1,2
        X33=K3-1
        DO 1 L3=1,2
        X43=L3-1
        DO 1 M3=1,2
        X53=M3-1
        IF(800000*X11+600000*X21+1100000*X31+450000*X41+
       A1900000*X51.GT.2000000) GO TO 1
        IF(800000*X12+600000*X22+1100000*X32+450000*X42+
       A1900000*X52.GT.2000000) GO TO 1
        IF(800000*X13+600000*X23+1100000*X33+450000*X43+
       A1900000*X53.GT.2000000) GO TO 1
        P=8000000*X11*.10*1**1.5
        A+600000*X21*.12
        A+1100000*X31*.05*1
        A+4500000*X41*.03*1
        A+1900000*X51*.06
        A+800000*X12*.10*2**1.5
```

```
      A+600000*X22*.12
      A+1100000*X32*.05*2
      A+450000*X42*.03*2
      A+1900000*X52*.06
      A+800000*X13*.10*3**1.5
      A+600000*X23*.12
      A+1100000*X33*.05*3
      A+450000*X43*.03*2
      A+1900000*X53*.06
       IF(P.GT.PMAX) GO TO 2
       GO TO 1
   2   IX11=X11
       IX21=X21
       IX31=X31
       IX41=X41
       IX51=X51
       IX12=X12
       IX22=X22
       IX32=X32
       IX42=X42
       IX52=X52
       IX13=X13
       IX23=X23
       IX33=X33
       IX43=X43
       IX53=X53
       PMAX=P
   1   CONTINUE
       WRITE(108,3)IX11,IX21,IX31,IX41,IX51
   3   FORMAT('0',5I5)
       WRITE(108,4)IX12,IX22,IX32,IX42,IX52
   4   FORMAT('0',5I5)
       WRITE(108,5)IX13,IX23,IX33,IX43,IX53
   5   FORMAT('0',5I5)
       WRITE(108,6)PMAX
   6   FORMAT('0',F15.2)
       STOP
       END


      THE PRINTOUT IS

       1  1  0  1  0

       1  0  1  0  0

       1  0  1  0  0

        1082466.00
```

Therefore, the Algoma Central Company should invest in projects 1, 2, and 4 the first year, projects 1 and 3 the second year, and projects 1 and 3 the third year. This will yield a maximum return of $1,082,466 during the three years.

EXAMPLE 9

The Medford Insurance Company wants to invest no more than $900,000 in blocks of $100,000 in five different securities. Their returns are listed below:

Security	Return (%)	Amount Available ($)
1	8	200,000
2	12	300,000
3	15	200,000
4	7	100,000
5	9	100,000

Government regulations state that at least 50% of the investment must be in securities 1, 4, or 5 because their risks are lower and hence won't jeopardize the policyholders' reserves; and company policy says that at least 100,000 of each security must be purchased. What investment plan will maximize the return under these conditions? The program follows:

```
C    INSURANCE  REGULATED  INVESTMENT
       INTEGER X1,X2,X3,X4,X5,PMAX,P
       PMAX=-999999
       DO 1 I=1,2
       X1=I*100000
       DO 1 J=1,3
       X2=J*100000
       DO 1 K=1,2
       X3=K*100000
       DO 1 L=1,1
       X4=L*100000
       DO 1 M=1,1
       X5=M*100000
       IF(X1+X4+X5.LT..5*(X1+X2+X3+X4+X5)) GO TO 1
       P=.08*X1+.12*X2+.15*X3+.07*X4+.09*X5
       IF(P.GT.PMAX) GO TO 2
       GO TO 1
   2   IX1=X1
       IX2=X2
       IX3=X3
       IX4=X4
       IX5=X5
       PMAX=P
   1   CONTINUE
       WRITE(108,3)IX1,IX2,IX3,IX4,IX5,PMAX
```

```
3    FORMAT('0',5I10,I12)
     STOP
     END
```

```
                    THE PRINTOUT IS

   200000    200000    200000    100000    100000        85999
```

Therefore, the company should buy \$200,000 worth of Security 1, \$200,000 of Security 2, \$200,000 of Security 3, \$100,000 of Security 4, and \$100,000 of Security 5. The return will be \$85,999.

EXAMPLE 10

An enclosed structure of capacity 25,000 cubic meters is to be built so as to minimize the cost of the building materials. It is to be rectangular with floor and roof size XY at \$30 and \$17 per square meter cost, respectively. The two XZ sides and the two YZ sides cost \$12 per square meter. Also, the height can be no more than 50 meters, due to a zoning ordinance, and the sides must be at least 20 meters wide.

Therefore, we seek to minimize $C = 30XY + 17XY + 24XZ + 24YZ$ subject to $X \geq 20$, $Y \geq 20$, $0 \leq Z \leq 50$, and $XYZ = 25,000$ cubic meters.

As in all these problems, we will use our search all possible techniques. We go by increments of one meter, but a finer mesh could be used if desired. The program follows:

```
C   MINIMIZE COST OF BUILDING STRUCTURE
        INTEGER Y,Z
        CMIN=999999
        DO 1 I=1,50
        Z=I
        AK=25000./Z
        K=AK
        DO 1 J=20,K
        Y=J
        X=25000./(Z*Y)
        C=30*X*Y+17*X*Y+24*X*Z+24*Y*Z
        IF(C.LT.CMIN) GO TO 2
        GO TO 1
    2   CMIN=C
        IZ=Z
        YY=Y
        XX=X
    1   CONTINUE
        WRITE(108,3)XX,YY,IZ,CMIN
    3   FORMAT('0',2F10.2,I10,F10.3)
        STOP
        END
```

```
THE PRINTOUT IS

23.63   23.00   46    77022.375
```

Therefore, $X = 23.63$, $Y = 23$, $Z = 46$, and $C = 77,022.38$. So the structure should be 46 meters high and 23.63 by 23 to give a minimum cost of $77,022.38.

EXAMPLE 11

A farm silo of cylindrical shape with a half-dome top is to be built to have a capacity of 300 cubic meters. The height of the cylinder is to be between 10 and 80 meters. The radius of the cylinder (and half-dome, too) is to be greater than or equal to 1. Cylinder volume and dome volume = 300 cubic meters. Therefore,

$$\pi r^2 h + .5\tfrac{4}{3} \pi r^3 = 300$$

Solving for r, we see that r must be less than or equal to 3.1 meters. We will vary r by hundredths of a meter. The sides, floor, and roof cost $20, $12, and $30 per square meter, respectively.

Therefore, we seek to minimize $C = 2\pi rh(20) + \pi r^2(12) + .5(4\pi r^2)(30)$ subject to $1 \le r \le 3.1$, $10 \le h \le 80$, and $\pi r^2 h + .5\text{-}4/3 \pi r^3 = 300$. The program follows:

```
C  MINIMIZE COST OF BUILDING FARM SILO
      CMIN=999999
      DO 1 I=1,211
      R=1+(I-1)*.01
      H=(300-.666667*3.14159*R**3)/(3.14159*R**2)
      IF(H.LT.10.OR.H.GT.80) GO TO 1
      C=40*3.14159*R*H+12*3.14159*R**2+60*3.14159*R**2
      IF(C.LT.CMIN) GO TO 2
      GO TO 1
    2 RR=R
      HH=H
      CMIN=C
    1 CONTINUE
      WRITE(108,3)RR,HH,CMIN
    3 FORMAT('0',3F10.3)
      STOP
      END


      THE PRINTOUT IS

   2.830   10.037    5380.898
```

Therefore, $r = 2.83$, $h = 10.037$, and $C = 5380.90$. So the silo should have a radius of 2.83 meters and a height of 10.037 meters to yield a minimum cost of $5,380.90.

EXAMPLE 12

A container with a base and top that are equilateral triangles and rectangular sides is to be made to hold 2000 cubic centimeters. The surface area is to be minimized. This will minimize the cost as all five sides are made from the same material. The side of the triangle S must be between 2 and 20 centimeters and the length (L) of the rectangular side must be between 10 and 100 centimeters. The height of the triangle (h) equals $\sqrt{3}/2\ S$.

Therefore, we seek to minimize $A = .5Sh(2) + 3SL$ subject to $2 \leq S \leq 20$, $10 \leq L \leq 100$, and $.5ShL = 2000$. We vary S by hundredths of a centimeter. The program follows:

```
C  MINIMIZE COST OF TRIANGULAR CONTAINER
       AMIN=999999
       REAL L
       DO 1 J=1,1801
       S=2+(J-1)*.01
       H=SQRT(3.)/2*S
       L=2000/(.5*S*H)
       A=S*H+3*S*L
       IF(A.LT.AMIN) GO TO 2
       GO TO 1
    2  SS=S
       HH=H
       RL=L
       AMIN=A
    1  CONTINUE
       WRITE(108,3)SS,HH,RL,AMIN
    3  FORMAT('0',4F15.3)
       STOP
       END


                   THE PRINTOUT IS

      20.000    17.320    11.547      7143429.000
```

Therefore, $S = 20$, $h = 17.32$, $L = 11.547$, and $A = 7,143,429$. So with equilateral triangle sides of 20 centimeters and rectangular sides of length 11.547 centimeters, we minimize the surface area of the container under our constraints.

EXAMPLE 13

Minimize $A = 2hW + 4hL$ subject to $2 \leq h \leq 20$, $3 \leq W \leq 20$, and $hWL = 3,000$ cubic centimeters.

From the program below we can see that a height of 2 centimeters, a width of 20 centimeters, and a length of 75 centimeters will minimize the surface area.

```
C   MINIMIZE AREA OF RECTANGULAR CONTAINER
        INTEGER H,W
        REAL L
        AMIN=999999
        DO 1 I=2,20
        H=I
        DO 1 J=3,20
        W=J
        L=3000/(H*W)
        A=2*H*W+4*H*L
        IF(A.LT.AMIN) GO TO 2
        GO TO 1
    2   HH=H
        WW=W
        RL=L
        AMIN=A
    1   CONTINUE
        WRITE(108,3)HH,WW,RL,AMIN
    3   FORMAT('0',4F15.3)
        STOP
        END
```

                    THE PRINTOUT IS

        2.00   20.000   75.000   680.000

EXAMPLE 14

A company will be making regular shipments of its product by containerized boxes of dimensions (inside) 2 by 3 by 8 meters. The company's product is put in a box with 10,000 cubic centimeters volume. Then the boxes are stacked in one of the six basic stacking formations (depending on which dimensions of the box go up, down, or across the containerized box) in the 2 by 3 by 8 meter box.

The company will make the 10,000 cubic centimeter boxes. The shipping charges are substantial, so it is desired to find the dimensions for the 10,000 cubic centimeter boxes that will allow the company loaders to put the maximum number in each container, using one of the basic stacking formations, and hence reduce shipping costs.

The height and/or width of the box cannot exceed 50 centimeters. Each box dimension must be at least 4 centimeters. Also, the walls of the boxes are ½ centimeter on all six sides.

The program below looks at all combinations of heights and widths (by one centimeter increments; more accuracy could be obtained from a finer mesh) and all stacking formations for each. It saves and prints the optimum dimensions and stacking formation.

```
C   A PROGRAM TO FIND THE
C   DIMENSIONS FOR A RECTANGULAR
C   BOX OF VOLUME 10,000 CUBIC
C   CENTIMETERS SUCH THAT THE
C   MAXIMUM NUMBER OF THESE BOXES,
C   THAT CAN BE STORED IN A
C   CONTAINER 2 BY 3 BY 8 METERS,
C   WILL BE ACHIEVED.
C   SIDE CONDITIONS: THE HEIGHT
C   AND/OR WIDTH OF THE BOX
C   CANNOT EXCEED 50 CENTIMETERS
C   ALSO THE WALLS OF THE INDIVIDUAL
C   BOXES ARE ONE HALF CENTIMETER
C   ON ALL SIX SIDES.
C   UNIFORM STACKING OF THE BOXES,
C   WITH ONE OF THE SIX BASIC
C   STACKING CONFIGURATIONS, IN
C   THE CONTAINER IS ASSUMED.
C   EACH DIMENSION MUST BE AT
C   LEAST 4 CENTIMETERS.
        INTEGER H,W
        REAL L
        MAXNUM=-999999
        DO 1 I=5,51
        H=I-1
        DO 1 J=5,51
        W=J-1
        L=10000./(H*W)
C   H INTO 200 W INTO 300
        N200=200/(H+1)
        N300=300/(W+1)
        N800=800/(L+1)
        M1=N200*N300*N800
        IF(M1.GT.MAXNUM) GO TO 2
        GO TO 100
      2 IN200=N200
        IH=H
        IN300=N300
        IW=W
        IN800=N800
        RL=L
        MAXNUM=M1
  100   CONTINUE
C   W INTO 200 H INTO 300
        N200=200/(W+1)
        N300=300/(H+1)
        N800=800/(L+1)
        M2=N200*N300*N800
        IF(M2.GT.MAXNUM) GO TO 4
        GO TO 200
      4 IN200=N200
        IW=W
        IN300=N300
```

```
          IH=H
          IN800=N800
          RL=L
          MAXNUM=M2
  200   CONTINUE
C   L INTO 200 W INTO 300
          N200=200/(L+1)
          N300=300/(W+1)
          N800=800/(H+1)
          M3=N200*N300*N800
          IF(M3.GT.MAXNUM) GO TO 6
          GO TO 300
      6   IN200=N200
          IH=H
          IN300=N300
          IW=W
          IN800=N800
          RL=L
          MAXNUM=M3
  300   CONTINUE
C   W INTO 200 L INTO 300
          N200=200/(W+1)
          N300=300/(L+1)
          N800=800/(H+1)
          M4=N200*N300*N800
          IF(M4.GT.MAXNUM) GO TO 9
          GO TO 400
      9   IN200=N200
          IH=H
          IN300=N300
          IW=W
          IN800=N800
          RL=L
          MAXNUM=M4
  400   CONTINUE
C   H INTO 200 L INTO 300
          N200=200/(H+1)
          N300=300/(L+1)
          N800=800/(W+1)
          M5=N200*N300*N800
          IF(M5.GT.MAXNUM) GO TO 8
          GO TO 500
      8   IN200=N200
          IH=H
          IN300=N300
          IW=W
          IN800=N800
          RL=L
          MAXNUM=M5
  500   CONTINUE
C   L INTO 200 H INTO 300
          N200=200/(L+1)
          N300=300/(H+1)
```

```
      N800=800/(W+1)
      M6=N200*N300*N800
      IF(M6.GT.MAXNUM) GO TO 10
      GO TO 1
  10  IN200=N200
      IH=H
      IN300=N300
      IW=W
      IN800=N800
      RL=L
      MAXNUM=M6
  1   CONTINUE
      WRITE(108,3)IN200,IH,IN300,IW,IN800,RL,MAXNUM
  3   FORMAT('0',5I12,F15.3,I12)
C  DO THE DIVISIONS TO FIND OUT
C  WHICH DIMENSION IS WHICH.
      STOP
      END
```

THE PRINTOUT IS

8   14   20   24   26   29.762   4160

$IH = 14$ centimeters for height, and $14 + 1$ into $300 = 20 = IN300$. So the height of the box is 14 and lay that dimension across the 3-meter direction. $IW = 24$ centimeters for width, and $24 + 1$ into $200 = 8 = IN200$. So the width of the box is 24 and lay that dimension across the 2-meter direction. This leaves $RL = 29.762$ centimeters for the length to be stacked in the 8-meter direction. This will give $8 \times 20 \times 26 = 4,160$ boxes per container.

EXAMPLE 15

The demand curve (price-quantity curve) of a product is $P(q) = 6 + 1200/q$. The cost curve is $7 + .8q$. And no more than 100 units per day can be produced.

Therefore, we seek to maximize $P = 6q + 1200 - 7q - .8q^2$ subject to $0 \leq q \leq 100$. From the printout we can see that the company should consider stopping production of this product unless it can improve its price and/or cost curves.

```
C  MAXIMIZE PROFIT TAKING DEMAND
C  CURVE AND COSTS INTO ACCOUNT
      INTEGER Q
      PMAX=-999999
      DO 1 I=1,101
      Q=I-1
      P=6*Q+1200-7*Q-.8*Q**2
      IF(P.GT.PMAX) GO TO 2
      GO TO 1
```

```
2   IQ=Q
    PMAX=P
1   CONTINUE
    WRITE(108,3)IQ,PMAX
3   FORMAT('0',I10,F15.3)
    STOP
    END
```

THE PRINTOUT IS

```
    0     1200.000
```

EXAMPLE 16

The cost curve of a product is \$22 + \$.85q + \$.02$q^{1.4}$. The price curve is \$200 − \$.6q. Also, we can produce no more than 1,000 units per day.

Therefore, we seek to maximize Profit $= (200 - .6q)q - (22. + .85q + .02q^{1.4})q$ subject to $0 \le q \le 1000$ units per day.

The printout shows that 57 units per day will maximize the profit.

```
C   MAXIMIZE PROFIT TAKING DEMAND
C   CURVE AND COST INTO ACCOUNT
    INTEGER Q
    PMAX=-999999
    DO 1 I=1,1000
    Q=I
    P=(200-.6*Q)*Q-(22.+.85*Q+.02*Q**1.4)*Q
    IF(P.GT.PMAX) GO TO 2
    GO TO 1
2   IQ=Q
    PMAX=P
1   CONTINUE
    WRITE(108,3)IQ,PMAX
3   FORMAT('0',I10,F15.3)
    STOP
    END
```

THE PRINTOUT IS

```
   57      5107.512
```

EXAMPLE 17

We seek to maximize $N = 25L^4 C^2$ where N is the number of units of production and L and C are labor and capital. Each laborer costs 500 cents per time period. There must be at least 10 laborers. Capital is spent in units of 100 cents. There is a \$10,000 budget available. So $500L + 100C = 1,000,000$ cents.

The printout shows that \$8,335 and 333 laborers will maximize production.

```
C   MAXIMIZE PRODUCTION AS A FUNCTION
C   OF LABOR AND CAPITAL UNDER CONSTRAINTS
        INTEGER L,C
        REAL N,NMAX
        NMAX=-999999
        DO 1 I=1,10001
        C=I-1
        L=(1000000-100*C)/500
        N=25*L**.4*C**2
        IF(N.GT.NMAX) GO TO 2
        GO TO 1
    2   IC=C
        RL=L
        NMAX=N
    1   CONTINUE
        WRITE(108,3)IC,RL,NMAX
    3   FORMAT('0',I10,2F15.3)
        STOP
        END


            THE PRINTOUT IS

    8335    333.    17730813952.000
```

EXAMPLE 18

Minimize the cost function $15 + 7x^2 + 3x + 9xy + y^2$ subject to $0 \le x \le 100$, $0 \le y \le 50$, and $xy = 2400$.

From the printout we see that if $x = 48$ and $y = 50$, we get a minimum cost of $40,387.

```
C   MINIMIZE COST FUNCTION UNDER CONSTRAINTS
        INTEGER X
        CMIN=999999
        DO 1 I=1,101
        X=I-1
        Y=2400/X
        IF(Y.GT.50) GO TO 1
        C=15+7*X**2+3*X+9*X*Y+Y**2
        IF(C.LT.CMIN) GO TO 2
        GO TO 1
    2   IX=X
        AY=Y
        CMIN=C
    1   CONTINUE
        WRITE(108,3)IX,AY,CMIN
    3   FORMAT('0',I10,2F15.3)
        STOP
        END
```

```
       THE PRINTOUT IS

48      50.000        40387.000
```

EXAMPLE 19

Minimize the cost function $12xy + 17xz + 4yz$ subject to $x \geq 0$, $y \geq 0$, $z \geq 0$, and xyz = 1000. This could be solved as a LaGrange Multiplier problem, but we use our easier techniques. The solution is $x = 21$, $y = 8$, $z = 5.952$ for a minimum cost of $6,093.12. More accuracy could be obtained if desired.

```
C  MINIMIZE COST FUNCTION UNDER
C  EQUALITY CONSTRAINT
C  NORMALLY SOLVED AS A
C  LAGRANGE MULTIPLIER PROBLEM
C  HOWEVER WE WILL USE OUR
C  NEW TECHNIQUES
       INTEGER X,Y
       CMIN=999999
       DO 1 I=1,1000
       X=I
       K=1000/X
       DO 1 J=1,K
       Y=J
       Z=1000/(X*Y)
       C=12*X*Y+17*X*Z+41*Y*Z
       IF(C.LT.CMIN) GO TO 2
       GO TO 1
2      IX=X
       IY=Y
       ZZ=Z
       CMIN=C
1      CONTINUE
       WRITE(108,3)IX,IY,ZZ,CMIN
3      FORMAT('0',2I10,F10.3,F15.3)
       STOP
       END
```

```
          THE PRINTOUT IS

21     8     5.952      6093.12
```

EXAMPLE 20

Maximize $P = 7x_1(3 - x_1) + 4x_2(4 - x_2)$ subject to $0 \leq x_1 \leq 30$ and $0 \leq x_2 \leq 15$. This is a dynamic programming problem. Our techniques work well on these problems, too. The answer is $x_1 = 1$, $x_2 = 2$, and $P = 30$.

```
C   WE SOLVE A DYNAMIC PROGRAMMING
C   PROBLEM WITH OUR TECHNIQUES
        INTEGER X1,X2,PMAX,P
        PMAX=-999999
        DO 1 I=1,31
        X1=I-1
        DO 1 J=1,16
        X2=J-1
        P=7*X1*(3-X1)+4*X2*(4-X2)
        IF(P.GT.PMAX) GO TO 2
        GO TO 1
    2   IX1=X1
        IX2=X2
        PMAX=P
    1   CONTINUE
        WRITE(108,3)IX1,IX2,PMAX
    3   FORMAT('0',3I12)
        STOP
        END
```

```
        THE PRINTOUT IS

        1       2       30
```

EXAMPLE 21

Maximize $P = 7x_1 + 3x_2 + 4x_3^2$ subject to $5 \le x_1 \le 20, 0 \le x_2 \le 11, 0 \le x_3 \le 5$, and $5x_1 + 9x_2 + 17x_3 \le 100$. The solution to this dynamic programming problem is $x_1 = 20, x_2 = 0, x_3 = 0$, and $P = 140$.

```
C   ANOTHER DYNAMIC PROGRAMMING PROBLEM
        INTEGER X1,X2,X3,PMAX,P
        PMAX=-999999
        DO 1 I=5,20
        X1=I
        DO 1 J=1,12
        X2=J-1
        DO 1 K=1,6
        X3=K-1
        IF(5*X1+9*X2+17*X3.GT.100) GO TO 1
        P=7*X1+3*X2+4*X3**2
        IF(P.GT.PMAX) GO TO 2
        GO TO 1
    2   IX1=X1
        IX2=X2
        IX3=X3
        PMAX=P
    1   CONTINUE
        WRITE(108,3)IX1,IX2,IX3,PMAX
    3   FORMAT('0',4I12)
```

```
STOP
END
```

```
THE PRINTOUT IS
```

```
20    0    0    140
```

APPENDIX E

The Impact of Computers on the Philosophy of Optimization

Since the beginning of mathematical thought, one idea has affected all mathematical theories. This idea was the realization that mathematics had to use sophisticated and intricate reasoning to obtain solutions to problems in a very few computation steps, because man was unable to do calculations with much speed or for long periods of time. Therefore, every piece of mathematical philosophy had to reflect this fact.

However, in literally just the last few years computers have become so fast, so inexpensive, and so accessible that now for the first time in history man can take the simple, uncomplicated approach to a problem and let the computer do the work.

John Kemeny has observed in his book *Man and the Computer* that man and the computer are rapidly forming a symbiosis that can be of enormous benefit to man. It is time for mathematical philosophers to take this reality into account when doing their creative thinking.

Certainly, calculus is here to stay. However, one of the major applications of calculus is optimization (through various derivative tests and Jacobian procedures). And these techniques can prove difficult if the problem is sophisticated enough. With this in mind, if the author's theories about the connectedness of sampling distributions of optimization problems are right (no isolated extreme points), then it can be believed that the coming debate over simulation versus calculus in optimization is a creditable one.

The author's purpose in all of this is not to announce our entry into the post-calculus world or to signal the end of the "simplex" era, but rather to point out that it is time to take statistical optimization seriously.

To paraphrase Dr. Kemeny, perhaps calculus and our Monte Carlo optimization techniques can form a new symbiosis for the greater benefit of science.

INDEX